PRECEDENTS

OF

AMERICAN NEUTRALITY,

IN REPLY TO THE SPEECH OF

SIR ROUNDELL PALMER,

ATTORNEY-GENERAL OF ENGLAND,

IN THE

BRITISH HOUSE OF COMMONS,

MAY 13, 1864.

BY

GEORGE BEMIS.

BOSTON:
LITTLE, BROWN AND COMPANY.
1864.

Entered according to Act of Congress, in the year 1864, by
GEORGE BEMIS,
In the Clerk's Office of the District Court for the District of Massachusetts.

WINTHROP PRESS, CAMBRIDGE:
ALLEN AND FARNHAM.

CONTENTS.

I. EXPULSION AND SEIZURE OF GENET'S PRIVATEERS IN 1793. — A PRIVATEER CONSIDERED A PUBLIC SHIP OF WAR 1

II. THE CASE OF THE CASSIUS 15

III. THE CASE OF THE SANTISSIMA TRINIDAD, AND JUDGE STORY ON NEUTRAL DUTIES 22

IV. JUDGE STORY'S DICTUM IN THE AMISTAD DE RUES CASE. — SUMMARY OF AMERICAN AUTHORITY 30

V. RETROSPECT OF THE ALABAMA CASE. — HER ESCAPE THE RESULT OF BRITISH TREACHERY AND OFFICIAL CONNIVANCE OR NEGLIGENCE 36

VI. AMERICAN TREATMENT OF FRENCH AND BRITISH ALABAMAS IN WASHINGTON'S ADMINISTRATION 48

APPENDIX. — EXTRACT FROM THE SPEECH OF MR. THOMAS BARING, AND THE SPEECH OF THE ATTORNEY-GENERAL IN FULL 68

PREFACE.

THE writer hopes that his use of the terms " Precedents of Neutrality," upon his title-page, will not deter any, who might otherwise be interested in his pamphlet, from looking further into it, through fear of encountering only something purely technical and legal. He does not use "Precedents" as if he were going to treat of "Pleading" or "Practice," but, in the broadest sense of the term, as *Historic Instances*, " teaching by example." In this sense he hopes that his compilation or summary of American Precedents will address itself favorably to Englishmen, for whom it is mainly intended, as appealing to that well-known English element of action which rejoices in taking what is good in the past for a rule of conduct for the future.

Would that the instances which he collects of American neutral conduct belonged to English history, and made part of the British national code! Then, certainly, if there were any of its old sense of honor and magnanimity left in the nation, we should see no such paltering course of action as has marked the Alabama and Alexandra cases, and, more recently, has displayed itself in this Georgia decision, to which the writer more immediately addresses himself.

In treating of these American precedents, as thus defined, the writer desires it to be understood that he does not intend to cover the ground of citing *all* the American precedents, but only such part of them as belongs to this review of the Attorney-General's late speech; and, even in this limited undertaking, he for the most part omits all that have ever been before adduced or generally commented on. Thus he intends his short summary to be *in addition* to such historical memorials as have appeared, on the other side of the water, in the letters and criticisms of "Historicus" (Mr. William Vernon Harcourt), and the compend of American Neutral History by Mr. Frederick Waymouth Gibbs; and, on this side of the water, in the pamphlets of Mr. Grosvenor P. Lowrey, Mr. Charles G. Loring, and others.

So far as the writer is to find readers among his own countrymen, he cannot but commend to their notice the attempts made by certain candid and high-minded Englishmen to bring the force of American Neutral History to bear upon current English conduct. Leaving out of view English parliamentary and official utterances, and confining the suggestion for the present to strictly historical and legal publications, the writer would especially commend to American attention the efforts of the two Englishmen just named — Messrs. Harcourt and Gibbs — to impress upon their countrymen the just importance of our early neutral statesmanship and jurisprudence. He ventures to call their productions in this line — though widely differing from each other — admirable, and such as would do credit to the best-educated American. That these writings have not been reproduced and extensively read in this country, for *American information*, is to him almost a matter of complete surprise. He can only explain it upon the idea that the absorbing nature of our domestic struggle, and the preconceived prejudice against England at an early day for her apparent lukewarmness or even hostility towards our national well-being, have rendered us comparatively indifferent to whatever bears the name of English. .

And yet, in characterizing the writings of Historicus and Mr. Gibbs in these terms, the writer begs that it may not be supposed that he has overlooked the fact that one of them — the former — is thoroughly and bitterly English in his prejudices, — apparently believing that no good can come out of a republican form of government, and that the highest art in American demagoguism consists in getting up a war against England; and that the latter (Mr. Gibbs) sees no other end to our civil struggle but failure on the part of the North.

Of course, in instancing English notice of American neutral history, the discussion which it underwent in the judicial hearing of the Alexandra case cannot be overlooked. Though that trial, as his American readers are well aware, ended in a ridiculous abortion, the writer cannot but regret that the masterly review and analysis of American neutral decisions at the bar of the Court of Exchequer — to say nothing about the able, acute, and highly interesting, though sometimes wrong-headed, comments upon them on the part of the bench — have not, as yet, been reproduced and read in this country. As a matter of historic interest, he doubts if the annals of the English law afford such another exhibition of the highest order of cultivated legal ability as this same Alexandra law-hearing displays on the part of the respective counsel engaged, particularly in the leaders, — Sir Roundell Palmer on the one side, and Sir Hugh Cairns on the other.

Oh that such a discussion could have ended in a judgment pronounced by a Kent, a Story, or a Marshall! Then England would have established for herself another precedent worthy of the world's imitation, and serviceable for her own future guidance to all time. But now! — The writer will say nothing further here of the Alexandra case, except that the dissenting opinions — as they may be called — of Barons Channell and Pigott read worthily of English judicature.

BOSTON, June, 1864.

PRECEDENTS OF AMERICAN NEUTRALITY.

I.

EXPULSION AND SEIZURE OF GENET'S PRIVATEERS IN 1793-4. — A PRIVATEER CONSIDERED A PUBLIC SHIP OF WAR.

THE late speech of the Attorney-General of England, Sir Roundell Palmer, made in the debate in the British House of Commons on the 13th ultimo, on the question of admitting the Confederate ship Georgia into the port of Liverpool, contains so many misrepresentations, or misstatements concerning American law and statesmanship — based, for the most part, on the pretended authority of Mr. Justice Story — that, as one interested in the just record of his country's history, and in the correct appreciation of the opinions of that eminent jurist and publicist, the writer feels impelled to notice and to reply to them.

He is well aware that it is a thankless task to endeavor to enlighten or persuade most Englishmen of rank or station as to the law, or the morality of our struggle. But as the Attorney-General, on various occasions, has shown himself so well disposed toward our cause, and, in the matter of International law in particular, has so often manifested such a high-toned candor in submitting to be instructed by American precedents, and in urging them upon the consideration of English judges and legislators, it may not be labor lost to endeavor to convince him, and through him, impartial Englishmen, that he has not yet read aright an important chapter in our national politics and jurisprudence, and that the next time he invites the British House of Commons to follow the lead of American authority, it should be to a practical result, diametrically opposite from that arrived at on the occasion referred to.

To state the proposition put forth and advocated by Sir Roundell Palmer, would be, to all well-informed Americans, to answer it. He contended — in the debate referred to, which ensued on Mr. Thomas Baring's motion, that the Georgia should be ordered away from British ports — that the Americans themselves would not have ordered away a vessel, circumstanced like the Georgia, under their precedents of 1793, nor, under the practice established by the later decisions of the United States Supreme Court. "Why!" — an American would reply: — "They not only *would* order away a vessel like the Georgia, but they *did* do it, time and time again. Did they not arrest and try Gideon Henfield for enlisting on board the Sans Culottes, long before there was any Foreign Enlistment Act? Did they not seize the prizes brought in by Genet's privateers, as fast as they appeared in American ports? Did they not seize French privateers, themselves, while in the process of arming, and compel them to dismantle or undergo confiscation? Did they not finally take the British minister's list of French privateers illegally fitted out in American ports, the Sans Culottes, the Citoyen Genet, and all that tribe, and give them notice, one and all to quit, and never show themselves again? Here was the very thing itself; a matter of common notoriety. Why raise a question whether the Americans *would* do it."

We can hardly suppose that these well-verified facts of history have escaped the attention of the Attorney-General; especially as the letters of Mr. Jefferson, detailing them to the British and French ministers of that day, have often been reproduced and commented on. But by way of fixing them in the public mind, and of refreshing Sir Roundell Palmer's memory, if he happens to have forgotten them, we will briefly recall a few of the leading precedents, diplomatic and judicial, belonging to the periods referred to, and bearing upon the issue which the Attorney-General raises with this country. We shall select only those, for the most part, which it is believed have not yet caught the English eye, or been adequately noticed on the English side of the water.

We commence with two Circulars, addressed by Washington's Administration to the Governors of the several sea-board States, directing the enforcement by them of the orders of exclusion of these same privateers of Genet's, within the limits of their respective States. They happen to be addressed in this instance to the Governor of Massachusetts, and are to be found in the Massachusetts State archives, where we copied them, under the general right of access permitted to the public at large:

From the Secretary of War, General Knox, to Governor Hancock.

"WAR DEPARTMENT, Aug. 16, 1793.

"To HIS EXCELLENCY, THE GOVERNOR OF MASSACHUSETTS:

"SIR, — It has, heretofore, been made known, that the fitting out of privateers, in the ports of the United States, was considered as incompatible with our present state of neutrality.

"The Executive, after trying other measures, in vain, to prevent a continuance of the practice, finds itself, at length, constrained to resort to means more decisive than have been hitherto employed. To avoid, therefore, a further infraction of our rights, and a further commitment of our peace, the President of the United States, after mature deliberation, has decided that no armed vessel, which has been, or shall be, originally fitted out in any port of the United States as a cruiser, or privateer, by either of the parties at war, is to have asylum in any ports of the United States.

"I am directed to inform your Excellency of this decision, and to request that in case any vessel, within the foregoing description, should arrive in any port, or harbor, in the State of Massachusetts, that you would cause her to be ordered to depart immediately; and in case of her refusal, that you would take effectual measures to oblige her to depart.

"It is, at the same time, the desire of the President, that force may not be resorted to, until every proper effort has been previously made to procure the early departure without it. And the President has further directed me to request that, in case any such vessel shall have sent, or brought, subsequent to the 5th inst., or should hereafter send or bring, any prize or prizes into any port or harbor of your State, that you would cause such prize or prizes to be immediately secured by the militia, for the purpose of being restored to the former owners.

"It is also requested, that you would please to transmit, in writing, all the cases and the evidence thereon, which may occur in pursuance of this communication. The following are the names of the privateers, comprehended within the meaning of this letter, that have hitherto come to the knowledge of the Government:

Citizen Genet,
Sans Culottes, } fitted out at Charleston, S. C.
Vainqueur de la Bastille,
Petit Democrat, " " Philadelphia.
Carmagnole, " " Delaware.

"I have the honor to be, &c.,
"KNOX, *Secretary of War.*
"His Excellency, JOHN HANCOCK."

From the Secretary of the Treasury, General Hamilton, to the Governor of Massachusetts.

"PHILADELPHIA, Aug. 18, 1794.

"SIR, — The Secretary of War being absent from the seat of Government, I am directed by the President to write to you on the subject of those French privateers, fitted out in our ports, which you have heretofore been informed were to be denied asylum within the United States, except upon the condition of being dismantled of their military equipments.

"The subsequent conduct of some of these vessels, is a matter of real embarrassment and dissatisfaction. By running from one port to another, they have, in effect, enjoyed the asylum which it was intended to deny them, and have thereby placed the Government in the unpleasant situation, not only of seeing itself trifled with, but of being liable to the suspicion of connivance in an evasion of its positive assurances to foreign powers.

"It is inadmissible that such a state of things should continue, and therefore, the President has come to a resolution, to cause every such vessel, which, since the promulgation of his instruction to refuse them asylum, shall have been in a port of the United States, so as to have had an opportunity to acquire a knowledge of that instruction, and which shall hereafter be found in any port or district of the United States, to be deprived of her military equipments. I have it in instruction from him to communicate this resolution to you, and to request your effectual coöperation in carrying it into execution within the State of Massachusetts. While the reasons which have been assigned beget a solicitude in the President, that the measure may be punctually and completely executed, there are weighty considerations which induce him to wish that it may be found practicable to accomplish it in each case, without bloodshed. To this end, it will be useful that any force which may be employed for the purpose, should be such as will control a disposition to resist.

" With perfect respect,
" I have the honor to be, &c.,
" ALEXANDER HAMILTON, *Secretary of Treasury.*
" His Excellency, The Governor of Massachusetts."

Now, if the Attorney-General did not need the reminder of such documents as the above, to refresh his recollection of how the Americans dealt with French cruisers in 1793-4, we can only characterize as disingenuous, the turn by which he sought to do away with the force of those precedents, when Mr. Baring quoted Historicus's deductions from them, to the same effect, as we have above intimated. Historicus's letter to the London Times, of February 17th, as our readers may be aware, had unreservedly insisted that the British Government could do no less than exclude such vessels as the Alabama and Florida from English ports, on *the authority of what the Americans themselves had done on former occasions.* But the Attorney-General, without noticing Historicus's frank and honorable concession, invents a formula, or, as the lawyers would call it, frames a special plea, by which he hopes to " avoid," without even " confessing," the merits of these American precedents. According to the elaborate report of his speech in the *Times,* of May 14th, which we suspect must have been submitted to Sir Roundell's personal revision, he says:

" I do not find that the United States, which have really settled all the doctrines of law applicable to this kind of neutrality, by fitting out vessels in their ports for belligerent na-

1 *

tions, ever adopted the practice of inquiring into the previous history of *public* ships of war, which labored under the suspicion or allegation of having been fitted out in their ports in violation of their neutrality. In the cases of the Santissima Trinidad and the Cassius, the particulars of which were similar to those of the Georgia, Mr. Justice Story said," &c.

It is in that word "*public*," which *we* italicize (not *Sir Roundell Palmer*, nor the *Times*), that the disingenuousness and plea in avoidance, which we have referred to, consist. The Sans Culottes, &c., were privateers? So Sir Roundell Palmer intends to dispose of them by inquiring after "public ships of war." As if public ships of war of France or England would have been likely to be built in the United States, in 1793, when the Government was but four years old, and did not own a single ship of war, itself!

But is the Georgia, herself, a public ship of war, or only a privateer? Mr. Cobden put some searching suggestions on this point to the Attorney-General, when he quoted, in reply to him, that the *Moniteur* had made an official slip-down in calling the Florida "a privateer," and that Mr. Dayton and Mr. Seward had very justly argued thereon, that the declaration of the European Congress of 1856, in regard to abolishing privateering, became mere moonshine in view of the action of the Federal Government.

We will concede, however, for argument's sake, that the Georgia is a public ship. — [A queer public *Confederate* ship, however, while sailing for the first two months of her piratical career under a *British* register!] But is the Attorney-General ignorant, that the American authorities, which he relies on, have expressly held that a privateer stands on the same footing as a regular ship of war, in the particular of being exempted from neutral interference and jurisdiction while in a neutral port? Has he forgotten, that the *L'Invincible* (1 Wheat. 238), a French privateer, brought into an American port, and libelled for a maritime tort, was expressly exempted from judicial procedure, on the score of being a national armed vessel? If he has happened to overlook this important landmark in American international jurisprudence, in the press of his numerous and burdensome official engagements, we beg to call it to his notice. Here is Mr. Justice Curtis's marginal abstract of the case : " The exclusive cognizance of prize questions belongs in general to the capturing power, and the courts of other countries will not undertake to redress alleged maritime torts committed by public-armed vessels in assertion of belligerent rights. This applies to privateers duly commissioned. But our courts of admiralty will take jurisdiction to inquire if the alleged wrongdoer is duly commissioned, or has, by the use of our territory to increase his force, trespassed on our neutral rights." We commend this last ruling to Sir Roundell's attention, in connection with another statement of his which we shall hereafter examine.

Our readers will excuse our quoting a few lines from the opinion of the court, delivered by Mr. Justice Johnson, with a view of clearing up this distinction between a privateer and a public ship : " It would be difficult to distinguish this case in principle from those of *The Cassius* (3 Dall. Rep. p. 121), and *The Exchange* (7 Cranch, p. 116), decided in this court. The only circumstance in which they differ, is, that in those cases the vessels were the property of the nation ; in this, that it belongs to private adventurers. But the commission under which they acted was the same ; the same sovereign power which could claim immunities in those cases, equally demands them in this ; and although the privateer may be considered a volunteer in the war, it is not less a part of the efficient national force, set in action for the purpose of subduing an enemy."

This decision, we beg it to be noted, was an affirmance of the ruling of Mr. Justice Story in the Circuit Court below, and expresses, therefore, with repeated emphasis, his opinion, that a privateer enjoys the same degree of exemption from local jurisdiction, as a full commissioned ship of war ; an opinion which the same eminent judge a third time reiterated, with the sanction of the whole court, in the case of *The Santissima Trinidad*, and with which it ought to be presumed, therefore, that Sir Roundell Palmer is by this time familiar.

But it so happens in regard to the '93 precedent, unfortunately for the Attorney-General's proposition, that one vessel at least of the proscribed French cruisers — the Little Democrat of historic fame, the same which Hamilton and Knox proposed to blow out of water with a land battery, if she undertook to leave the Delaware, in further prosecution of her attempted violation of American neutrality — was in all senses a public ship of war. Here is the impudent note of the French minister of that day, Genet, to the American Government, fully proving it:

"*The citizen Genet, Minister Plenipotentiary of the French Republic, to Mr. Jefferson, Secretary of State* (1 Am. State Pap. 163)."

"PHILADELPHIA, July 9, 1793.

"SIR, — You required of me details relative to the brigantine La Petite Democrate, heretofore La Petite Sarah, at present armed and ready to go out of the Delaware. They are as follows : This vessel, Sir, of English property, armed by our enemies with four cannons and other arms, was taken by the Embuscade frigate, belonging to the Republic of France, and sent into Philadelphia. Her construction being elegant and solid, her bottom coppered, and a swift sailer, her masts and rigging being in a good condition, I have thought — on the report of the captain of the Embuscade and other enlightened mariners — that the acquisition of this vessel would be advantageous to the marine of the Republic; and this consideration, joined to the desire I had of finding employment for a great number of French marines, who were here, exposed to the dangers which often attend idleness, and to misery, determined me to take her on account of the State.

"I have had her repaired. I have completed her armament with cannon which I found on board of four French vessels, and given the command of her to citizen Amiot, ensign of the Republic; and when ready, I shall despatch her with a commission of the Executive Council, and with my particular instructions. I shall confine myself, Sir, to represent to you these facts, which require no discussion on my part, and which cannot create any difficulty on that of your Government. When treaties speak, the agents of nations have but to obey.

"Accept, Sir, my esteem and respect,
"GENET."

We commend this precedent to the Attorney-General's notice on another point, where he says, " I can find no instance of any prohibition or exclusion from any port [of the United States] of any prize, after her conversion into a ship of war." Was not this Little Democrat a prize? Was she not converted into a ship of war? and was she not prohibited from the ports of the United States? As to her absolute exclusion from those ports, of course we need not explain to the Attorney-General, that it was physically impossible for the United States to keep her and her associate cruisers away from the bays and harbors of the Union, if they persisted in coming in at the risk of an infraction of the national peace. He knows, as well as we do, that the new formed Government had to rely on its State militia for the enforcement of any of its orders; and that, at that early day of its existence, it had not a soldier, nor a sailor, — much less, a ship of war, — of its own, at command.

But we suspect that the Little Democrat was not the only one among the fleet of French cruisers which infested our waters in 1793-4, and which were repeatedly ordered off, that might in strictness rank under the head of public ships of war. Here is another note of Genet's, in which he expresses his disgust at American interference with what he calls a French " advice " (or mail) " boat," the *Carmagnole* or *Columbia*, which Gov. Clinton, of New York, had required him to dismantle. The reader will have remembered her name among the proscribed French cruisers of Secretary Knox's list. We give Gov. Clinton's letter, as prefatory (1 *Am. State Pap.* p. 186):

"*Mr. Clinton, Governor of New York, to Mr. Genet, Minister Plenipotentiary of France.*

"NEW YORK, Nov. 21, 1793.

" SIR, — As by your letter of the 11th instant, I am informed that the vessel therein mentioned, now repairing at the wharf in the East River, is called the Carmagnole, and that she was fitted out as a privateer in the Delaware, I conceive it proper to transmit to you a copy of a letter, which I have since received from the Secretary of War, dated the 15th instant, in answer to one from me to the President of the United States, informing him of your having withdrawn the commissions granted to certain privateers, fitted out in the ports of the United States, by which you will perceive it to be the sense of the President, that this vessel should be entirely divested of her warlike equipments, and which, from the readiness you are pleased to express to conform to the views of the Federal Government, I cannot doubt, will, on the receipt hereof, be complied with ; and that, until this is effected, you will not permit her to leave the harbor.

"I am, &c.,
"GEORGE CLINTON."

"*Citizen Genet, Minister Plenipotentiary from the French Republic, to General Clinton, Governor of the State of New York.*

"NEW YORK, Nov. 23, 1793,
2d Year of the French Republic.

"SIR, — I have received the letter which you did me the honor to write me, the 21st instant, as also the copy annexed to it of a letter from the Secretary of War.

"The fresh requisitions which have lately been transmitted to you, respecting the schooner *Columbia*, formerly called the *Carmagnole*, are only a continuation of the system which has been observed toward me, from the very commencement of my mission, and which evidently appears to be calculated to baffle my zeal, to fill me with disgust, and to provoke my country to measures dictated by a just resentment, which would accomplish the wishes of those whose politics tend only to disunite America from France, the more easily to deliver the former into the power of the English.

"Warned by this conjecture, which is unfortunately but too well founded, instead of proving to you as I could easily do, that the orders which have been given to you are contrary to our treaties, to the conduct of the Federal Government even toward the British nation (whose packets, and a great number of merchant vessels, I am well informed, have been permitted to arm for their defence in their ports), to the bonds of friendship which unite the people of both republics, and to their mutual interests, since the vessel in question is intended to serve as an advice boat in our correspondence with the French islands, which by our treaties you are bound to guaranty, and in whose fate your property is no less interested than ours, I will give orders to the consul and the French commodore of the road [harbor], to con-

form themselves to every thing that your wisdom may think proper to direct. " Accept, Sir, &c.,
"GENET."

It seems, that, after all, Genet did not keep his word about dismantling the Carmagnole, and Mr. Randolph, who had succeeded Mr. Jefferson as Secretary of State, had to quicken the diplomatic conscience of Mr. Fauchet, Genet's successor as French minister, into a better observance of international duties, by compelling her disarmament or her prompt departure from American waters. Two sharp letters of his to Mr. Fauchet on this subject, which seem to have had the effect to finally rid the American coast of this truculent privateer, or public ship of war (for we are not clear that Genet's pretence of her being a mail-packet was not — like his promise to dismantle her — a diplomatic falsehood), will be found in 1 Am. State Papers, p. 600, under dates of August 14th and August 20th, 1794. In the first of these letters, that of the 14th, Mr. Randolph credits the French minister with another case of dismantling, *actually executed*, which we suppose refers to still another of Genet's cruisers.

We have not space for all the correspondence at this particular stage of the enforcement of President Washington's order of expulsion of these cruisers; but as a specimen of it, we commend to the attention of the Attorney-General the following reply of Mr. Fauchet to Mr. Randolph, under date of August 21, 1794 (1 Am. St. Pap. p. 600); both as showing the urgency with which the order was insisted on by the United States, and the reasons given by the French minister for not better complying with it. We hope that the French minister's complaint of undue partiality on our part toward the English, in this matter, will not detract from the binding efficacy of the precedent otherwise, at this juncture:

"*Joseph Fauchet, Minister Plenipotentiary of the French Republic, &c., to Mr. Randolph, Secretary of State, &c.*

"PHILADELPHIA, August 21, 1794.

"SIR, — I told you verbally, and repeat it in writing, that the Cornelia and Columbia had sailed for France. Then my intention was, that they should not return into the ports of the United States. But they were compelled to take shelter, by the pursuit of the English vessels of war, which at this time block up all your ports. It would be as unjust as unreasonable to impute to them as a crime this return, which was rendered necessary by so unhappy a circumstance, — unless it should be wished that these two vessels should become the prey of the English, and I avow it with profound sorrow, that I have been tempted to entertain this opinion, when I learned, that at New York, orders had been given to the Cornelia immediately to quit that port, although it was known that two English frigates were to have seized her on her departure. But, Sir, it is too painful to me to harbor a doubt injurious to the public officers of a free nation, to give myself up to this impression; and at the same time, it is too grateful to me to prove with what strictness we fulfil our treaties and our engagements, to omit giving you the following details:

"The first of these two vessels, the Cornelia, which is at New York, is about to go to Boston, to be there completely dismantled. The second, the Columbia, which was in the Delaware, departed thence on the 11th of this month. I am surprised, Sir, that you were not informed of her departure, with as much care as you were of her arrival. Perhaps it was not the duty of the same person to give the two advices, which might have prevented your complaint. But, Sir, when the Federal Government fulfils with so much exactness the new obligations which it has imposed upon itself, in relation to England, is it not just to require from it the same scrupulous observance of sacred treaties, which it has long since contracted with France? Why, then, is an asylum refused to an unfortunate barque, which, in her flight, had thrown into the sea some of her cannon and of her water (?), when it is given, though against the tenor of these very treaties, to the vessels of war which have taken prizes from the citizens of the republic? Without doubt, Sir, this violation, which is so fatal to us, takes place through forgetfulness only. It would be horrible to me to attribute it to any other motive; therefore, I content myself with subjoining here an extract of the 17th article, in order to recall it to your remembrance.

"'Art. 17th. And on the contrary, no asylum or retreat shall be given in their ports or harbors to those who shall have taken prizes from the subjects of his Majesty or the said States; and if they are compelled to enter them by tempest or the danger of the seas, they shall be obliged to depart as soon as possible.'

"Neither tempest nor the danger of the seas have compelled the

the English vessels of war to enter your ports; notwithstanding they have been there supplied; notwithstanding they remain there to interrupt your commerce and our supplies; and notwithstanding we are your nearest allies. "Accept, Sir, &c.,

"JH. FAUCHET."

We commend also to Sir Roundell Palmer's notice, the following letter from Genet to Jefferson, of the date of July 8, 1793, showing how *Le Vainqueur de la Bastille*, another of Genet's squadron, came to grief, with one of her prizes, at an early day of Mr. Genet's experiment on American forbearance. It will be noticed in this case, that the commander of the French "Georgia" had the grace to send back his American register, before entering upon his career of privateering. But even this pretence toward decency (which it seems did not suit the impertinent Genet), did not exempt him and his vessel from a taste of the law. (1 *Am. State Papers*, p. 163.)

The Minister of the French Republic to Mr. Jefferson, Secretary of State.

"PHILADELPHIA, July 8, 1793.

"SIR, — The French armed vessel *Le Vainqueur de la Bastille*, of American construction, and heretofore bearing the name of Hector, has sailed from Charleston, furnished with a French commission and her old American register, which the commander Hervieux, sent to the Custom House, after having cleared the bar of that port. This conduct, condemnable only for its timidity, has led the Custom House of Charleston to require the Government of South Carolina to cause him to be arrested; and in consequence, *Le Vainqueur de la Bastille* has been seized at Wilmington, together with a prize which she took in there. The laws of the United States inflict no punishment in the present case, only where there has been an intention of avoiding the duties imposed by the United States; and as it (is) proved by the war-commission, and by the instructions in Captain Hervieux's possession, that he went out of the port of Charleston only to resist, as much as possible, the unjust attacks of our enemies — a duty which all the treaties authorize him to fulfil, and which no law of the United States, and consequently no order of the Executive of these States, can forbid him to fulfil — I request you, Sir, to desire of the Federal Government the liberation of Captain Hervieux and of his crew of the *Le*

Vainqueur de la Bastille, and of her prize, now detained in the port of Wilmington, North Carolina.

"GENET."

We are unable to trace the history of this case to its termination. We suppose that, as was usual in such cases, the prize was retained by the Federal Government and turned over to its original owners, and the illegally-equipped cruiser, after undergoing a reduction of her armament, allowed to go to sea again on a promise of never repeating her offence; a promise which, perhaps, she in some sense kept, by only arming anew in some French, instead of an American port, and then returning to her old business of privateering.

But taking the case as one of actual seizure by the American Government in the first instance, though followed by a subsequent liberation on some terms or other, can Sir Roundell Palmer doubt, after reading it, that Washington's Government put a black mark against the Georgias of that day, which was noticed and acted upon when the offenders sought a second time the hospitality of our harbors? And if he cannot draw a distinction between a privateer and a public ship (as Judge Story and the United States Supreme Court could not), had he not better look further into American history, before repeating his assertion that he cannot find that the United States "ever adopted the practice of inquiring into the previous history of public ships of war, which labored under the suspicion or allegation of having been fitted out in violation of their neutrality," and, "that we are not therefore warranted, upon the authority of the United States, in excluding this vessel [the Georgia] from our ports?"

II.

THE CASE OF THE CASSIUS.

But in the cases of *The Cassius* and *The Santissima Trinidad*, the Attorney-General feels confident that the Americans gave proof of an established practice of theirs, to let ships of war go free of molestation, however illegal might be their antecedents in regard to a violation of neutrality. After quoting the *dictum* of Judge Story's in *The Santissima Trinidad*, with which we stopped short in our former citation from his speech, and making some comments on it, he goes on to say: " The Santissima Trinidad and the Cassius were both received into the ports of the United States, held not to be amenable to courts of law, and never ordered by the Government to leave any port."

We confess that when we read this statement of the Attorney-General's, we could hardly help suspecting that the London Times had made some mistake in reporting his remarks, particularly so far as concerned the Cassius, and that the reporter had mixed up the two cases referred to, *The Cassius* and *The Santissima Trinidad*, in a way which Sir Roundell Palmer had never intended. But on reflection, considering how similar the conduct of the argument was to the turn played upon *public ships*, which we have before alluded to, and remembering the elaborate completeness of the legal citations and many of the legal deductions, we inclined to the belief that it was a genuine report. Accepting it as such, we would venture now to call Sir Roundell's attention, briefly to the legal and diplomatic history of the Cassius, and to inquire of him respectfully, in conclusion, if he has not too hastily adopted the opinion of some junior as to its bearing.

Here is a brief summary of the early history of this vessel, as stated in a despatch from Mr. Pickering, American Secretary of State, to Mr. Pinckney, our minister at the French Republic, dated January 16, 1797, and published in 1 American State Papers, p. 564. The despatch is intended for a formal replication to a series of unfriendly complaints on the part of the French minister, Adet, among which the charge of unhandsome treatment of France, in this affair of the Cassius, plays a conspicuous part: [1]

"The Cassius, under the name of Les Jumeaux, was fitted and armed for a vessel of war in the port of Philadelphia, in violation of the law of the United States. In December, 1794, having escaped from the port to descend the river, orders were given to the militia of the State of Delaware to intercept her. The attempt was made, and failed. The crew of Les Jumeaux, which was unexpectedly found to be very numerous, resisted the officers who went on board, manned their cannon, and brought them to bear on the cutter in which the militia, about forty in number, were embarked. Their force being inadequate to the enterprise, they retired with an intention to return the next day with a reinforcement. They did so, but Les Jumeaux had sailed and gone to sea. The agent, Mr. Guinet, by whom Les Jumeaux had been fitted out, was tried at the circuit court in Philadelphia, convicted of the offence, and received sentence of fine and imprisonment." [2]

So far the American Secretary of State's narrative of the antecedents of the Cassius.

We next give, in the chronological order of events, another

---

[1] This State paper of Mr. Pickering, constitutes, in our judgment, one of the best productions of Washington's administration, particularly in that part which meets and disposes of the eternal claim, on the part of France, upon American gratitude, for helping the United States to achieve their independence, so perpetually harped upon by the French envoys and statesmen of that day.

[2] This important State trial, reported under the name of *United States* v. *Guinet*, in Wharton's State Trials, p. 93, and 2 Dall. Rep. p. 321, being the first that arose after the passage of the earliest American Foreign Enlistment Act of 1794, is, of course, very familiar to the Attorney-General, as it was cited and commented on at large, in the Alexandra law-hearing. It may be new to him, however, that the Cassius was the vessel which the defendant in that case was "concerned in equipping."

State paper, which probably has never met the eye of Sir Roundell Palmer, but which fell under our notice for the first time the very day that we read his speech, and which helps to throw light upon the character of the American " reception " of this vessel. It is another circular from Mr. Pickering, when Secretary of War, to the Governors of the maritime States (in this case addressed to the Governor of Massachusetts), ordering the seizure of the Cassius, if she should come into any port of the United States to complete her equipment. It will be noticed that the parallelism of this case with the Georgia is complete, in the particular of both vessels intending to arm after they should have got away from their place of equipment. It also answers the assertion or suggestion, repeated twice at least, we believe, by Earl Russell, that the Americans never had to deal with a case where the violators of their neutrality attempted to practice concealment and deception toward them in the manner that the builders of the Alabama had done toward the English. We copy the document, as before, from the Massachusetts State-archives:

Mr. Pickering, Secretary of War, to Governor Samuel Adams.

"Department of War, January 6, 1795.

"Sir, — A ship called Les Jumeaux (or the Twins), Captain Rualt, armed and equipped in the port of Philadelphia as a cruiser, contrary to our neutrality and the laws of the United States, in such case provided, has lately escaped from the Delaware. It appears by the report of the officer employed to seize her, that she sailed from Bombay Hook, the 2d inst. The proof is positive that the ship has been unlawfully fitted out as above mentioned. A description of her and her equipments, so far as is known, is enclosed. As the necessity of concealment prevented her completing her equipments in such manner as to commence an immediate cruise, it is probable, that in order to complete them, she will put into some port of the Chesapeake, or other port in the United States. It is, therefore, the request of the President of the United States, that you will cause the requisite measures to be taken for seizing the above-mentioned ship, with her tackle, furniture, and stores, and also for apprehending the captain, together with such of his officers and men as have participated with him in violating the laws of the United States.

"I have the honor to be, &c.,

"TIMOTHY PICKERING, *Secretary of War.*

"His Excellency, Samuel Adams."

Getting warning, doubtless, of this circular, the Cassius never ventured into an American harbor, till she had effected such a change in her condition as she thought would put her beyond the danger of interference in case of return. She went to a French port in Saint Domingo (then a French possession), was there regularly transferred by a bill of sale to the French Government [*See* the French minister's voucher for this, 1 Am. State Papers, pp. 635, 636], and having received a public commission, boldly ventured back to Philadelphia. It is true that the American Government did not thereupon enforce upon her the threats of Mr. Pickering's circular. But they did another thing which showed, as plainly as any seizure would have done, their disposition to enforce the laws of neutrality, as far as lay in their power. Civil suits having been commenced against the Cassius, and her captain arrested, immediately upon her arrival at Philadelphia, by parties who had before sustained pecuniary damage by her illegal proceedings (as detailed in 1 Am. State Papers, p. 564, *ut supra*), the United States' Executive *backed up the authority of the Federal tribunals in taking cognizance of those suits*, and two several proceedings having been dismissed on technical grounds, *a final condemnation of forfeiture in a* "qui tam" *suit was pronounced, and* (we have no doubt) *enforced under national auspices.*

The length which the American Government went, on this occasion, in vindicating their neutrality, can, in some degree, be inferred, from the tone of complaint adopted in regard to it by the French minister of that day, Adet, addressing the American Secretary of State in a violent reclamation for indemnity and satisfaction. His memorial will be found in American State Papers, vol. 1, pp. 579–586. Further angry correspondence, relating to this vessel, showing that we carried the assertion of our neutral independence, and sense of international justice, to the very verge of a war with France, will be found in 1 Am. State Papers, pp. 629–639. Our limits only permit a brief citation from Mr. Adet's memorial, at p. 586:

"The undersigned, Minister plenipotentiary, made new representations to the Secretary of State of the United States upon the foregoing facts. Mr. Pickering, then Secretary of State, in his answer of 1st August, 1795, repeats this phrase of Mr. Randolph: 'As long as the question is in the hands of our courts, the Executive cannot withdraw it from them;' adding thereto this remarkable expression: 'and, therefore, is not chargeable with suffering a violation of the treaties subsisting between the two republics.' The undersigned complained that the new suit commenced against the Cassius had been carried to an incompetent tribunal, and in the same letter of August 1, 1795, the Secretary of State replied on this head to the undersigned, 'the counsel, who have told you that such is the law, have led you into an error,' &c.; maintaining the competency of the tribunal.

"The undersigned, minister, in these circumstances, saw himself obliged to disarm the vessel; to discharge the crew, which, during these transactions he had supported at great expense, and abandoned the Cassius to the Government of the United States, protesting against the illegality of her arrest.

"The undersigned, minister, is not acquainted with the details of what happened since that time relative to this affair; he only knows that in the month of October last, the Circuit Court declared itself incompetent, notwithstanding the assertion of the Secretary of State, and quashed all the proceedings. In consequence, the Secretary offered him the Cassius; as if, after having retained, in contempt of treaties, a state vessel, after having left her to rot in port, the Government of the United States were not to answer both for the violation of the treaties, and for the damages the Cassius has sustained.

"ADET."

It was, doubtless, after the date of this despatch (Nov. 15, 1796), and in consequence of the abandonment by the French Government of any further interest in the Cassius, that the *qui tam* suit for a forfeiture proceeded to judgment. Mr. Justice Johnson, in his opinion in the *L'Invincible* (1 Wheat. p. 253), already quoted, and who grounds that opinion, as we have seen, in great part upon the precedent of the Cassius, is our authority for saying that she was finally condemned for a forfeiture. Of course, he would be exact in his statement of that part of the history of the case, since the idea of her ultimate forfeiture would apparently militate with the point to which he was citing her precedent; — namely, that a public ship of war was ordinarily exempt from local jurisdiction. This same fact of her forfeiture was also largely commented on in the case of *The Nereyda* (8 Wheat. 108), and was accepted on all hands by the bench and the opposing counsel — after a double argument of the Nereyda case, in which this Cassius precedent was treated as the controlling one — as an established verity.

We know that "Historicus" attempts to raise a question of the ultimate forfeiture of the Cassius, in his letter to the London Times of Nov. 7, 1863. But it seems to us an improbability bordering upon absurdity, to contend that men of the eminence and habits of accuracy of Mr. Justice Johnson, Chief Justice Marshall, and Mr. Justice Washington, all of whom were upon the stage of public life at the time of the occurrence of the national controversy about the Cassius, should not have been well informed as to her ultimate fate. Her final adjudication must have occurred in Mr. Justice Washington's circuit in Pennsylvania, at or about the time of his coming upon the bench, and Chief Justice Marshall, as one of the American envoys to the French Republic in 1798, had had occasion to pen or concur in a despatch in which this same affair of the Cassius occupied a prominent position. [*See* 2 Am. State Papers, p. 193.][1]

Now, with such a record as this in this case of the Cassius, we should hardly think that Sir Roundell Palmer would again advisedly repeat his declaration, that she " was received into

---

[1] In the report of the judgment of the Circuit Court of Pennsylvania in 1796, dismissing the second suit, it will be noticed by a foot-note of the reporter's (2 Dallas, p. 369), that the counsel for the prosecution said that he should commence a new (third) action in the *District* Court — the proper tribunal for it, as the Circuit Court had just decided. It was doubtless in this *third* suit that the forfeiture took effect.

the ports of the United States, held not to be amenable to courts of law, and never ordered by the Government to leave any port."

Whether the American Executive showed political sagacity and the American courts judicial discretion in their dealings with the Cassius, is no part of our thesis; but that, as a matter of fact, the American nation dealt with her in a manner diametrically opposite from that stated by the Attorney-General, and in a spirit which should have prevented her case ever being likened to that of the Georgia or quoted to American disparagement, is, we submit, one of the clearest demonstrations of history.

If, perchance, any doubt hangs over the final result of the suit for a forfeiture, all we have to say, is, that we shall be content to have the British nation act toward the Georgia, and all that tribe, in the spirit of the Cassius precedent; — *leaving out the forfeiture.* When the British Government have sent an armed force to prevent the escape of another Georgia, as soon as they are informed of such an expedition being meditated in their ports; — when they have indicted, *convicted,* and PUNISHED her builders and equippers, in case she *has* escaped; — when they have sent orders to all the ports of the British empire to seize her, in case she makes her appearance again before going into a Confederate port to procure a legitimate transfer and a national commission; — when, after having fortified herself with a (so-called) national character, and having again come within British jurisdiction, they shall have upheld and justified civil and penal proceedings against her at the risk of a war with as powerful a nation as France, and which proceedings shall have detained her till she rots at the wharf and is abandoned in disgust by her belligerent equippers — for one, we shall confess ourselves satisfied with British administration of International law. Until then, we shall hope never to hear this precedent of the Cassius again drawn forth from the file, as an arrow from the quiver of an enemy.

III.

THE CASE OF THE SANTISSIMA TRINIDAD, AND JUDGE STORY ON
NEUTRAL DUTIES.

But there remains the case of *The Santissima Trinidad* for Sir Roundell Palmer to fall back upon. This is the American case which has afforded so much capital to English Confederate-sympathizers in parliament and the courts: this is the case upon which Lord Chief Baron Pollock, at the jury-trial of the Alexandra case, broke out in eulogy upon American jurists, as having rendered "the pursuit of the law almost captivating," and then based his main ruling (if the Chief Baron can be got to admit that there was any ruling in that case) upon an unfairly-selected definition from Webster's Dictionary: this is the case which helped inspire Baron Bramwell with so much joy for the "fearless and honest principles" on which law was administered in America ("the same fearless and honest principles as those on which, I venture to say, law is administered here" in England), and which showed its fruits thereupon in a judgment of his, avowedly sanctioning "an evasion" of the British statute; and this, finally, is the case from which the Parliamentary advocates of the Rebellion, from Sir Hugh Cairns down to Mr. Roebuck, have derived an inexhaustible fund of argument and law, based upon the *dicta* of the (so-called) "great American jurist."

The Attorney-General, we believe, has not indulged in any praise of Mr. Justice Story in this speech, in the course of his various citations from his opinions. We are almost disposed to thank him for this; so common has it become for Englishmen to begin their hostile citations of American authorities with a preliminary eulogy of American judges and statesmen. We are now so accustomed to this, that instead of " timeo Danaos et *dona ferentes*," we may well change the poet's sentiment into *laudes* " ferentes." There are, to be sure, honorable exceptions to this practice; among which we would particularly specify " Historicus; " and, we desire to add, in all sincerity, the Attorney-General, himself. We do not hesitate to say, that we regard his praise as generally sincere; and that, when bestowed, it falls within the classic postulate of value, as coming from a " laudato viro." Perhaps his admission, in the present connection, of the " United States having really settled all the doctrines of law applicable to this kind of neutrality, *by fitting out vessels in their ports for belligerent nations*," is (in the italicized portion) intended for a Parthian arrow; but we prefer to accept it in a friendly sense, and to take back nothing from our expression of respectful esteem.

Coming now to *The Santissima Trinidad* decision, and the weight of *praise* which Judge Story has had to bear for having pronounced it, we have to say, in the first place, that it was not the case of a vessel — so far as we have any light about it — which, according to Sir Roundell Palmer's allegation, " had violated the United States' Foreign Enlistment Act over and over again." We are not aware that the Independencia (which was the aggressive belligerent; the name of the case, " The Santissima Trinidad," being borrowed from the aggrieved vessel,) ever had any other reputation than what she got from this judicial proceeding. She does not figure in diplomacy, was never made the subject of ministerial complaint, that we are aware of, nor do we ever remember to have seen her name connected with any of the numerous cases of illegal capture in violation of the American Foreign Enlistment Act, which filled the United States Supreme Court about the period of her adjudication; — *The Gran Para, The Arrogante Barcelones*, &c. She appears to have been one of the ordinary run of Buenos-Ayrean privateers, whose illegal equipment in an American port, at the time of the South American struggle for independence, consisted not in an original outfit, but only in an increase of armament or force; an important distinction, as the Attorney-General is aware, which has always been observed in American legislation and diplomacy, which justly marks, in the latter case, a much more mitigated degree of culpability. A very good statement of this distinction (if the Attorney-General has not considered it), will be found in Mr. Jefferson's letter to Mr. Hammond, of Nov. 14, 1793, published in 4 *Jefferson's Writings*, p. 78, (H. A. Washington's ed. 1861), which is not contained in the American State Papers.

If, in the next place, Sir Roundell Palmer means to imply " by [the Santissima Trinidad] never being ordered by the Government to leave any port," that the American Government ever knew of her presence in an American port, — much more that such presence was ever brought to their notice either judicially or diplomatically, we should be glad to have him furnish any proof of the fact. What is stated in the report of facts in the 7th volume of Wheaton, about her coming back to the United States in 1817, after her voyage out to Buenos Ayres, refers to a period of time, some five years antecedent to the decision of the case in 1822. If Sir Roundell Palmer supposes that, at this latter date (1822), when for the first time the Federal Court decided that she had offended against American law by an increase of her force, the Independencia still lay in the port of Baltimore, we should be glad to be apprised of any evidence establishing the fact. Again, if there is any force in saying that the Santissima Trinidad [the Independencia, rather,] was " held not to be amenable to courts of law," in a case where nobody sought to make her amenable to a court of law, — since no proceeding, either civil or criminal, was ever commenced against the capturing vessel, herself, the Independencia, but only against her prize — we have to reply — that so far as the adjudication upon that prize is concerned, the directly-opposite statement is the true one : — The Independencia *was* " held amenable to the law," and her prize, the Santissima Trinidad's cargo, *was* taken away from her, notwithstanding that the captors set up that she was a public ship of war, and that her doings could not be inquired into. Let us try to make this plain by epitomizing the facts :

The Independencia (treated by the court as a public ship of war of the Buenos-Ayrean Government), brings into Baltimore certain prize-property captured on the high seas from two Spanish vessels, the Santissima Trinidad and the St. Andre; and the prize-property (not the capturing ship) being libelled by the Spanish owners (or on their behalf by the Spanish Consul) in a *civil* suit, on the ground that the Independencia had had her force increased in an American port, the captors set up in bar, that the Federal Court cannot take jurisdiction of the subject-matter, because the Independencia is a public ship of war. But the Court decide, that— *though the Independencia is a public ship of war* — she is as liable as any privateer to have her illegal prizes, when brought into American jurisdiction, taken away from her, if she has violated the Foreign Enlistment Act; and the court having inquired into that matter, and found, that on a certain occasion she has increased her force illegally in an American port, do thereupon take the prize-property away from her and give it back to the Spanish claimants.

If this is not holding her amenable to the law, we do not know what to call it; nor can we understand how the Attorney-General could ever have uttered the sentence attributed to him in the Times, implying the contrary.

The reader can judge for himself, also, whether this case, as thus stated, is any authority for Sir Roundell Palmer's other proposition, "that the United States never adopted the practice of inquiring into the previous history of public ships of war." Here the Federal Supreme Court, after solemnly deciding that the capturing ship was to be treated as a public ship of war, proceeded deliberately to inquire whether she had been originally equipped in an American port in violation of neutrality, or had ever increased her force in the same violation, and finding the evidence sufficiently decisive under the latter head, condemned her prize-property and restored it to its original owners.

This ruling of the Supreme Court was but a confirmation of their doctrine in the case of the *L'Invincible*, in the first of Wheaton, to which we have already referred. Judge Curtis's marginal abstract of that case, in one section, as will be remembered, was: "But our courts of admiralty will take jurisdiction to inquire if the alleged wrongdoer is duly commissioned, or has, by the use of our territory to increase his force, trespassed on our neutral rights." And since Judge Story has been vouched in so repeatedly for what is put forth for the opposite doctrine, by the Attorney-General, we desire to call Sir Roundell's attention to some other cases in which that highly coveted authority has unmistakably defined his position as to this point.

In the first place, we would respectfully inquire of the Attorney-General, if he has omitted to notice that Mr. Justice Story made one of the court, which at the same term and the day after the decision of the Santissima Trinidad, decided also *The Gran Para* (7 Wheat. 471)? — He will remember the case, by the now familiar citation from Chief Justice Marshall's opinion, ending thus: " this would indeed be a fraudulent neutrality, disgraceful to our own government," &c., — the fraudulent neutrality, that was to say, of allowing itself to be cheated out of administering international justice, by a *bogus* commission. Does that case, we would ask, look much as if Judge Story would have dropped the jurisdiction of the Georgia, if he had had her to dispose of judicially, the moment that it was intimated to him that she was a public commissioned vessel?

At the same February term of the Supreme Court, 1822, with the Santissima Trinidad decision, was also the decision of the cases of *The Monte Allegre* and *The Rainha de los Anjos* (7 Wheat. 520), participated in by Judge Story, in which the court threw aside another of these pseudo-commissions to enforce the provisions of the American neutral statute. In February, 1823, it was Mr. Justice Story (in *The Experiment*, 8 Wheat. 261), speaking for the whole court, who disposed of another of these same commissions by pronouncing it invalid, as obtained by deception toward the granting power; and, finally, — not to multiply cases, — it was Mr. Justice Story, at the same February term of the court, 1823, on behalf of the full bench, who took away from a privateer, illegally equipped within our jurisdiction, a Spanish *public ship of war*, which the privateer, after capturing, had converted into another privateer, and had sent back into our ports fortified with a Venezuelan commission, which commission she defied the American court to interfere with. (*The Nereyda*, 8 Wheat. already cited.)

As this case indirectly hits another of Sir Roundell's pet propositions, that he " can find no instance in which a prize, converted into a ship of war, has been excluded from our ports," we briefly cite its leading facts: The Spanish warship, the Nereyda, had been captured by the privateer, the Irresistible — doubtless the same Buenos-Ayrean buccaneer that figures as the capturer of the Gran Para, and by whose pretended commission Chief Justice Marshall thought it would be disgraceful for our government to be hoodwinked.[1] This time the Irresistible came before the court under the colors of the " Oriental Republic." She had fought and captured the Nereyda on the high seas, and having carried her prize into an allied port of a South American republic, had had her condemned in a so-called prize-court as capture of war, and sold at public auction. The prize-vessel, the Nereyda, had next adopted a Venezuelan commission, and afterwards ventured into Baltimore under the Venezuelan flag. The Spanish consul having detected his master's ship of war in the disguised privateer, libelled her on behalf of the Spanish crown, alleging that her capturer, the Irresistible, had violated the neutral laws of the United States by an illegal original outfit in an American port. The Supreme Court (Mr. J. Story giving the opinion), notwithstanding the show of the Venezuelan condemnation-in-admiralty and the Venezuelan commission as a privateer, and notwithstanding *that the capture had been made on the high seas*, restored her to the possession of the king of Spain, on admission of the original violation of the American law by the outfit of the Irresistible.

---

[1] The Attorney-General will find that this vessel was proceeded against for a forfeiture under the United States temporary Neutrality Act of 1817, ch. 58, in 7 Wheat. Rep. p. 551. She escaped punishment by the expiration of the statute under its own limitation, before final adjudication.

After reading this case, if his attention has not before been called to it, the Attorney-General, we fancy, will say less of Judge Story's high regard for commissions to belligerent ships of war. He will probably think less also of the doctrine of a commission's always superseding the necessity of a bill of sale, in the case of a public ship of war; — the only point to which Judge Story intended that his long *dictum*, beginning " in general the commission of a public ship . . . is complete proof of her public character," should apply.

No doubt the doctrine is true, " in general," as the learned judge lays it down, that a commission, duly authenticated, is evidence enough of nationality, without a bill of sale or other usual documentary papers of a private-owned ship. But if Sir Roundell Palmer will examine the cases adduced, and numerous others which can be instanced, he will find that the whole court, in general, and Judge Story more especially, in particular, time and again, when inquiring into the antecedents of suspicious belligerents, regularly brought before them for adjudication, have set aside commissions, as well where there were bills of sale as where there were none, when satisfied that such commissions were fictitious and collusive. The Independencia, for a rarity, happened to be able to show a *bona fide* commission, and to establish a changed nationality.

We do not propose at present to go into the other famous dictum of Judge Story's in this Santissima Trinidad case, about there being " nothing in our laws to forbid our citizens from sending armed vessels to foreign ports for sale," &c., which the Attorney-General does *not* cite. We suppose that the most captious critics of American neutrality among our English friends will admit that there *can* be such a thing as a *bona fide* transfer of a ship of war by neutrals to a belligerent; or if they cannot admit as much, we ask them how they hold upon the conduct of their own government in selling the Victor, *alias* the Rappahannock, to the Confederates ? When Judge Story, then, was talking about " a commercial adventure," &c., we will only ask for so much charity on his behalf, as to have it believed that he had in mind a transaction of at least as fair and above-board a character as that of the British transfer alluded to.

We drop the Santissima Trinidad case here; believing that it will hardly be thought worth the Attorney-General's citing again, when he has to advocate another Georgia reception, and hoping that if the favorers of the Lairds and the Millers of England think that they can make capital out of any of the *dicta* of Judge Story's contained in it, they will remember that that eminent and patriotic publicist has put himself too much at large upon the record of public law, to be set wrong by what can be misapplied from his readings in this single case.

IV.

JUDGE STORY'S DICTUM IN THE AMISTAD DE RUES CASE. — SUMMARY OF AMERICAN AUTHORITY.

THERE is one more citation from Judge Story in Sir Roundell Palmer's speech, namely, that from the case of *La Amistad de Rues* (5 Wheat. 385), which we feel constrained to notice. It is after the Attorney-General has got upon the Alabama case, and is trying to lay the ghost of the Governmental offence in that matter. He is able to find thus much in Judge Story's opinion in the Amistad de Rues case, which he thinks helps him out in his official task of justifying his Government for continuing to extend the hospitality of British harbors to the Alabama, and for refusing to make compensation for her past depredations upon American commerce:

"Mr. Justice Story thus lays down what is the limit of the obligation which the neutral owes to the belligerent in this matter: — ' When called upon by either of the belligerents to act in such cases, all that justice seems to require is, that the neutral nation should fairly execute its own laws, and give no asylum to the property unjustly captured. It is bound, therefore, to restore the property if found within its own ports; but, beyond this, it is not obliged to interfere between the belligerents.' "

On which the Attorney-General remarks (*inter alia*): "He [J. Story] does not say that an asylum may not be given to public ships of war, whatever their public history. . . . The authority of Mr. Justice Story, therefore, distinctly excludes the proposition that belligerents have any rights entitling them to require interference by the neutral, to the extent of excluding absolutely from her ports ships of this description, if it does not seem to the neutral, herself, necessary so to do. I say, then, we have done all that authority requires us to do."

Now, to pin any such inference as this from the Amistad de Rues case, and what Judge Story says or omits to say in it, upon the Alabama or Georgia question, is, to our thinking, a more disingenuous proceeding, if possible, on Sir Roundell's part, than to attempt to distinguish between a privateer and a public ship of war, in the way we have noticed. What the American court had before it was as if the Alabama — supposing her to have been illegally equipped in British territory — had voluntarily carried one of her prizes into Liverpool, and then the American owner of the prize having reclaimed her *with damages*, the question had arisen in the English court whether she should be restored simply, *in specie*, or with additional damages for detention and plunderage. Judge Story's decision (on behalf of the court) was, that it should simply be a restoration in specie; and he then goes on to say, that it is not for the neutral court to go into the question of wrongs, as between the belligerents, committed out of the court's jurisdiction, nor the grounds of the capture, &c.; — the court's business simply was to decide the question of restitution or non-restitution.

This being the attitude of the case in judgment, who could for a moment reasonably suppose that the presiding judge had in mind the question how the British crown, in its executive capacity, ought to deal with an Alabama or a Georgia, when a vessel answering to the antecedents of either should be making application for permission to re-enter the port of Liverpool? It was no more germane to the occasion for Judge Story to read a lecture about the international or executive duty of granting or withholding hospitality in the supposed case of application for asylum, than it would have been for the British judge, holding cognizance of the Alabama prize-question, as just suggested, to have gone off into a general disquisition upon the expediency of the Crown's observing neutrality at all between the two belligerents. All the business of the neutral tribunal in such case was, as Judge Story says, "to fairly execute its own laws, and give no asylum to the property unjustly captured." He speaks, to be sure, of "neutral *nation*" where we use "neutral *tribunal;*" but he is plainly treating of judicial, and not of executive functions, and by *nation* means the *courts* of a nation.

So interpreted, it seems to us a monstrous stretch of construction for the Attorney-General to find, in this *dictum* of Judge Story's in the Amistad de Rues case, any justification, either for admitting the Georgia into Liverpool, or for refusing to make indemnity for the piratical plunderings of the Alabama. Because in these six lines of Judge Story's — so runs the Attorney-General's reasoning — when he is treating of a wholly foreign matter, the learned judge is silent about stating the principles which should govern the cases of the Georgia and the Alabama, therefore the English are at liberty to do as they like in regard to both. As if, because the Lord's prayer omits to forbid stealing, therefore one may commit larceny at discretion ; or, to make the case more parallel to that of the Alabama, as if, because the ten commandments only forbid coveting a man's ox, &c., and are silent about a nation's coveting another nation's commerce, Great Britain is fully justified in helping herself to American commerce through the medium of the Alabama.

But supposing that we accept Judge Story's dictum as a generalization, and as one of the ten commandments of neutral law, is Sir Roundell Palmer prepared to argue, after his experience in the conduct of the Alexandra trial, that England herself has furnished a very notable specimen of "fairly executing her own laws," in that celebrated legal *mistrial*, or, as we might justly call it, *legal farce?* And had he no misgivings, when he dwelt upon the duty of "affording no asylum to property unjustly captured," that his Government might be held, by that formula, to a very different course of action from what it seems to have adopted, in regard to the Alabama's prizes, the Tuscaloosa and the Sea Bride ?

In truth, in all the Attorney-General's copious citations of American authorities, the Amistad dictum, as well as others, in justification of the reception of the Georgia, he seems to forget his own admission, contained in an earlier stage of his argument, that the question was not one of juridical duty, but of political expediency. "I have not the least doubt" — he emphatically asserts — " that we have a right, if we thought [should think] fit, to exclude any particular ship or class of ships ; " " but such power is simply discretionary," &c. Now, on his own view of the issue, as thus stated, for the Attorney-General to foist in such a dictum of Judge Story's as we have just considered, uttered when the only question under adjudication was of restoring a prize specifically, or of restoring her with damages, is, to our thinking, either making too much of the learned judge's declaration, or losing sight of the speaker's own argument.

We will only add, that " Historicus," to whom, perhaps, Sir Roundell Palmer is indebted for the first mention of the Amistad de Rues case, in his letter of November 7th, gives no such extended application of Judge Story's dictum as the Attorney-General elaborates, but simply classifies the decision in the case under the head of prize-procedure ; — a question of practice rather than of principle ; and that the case itself does not seem to have been thought worth citing at all, either by counsel or court, in the great case of *The Nereyda*, which we have just noticed, and where Judge Story spoke for himself, practically, about judicial interference between belligerents, in a manner flatly contradicting this supposed inclination of his authority.

Can Sir Roundell Palmer, then, in view of the American precedents, which we have cited in detail, or to which we have barely referred him, — in his capacity as a man or as a conscientious jurist, — adhere to his declaration, " I say, then, that we have done all that authority requires us to do," in not ordering the Georgia out of British ports ? Does he believe that such statesmanship as dictated the expulsion of the Little Democrat, the seizure of the Cassius, the indictment of Henfield, the punishment of Guinet, the dismantling of the Cornelia, the seizure of Le Vainqueur de Bastille, in Washington's Administration ; — or such jurisprudence as refused to be beguiled into " a fraudulent neutrality disgraceful to our government," by such shifts as were attempted in the cases of the Gran Para, the Monte Allegre, the Nereyda, &c., at the period of the South American contests, — would ever have refused to inquire into the antecedents of an illegally-equipped, British-registered Confederate rover, like the Georgia, where the only question was one of friendly and complimentary admission into a neutral port? Had we had upon our hands "the scandal and reproach" of an Alabama and a Florida outfit; had we had an Alexandra, a Pampero, and a Rappahannock case, all emanating from the lawlessness of this same meddlesome and aggressive belligerent Confederacy, to try our patience; — should we have had much hesitation in putting the Georgia upon the list of Genet's privateers, or issuing a second Cassius circular, commanding her instant seizure?

But American authority does not justify it, says the Attorney-General, and it is not worth while to inquire into what is right in the matter — "the question is only one of expediency." And then Sir Roundell Palmer goes off into a fictitious bill of grievances about Irish recruiting, and hopes that no irritation will be excited among the Americans by his attempting to make two *wrongs* equal to one *right*.

We suspect that the true key to this seeming blind perversity of thought and speech on behalf of the law-adviser of the ministry, is to be found in that phrase which the Attorney-General drops, when he says, "I must endeavor to show that the conduct which had been pursued by Her Majesty's Government has been that which the country had a right to expect." That was the task put upon him; — the official defence of the doings of his associates: — The same task which he undertook in his speech of March 27th of last year, when he was called upon to justify the escape of the Alabama; and a speech framed upon precisely the same model as this of May 13th. There, in like manner, the Attorney-General wondered at the irritation of the Americans at what Earl Russell has since admitted was "a scandal and a reproach;" and there, as here, we believe it was the troublesome shade of the Alabama — a ghost which will not down — that came athwart his mental vision to pervert his juridical conscience. The Alabama delinquency was a sin which he must by no manner of means confess; and so he takes especial pains here to say again that it was no sin at all.

We trust that Sir Roundell Palmer will not go through his political and official career (so far as he is called upon to advise upon American affairs), with this millstone of the Alabama reclamation about his neck. Let him abandon it for a bad job, and advising its settlement on some terms of compromise, or other, — admitting partial or accidental blame on the part of his Government — begin a new theory of American policy, worthy of his eminent abilities as a juridical statesman, and his high reputation for integrity and probity as a man. We have been led to expect as much from his manly and straightforward prosecution of the Alexandra case, and from his just — if not generous — tone toward American judges and jurists in many of his recent parliamentary and public speeches.

V.

RETROSPECT OF THE ALABAMA CASE.—HER ESCAPE THE RESULT OF BRITISH TREACHERY AND OFFICIAL CONNIVANCE OR NEGLIGENCE.

WE are sorry to pass under the shade of the Alabama case, again, in this Georgia discussion. We should not have done so, but for the Attorney-General's importing it into this speech — he, all the while, wondering at "the extraordinary and extravagant demands" of the Americans on account of damage done by the Alabama and similar vessels, which render it," as he says, "infinitely more difficult for us, at their request, to do any thing resting on our own discretion, and which we are not bound to do in law;" and also expressing the hope that this statement of his will not give offence to them "because," as he asseverates, "it is true, and because it is important that the matter should be understood."

Since Sir Roundell Palmer thus refers back to the old root of the Alabama bitterness, in part justification of the ministerial decision to admit the Georgia, we invite his attention to a grave error of his own, touching that same root of bitterness, which in our judgment goes to the very marrow of that controversy, and which we hope he will correct before wondering again at the irritation which Americans feel, when they hear that case cited as a specimen of British honor and neutral honesty. We once had occasion to notice the error in the columns of an American journal, and now reprint our former exposition of it, as appropriate to the present occasion. Sir Roundell Palmer's grave mistake consists in stating that orders were issued for seizing the Alabama on the 29th day of July (1862), the day of her escape, and in his not admitting at the same time — if this statement were true — that the

Collector of Liverpool had those orders in his pocket a day and a half, and never lifted a finger to execute them when the Alabama was within his reach, and when he was called upon by the American consul to prevent her escape. Here is the newspaper article:

THE CASE OF THE ALABAMA.

It is well known that the British ministry have made several elaborate attempts, both in State despatches and in Parliamentary debates, to throw off the blame of the escape of the Alabama, by showing that they issued an order to seize her, which reached Liverpool too late, or after the Alabama had already sailed. But we assert, in the face of this, that for more than thirty-six hours after the order for seizure is said to have been issued, she lay undisturbed within the control of the admiralty, and during that time shipped forty or fifty men for her crew, gunpowder and materials for gun-carriages, under the very eyes of the Custom-house authorities. Further, we assert, that, when she first made a show of getting out of the reach of the Custom-house jurisdiction, she did so in consequence of information, privately conveyed to her in advance, of the resolution of the Cabinet to detain her.

On the last point, to which we do not attach so much importance, because it rests upon a statement coming from a Confederate source, and therefore may be a Confederate lie, we will only say, that, in the published account of the cruise of the Alabama, written by one G. S. Fullam, entitled " Our Cruise in the Confederate States' War-Steamer Alabama — The Private Journal of an Officer," the writer, who is an Englishman, and who, we have seen it stated, is the son of an English clergyman, alleges, in reference to the hurried clearing out of the Alabama from her anchorage in Moelfra Bay (forty miles below Liverpool, on the Welsh coast, where she had dropped down on the morning of July 29, 1862), that " our unceremonious departure was owing to the fact of news being received to the effect that the customs' authorities had orders to board and detain us that morning." If this be true, who gave the news of the determination of the Cabinet? And what sort of neutrality is that, which forewarns a criminal offender that process is out after him and that he had better fly?

But the other point is more incontrovertible, and rests for its authenticity on published diplomatic papers, both English and American. The Solicitor-General, Sir Roundell Palmer (now Attorney-General), speaking in debate in the House of Commons on the 27th of March, 1863, and defending the Ministry with all his power from the charge of having been remiss in permitting the escape of the Alabama, says of Earl Russell's connection with the affair: "He told Mr. Adams on the 28th [of July] that the law-officers of the crown were consulted. He got their opinion on the 29th, and that very same day a telegraphic message was sent down to stop the ship." (*London Times*, March 28.) So, the new Solicitor-General, Collier, addressing his constituents at Plymouth, on the 17th of October following, says: "The government issued the necessary orders [for seizing the Alabama], but unfortunately the vessel escaped by stratagem on that very day." (*Times*, October 19.) Thus, the two legal representatives of the British ministry in the House of Commons say, and with the greatest exactness as to dates, in order to clear the government from imputation of negligence, that the order to seize the Alabama issued July 29, and that she unfortunately escaped that very day.

Now in the "History of the cruise of the Alabama," which we have just quoted, Second Officer Fullam states (p. 4): "At 9:15 A. M. of the 29th of July, 1862, we weighed anchor and proceeded slowly down the Mersey, anchoring in Moelfra Bay, having on board relatives and friends of the builders, both ladies and gentlemen. Our ostensible object in sailing was to go on a trial trip, and the presence of the ladies and gentlemen gave a certain color to the report. In the evening we transferred our visitors to a steam-tug. We remained here, shipping hands, &c., *until* 2 *A. M. of the* 31*st*, when we got under weigh, ostensibly bound for Nassau."

As further showing the whereabouts of the Alabama after

July 29th, there is, among the papers published in the English Blue Books for 1862, by order of the House of Commons, a letter signed W. H. Smith, Collector at Beaumaris [a Welsh town on Moelfra Bay], which states, that the Alabama lay at anchor in that bay *from* 7½ *P. M. July* 29*th, to about* 3 *A. M. July* 31*st*, and that during that time the steam-tug Hercules went alongside and put people on board the Alabama. There can be, therefore, no doubt, from official sources, that the Alabama lay at anchor upwards of thirty-six hours at Moelfra Bay, within the jurisdiction of the Collector of Beaumaris, and that during that time she was supplied with men from the tug Hercules, which, Fullam says, took up her pleasure party again to Liverpool.

Now, were the English government apprised of this, and did they take any steps to seize her in Moelfra Bay? Leaving out of view Fullam's statement, that, instead of being seized, they were apprised in advance that the order was coming, we ask our readers to consider whether the following letter from our vigilant consul at Liverpool — Thomas H. Dudley, Esq. — to the collector of that port, amounts to sufficient notice, or not, of the movements of the future pirate? This letter also appears in the published diplomatic documents of both countries:

"U. S. Consulate, Liverpool, July 30, 1862.

"Sir, — Referring to my previous communication to you on the subject of the gunboat 'No. 290,' fitted out by Mr. Laird at Birkenhead, I beg now to inform you that she left the Birkenhead dock on Monday night, (the 28th) and yesterday morning (the 29th) left the river, accompanied by the steam-tug Hercules. The Hercules returned last evening, and her master stated that the gunboat was cruising off Point Lynas, that she had six guns on board, concealed below and was taking powder from another vessel.

"The Hercules is now alongside the Woodside Landing Stage, taking on board men (forty or fifty), beams, evidently for gun carriages and other things, to convey down to the gunboat. A quantity of cutlasses was taken on board on Friday last.

"These circumstances all go to confirm the representations heretofore made to you about this vessel, in the face of which I cannot but regret she has been permitted to leave the port, and I report them to you that you may take such steps as you may deem necessary to prevent this flagrant violation of neutrality.

"Respectfully, I am your obedient servant,
"THOMAS H. DUDLEY, *Consul*.
"THE COLLECTOR OF CUSTOMS, Liverpool."

That nothing may be wanting to complete the chain of proof in our case, we will add, that Earl Russell, by a communication to Mr. Adams, dated July 4, 1862, had expressly authorized Mr. Dudley to communicate directly with the custom authorities at Liverpool.[1] So, then, if our readers follow us, the order to seize the Alabama (by telegraph) was in the hands of the Liverpool collector July 29. Mr. Dudley's letter, as above, was put into his hands the next day — July 30. The steam-tug Hercules was at that moment at the Birkenhead dock, and there she doubtless remained several hours, loading up with men and munitions of war, as indicated by Mr. Dudley. The Alabama herself lay, something like a day after this, only forty miles off, and within sight of the Welsh coast. The tug went down and delivered her consignment of men and munitions of war in due course, under the eyes of the Liverpool collector and with the order for her detention in his pocket, and not a finger was lifted to make the seizure; and now Earl Russell, without any reference to this last crowning act in the farce, admits that the rest of the case, up to that point, was "a scandal and a reproach."

Do not fair-minded Englishmen agree with us, that if ever a government ought to be affected with the consequences of culpable neglect of duty by its agents, here is a case for the application of the principle?

Since the appearance of the above article (probably with no reference whatever to it), Earl Russell has taken occasion to say in the House of Lords, in debate on the 29th of April last, that the first statement above put forth on the authority of the Alabama's historiographer is an undoubted fact: that informa-

---

[1] "Correspondence respecting the Alabama," &c., p. 5. Earl Russell to Mr. Adams, July 4.

tion of the proposed seizure of the Alabama *was* communicated in advance, and so, that she was enabled to escape. — " How the owner came to be informed of it," says his Lordship, according to the *Times* of April 30th, " it is impossible for me to say; there certainly seems to have been treachery on the part of some one furnishing the information."

Now, we submit to the Attorney-General, this puts an ugly aspect on the British side of the Alabama question, at the start ; that the Government, having decided that she ought to be seized, and having given the necessary orders for seizing her, are compelled to admit, that she escaped by treachery, official or ministerial.

But since penning the above article, a sight of the English Blue Books for 1863 — to which we then had not access, but as to which we borrowed our information from an English publication of " Correspondence relating to the Alabama," which we supposed complete — shows us a patent conflict of statement between the Attorney-General and the Liverpool Collector, Mr. S. Price Edwards, as to the date of the order for the seizure of the Alabama. We find Collector Edwards writing to the Commissioners of Customs, under date of August 1, 1862[1] : — " The ' 290 ' has left the port; but should an opportunity offer, she shall be seized in conformity *with telegram of yesterday*," [31st.]

So that, according to Collector Edwards, he did not get his order (*by telegram*) till July 31st. Is not this a pretty important variance from Sir Roundell's assertion, made with so much circumstance in the face of the British and American nations, that Earl Russell " got their [the law officers'] opinion on the 29th, and that very same day a telegraphic message was sent down to stop the ship?" Was it " treachery," again, we would inquire, that prevented the communication of this order to the Liverpool Collector for two days, or is there a question of veracity between the two Governmental officials?

We suspect that the Collector is in the right, and that Sir

---

[1] " The Alabama Correspondence between the Commissioners of Customs, &c., relating to the vessel No. 290, since known as the Alabama," — " printed by vote of H. C., March 24, 1863," p. 10.

Roundell has inadvertently made a mistake, which he will have at some day to correct; but with such a grave mistake lying at his door, we should hardly have expected him (in candor) to reiterate the error in this Georgia debate, and then hope to justify it by generalities from Judge Story, or by counter charges of Irish recruiting by the Kearsage. Had he read an able English criticism in the London Law Magazine for May, 1863, on the importance of these dates in this great international law-suit, to say nothing of the New York-journal article, which possibly may have been brought to his notice, we fancy he could not heedlessly have repeated his old error in such terms as he made use of in his late speech of the 13th of May:—
" As to the next ship, the Alabama, I need not repeat what was said upon a former occasion, as to the steps which were taken by the Government, after full consideration of the evidence laid before them, with a view to arrest that vessel. It is well known to the House and to the country, that orders to that effect were given, but the ship *in the mean time*, made her escape."

Is it true, that the Alabama escaped " *in the mean time?* " — i. e., as Sir Roundell would imply, between the issuing the order, and the time when it ought to have reached her?

We have already noticed, that Mr. Collector Edwards says that the order reached him (for the first time?) July 31st,— two days after she left the dock, and some hours after she had flown from Moelfra bay. Now, looking at the diplomatic correspondence which passed between the two governments relating to her, we find Earl Russell writing to Mr. Adams, under date of September 22, 1862,[1] " the report of the law-officers was not received until the 29th of July, and on the same day, a telegraphic message was forwarded to Her Majesty's Government, stating that the vessel had sailed that morning. [That is, news came *from* Liverpool, that she had already escaped.] Instructions were then despatched to Ireland to detain the vessel should she put into Queenstown, and similar instructions have been sent to the governor of the Bahamas in case of her visiting Nassau. It appears, however, that the

---

[1] " American Papers relating to Foreign Affairs," p. 200.

vessel did not go to Queenstown, as had been expected, and nothing has been since heard of her movement."

In the Blue Book for 1863, containing correspondence respecting the Alabama, &c., *ut sup.* we also find, at page 10, the following:

"31*st July*, 1862, *at about half-past seven*, *P. M.* Telegrams were sent to the Collectors at Liverpool and Cork, pursuant to Treasury Order, dated 31st July, to seize the gunboat (290) should she be within either of those ports.

"Similar telegrams to the officers at Beaumaris and Holyhead were sent on the morning of the 1st August. They were not sent on the 31st July, the telegraphic offices in those districts being closed."

Reading these two citations from the diplomatic documents, in connection with Collector Edwards' affirmation, that he did not receive his order to seize the Alabama till July 31st, we are compelled to conclude that the Attorney-General is wrong, and the Collector right, about the disputed and important fact in controversy. The telegraphic message was *not* " sent down to stop the ship on the 29th of July," and she *did not* " escape in the mean time." We trust, then, that the Attorney-General will take occasion the next time that he revives the Alabama contention, to correct his inadvertence (if it be such) as to the date of the first effort made to detain her, and not attempt to strengthen the case of his Government as to the use of due diligence, by the misstatement that the Government moved two days sooner than it did.

Having thus attempted to set right Sir Roundell Palmer's supposed inaccuracy, and so far seemingly admitted away the point of our own newspaper criticism, we are constrained to notice the still worse position, if possible, in which the correction leaves the Attorney-General's official principals, than the mistaken plea which he originally set up in their behalf. That plea left a heavy weight of responsibility at Collector Edwards' door: — " The ministry acted with due diligence and in good faith; but the Alabama gave the Custom-house authorities the slip," — was the tone of Sir Roundell Palmer's apology in March, 1863: — " The high officials were blameless."

Now let us look at the facts lying at the door of the high officials, and which Sir Roundell Palmer might justly imagine (without any great stretch of charity) would naturally irritate Americans, and without any "extravagant pretensions," lead them to think that they had a just claim for indemnity against England on account of the Alabama.

It is entirely conceded, on the new version of facts, that no telegram went off from the Treasury or the Foreign Office for any interference with the Alabama, for nine, or at least seven days, after a confessedly sufficient case had been laid before the Government by Mr. Adams.[1] The Ministry allege, in excuse, that she escaped the fifth day after; namely, the 29th, of which they admit full notice on that same day, and probably within a few hours. — What steps did they take, thereupon, to repair the error?

The vessel was expected to touch next at Queenstown, as Earl Russell says in his letter of the 22d of September, as we have quoted. Meanwhile, as was probable, she would linger on the North coast of Wales. Now, when was the telegraph put in motion to affect Queenstown, or the ports of Beaumaris, &c.? — The State paper, just quoted, affirms that it was not till *half past seven in the evening of the* 31*st*, that "telegrams were sent to the Collectors at Liverpool and Cork (Queenstown), pursuant to Treasury Order, dated July 31, to seize the gunboat (290), should she be within either of those ports. Similar telegrams to the officers of Beaumaris and Holyhead were sent *on the morning of the* 1*st August*. They were not sent on the 31st July, the telegraph offices to those districts being closed."

Now, was it "treachery" or "culpable slackness in the Executive" (within Historicus's admission of what would render England liable for the torts of the Alabama), which caused the neglect to send off the Welsh telegrams *for two days, — and till so late an hour of the second day, that the telegraph was not used till the third day,* — *after the information of the criminal's escape from legal process had been communicated*

---

[1] Mr. Adams, it will be remembered, had forwarded his preliminary proofs of the illegal outfit of the Alabama, as early as July 22, and "completed his evidence" including Mr. Collier's (now the Solicitor-General's) opinion of the plain duty of the British Government to stop her, and put it into Earl Russell's hands, as early as July 24.

to the authorities? Might not any American justly conclude, that those two entire days and part of the third, were designedly given as lee-way to the Confederate cruiser, to make sure her escape?

But looking more particularly to the pretended effort to cause her seizure at Queenstown or Cork (the former being, as is well known, the outer port to the latter), what dispassionate observer could fail to draw the inference, that the Ministry, or those who had the execution of the Ministry's orders in charge, intended that the Alabama should escape being seized, if she should touch at Queenstown?

Earl Russell says, in his letter of September 22, above quoted, that she was expected to go to Queenstown. On the morning of July 29, the Foreign Office are notified that she has quitted the Mersey; probably, for the Queenstown destination. The Treasury Order for her seizure is already made out; and telegraphic communication with that point is instantaneous: — How long will it take the Alabama to reach that port in the due course of steam navigation? — Something less than twenty-four hours, as is well known. Now, can the Attorney-General, or any other person in the Cabinet secrets, explain to us, how — consistently with an honest observance of neutrality — *there came to be a lee-way of a day and a half provided for the Alabama to reach Queenstown and get the news of the intention to seize her, before the message was sent off?*

It seems, as Earl Russell admits, that treachery conveyed a message to her down in Moelfra Bay; *did not Executive treachery, at head-quarters, take care, that a premonitory message of her danger should have time to reach her at Queenstown, before any arrival of the order for seizure could become possible?*

We admit that we are treading upon delicate ground in thus raising suspicions about the hidden motives for Cabinet action. But there stand the ugly facts on record: The Alabama escaped, — "a scandal and a reproach" to British neutrality. The order for her seizure was made out on the 29th day of July. No attempt to seize her was made while she lay a day and a half after that time, with full knowledge and within full control of the Government, in Moelfra Bay. It was expected that when she quitted Liverpool she would touch at Queenstown. No telegram was sent to that point to meet her for two days and a half! It was probable that she would linger along the Welsh coast; and no telegrams were sent to its two most important points, Beaumaris and Holyhead, for three days!

Surely, because the British Government have conducted themselves thus, in 1862, it should be no precedent for the smaller and gratuitous insult to the American people, in showing national hospitality to the Georgia, in 1864; and Americans are not to be blamed for feeling sore, that that precedent should be again evoked and held up as the probable constant rule of British action hereafter.

In thus characterizing the Georgia reception, we do not forget that Sir Roundell Palmer attempts feebly to suggest, that it " was afterwards stated that she was likely to be dismantled and sold." Have not the British Government had experience enough of Confederate pretences in speech and pretences in action, in the cases of the Gibraltar, the Florida, the Rappahannock, — to say nothing about the original escape of this same Georgia — to know that the market value of such statements or promises, on the part of the Confederate Government, stands very low? Had the Attorney-General forgotten what Earl Russell, the British Secretary of State for Foreign Affairs, had said in the House of Lords, only a fortnight before his own speech, about the latest case of these pretences, — the Lairds' disclaimer of building the iron-clads for the Confederates? We beg to remind Sir Roundell Palmer of it, if he attaches any weight to this promise of dismantling. Says Earl Russell, according to the report of his speech in the *Times* of April 30 :

" The only thing with which I should be disposed to reproach myself in the present case, is the degree of credulity with which I received the assurances that were made, that the iron-clads were not intended for the Confederate States. The Collector of Customs at Liverpool, Mr. Edwards, said he believed it was never intended to use them for that purpose. The law-officers, on his authority, took the same view. I was at first disposed to share that opinion; but evidence was poured in on me which there was no resisting; and I am convinced that the vessels were originally built for the Confederate States."

And again:

" I might have made a mistake [in causing the seizure of the rams], as it might happen that a policeman in the street, apprehending a man whom he sees quitting a house at three or four o'clock in the morning, with a sack-full of plate, might make a mistake, because it might turn out, singularly enough, that the man seized was the master of the house, who desired to go out at that early hour with a sack of plate on his back. That would be a singular occurrence, certainly; but no one would blame the policeman for having stopped the man."

By way of contrast with this Alabama precedent — to bring our protracted comments to a close — we desire to call the attention of the Attorney-General to three or four additional specimens of American neutrality, of the period of Washington's Administration, — showing our construction of that line of conduct, which, as he admits, ought to be binding on England. These precedents, we believe, will be quite new to most of our English readers; possibly, they may be so to Sir Roundell Palmer himself. At any rate, we are quite sure that he will find them utterly at variance with English action in both the instances of the Alabama and the Georgia.

VI.

AMERICAN TREATMENT OF FRENCH AND BRITISH ALABAMAS IN WASHINGTON'S ADMINISTRATION.

THE first precedent of this class, that we shall give, is stated on the authority of a letter from Mr. Randolph, Secretary of State, to Mr. Jay, our minister to Great Britain, dated August 11, 1794, and is to be found in the State Department at Washington, among the unpublished State documents, to which access is permitted to the public at large, on proper official application. Mr. Randolph's bold challenge of the facts stated in it, is, to our mind, a sufficient guaranty of their authenticity. Mr. Hammond, the British minister, to whom reference is made in the letter, had just received his letters of recall (July 28, 1794), and was then, it is presumed, on his way to England.[1]

"If" [says Mr. Randolph] "Mr. Hammond wishes any new evidence of our unchangeable neutrality, he may be told, — and the British Ministry likewise, — that the militia of Richmond in Virginia, actually marched at a moment's warning, between seventy and eighty miles to seize a vessel, supposed to be under preparation as a French privateer. Resistance was at first apprehended, but it was overawed, and the business completely effected."

Rather a contrast, this, — we submit, — of marching seventy or eighty miles "*at a moment's warning*," and seizing with military force a vessel " *supposed* to be under preparation," and "*completely effecting the business*," — to waiting from June 23d to July 29th, as the British Government did in the case of the Alabama, with Minister Adams and Consul Dudley, spurring them up with constant letters and affidavits of an *actual* equipment, sometimes weekly, but often almost daily or even hourly, and then the Government so " completely ! " effecting the busi-

---

[1] 11 Sparks' " Writings of Washington," p. 42.

ness, that the Alabama was notified of their intention to seize her beforehand, and had gone off before the necessary order issued, and then — when the evil might have been remedied by a subsequent order — postponing the sending of that order to Queenstown for two days and a half, and to the Welch coast for three days!

The next precedent which we shall cite, is one published quite at large in the historical and diplomatic publications of the day, but which does not seem to have attracted the attention it deserves. Its importance begins with its being a case of American neutral action before any Foreign Enlistment Statute had passed, and therefore proceeding upon purely international grounds. It relates to the French privateer, *Republican*, fitted out at New York, and seized by Governor Clinton with military force, on the 8th of June 1793. [The first Foreign Enlistment Act was passed June 5, 1794.]

Here is the fuming protest of the French Consul at New York, M. Hauterive, at the seizure, and his high-flying demand thereon for satisfaction upon Gov. Clinton, which we give as the first piece of this diplomatic history : (1 *Am. State Papers*, pp. 152-3.)

"NEW YORK, June 9, 1793.

"SIR, — I have just been informed, that last night a French vessel, armed for war and ready to hoist sail, has been arrested by authority, and that even the captain has not been permitted to go on board. This strange use of public force against the citizens of a friendly nation, who assemble here to go and defend their brethren, is a signal violation of the laws of neutrality, which I cannot impute but to a misconception which your attention and your equity will not fail to rectify, as soon as you shall be informed of it.

I require, Sir, the authority with which you are clothed, to cause to be rendered to Frenchmen and allies, and I must add, to freemen, of whatever nation they may be, the liberty of flying to the succor of their country. It is not in a country where Frenchmen have spilt their blood in the cause of humanity, that they ought to find in the laws, obstacles to their following yet again the most pleasing of their propensities, and to fulfil the most sacred of their duties.

"HAUTERIVE, — *Consul of the French Republic, New York.*
"To the Governor of the State of New York."

"CONSULATE OF NEW YORK.

" We, Alexander Hauterive, Consul of the Republic of France to the United States, at New York, certify, that in consequence of a requisition made by us to the Mayor of New York, and to the Governor of the State of the same name, dated 9th June current, to obtain a replevy of the detention, made by authority in this port, of a French vessel, called the Republican, belonging to Louis A. H. Caritat, and commanded by the citizen Orset, the Governor of the said State replied to us by a letter, under his signature, that it was in conformity to the injunction of the President of the United States, that he had ordered a detachment of the militia of this State to detain the said vessel, until the President of the United States should be informed of the circumstances of the facts ; upon which we have delivered to him an act certified and signed by us.

" Done in New York, the 10th June, 1793."

"HAUTERIVE,
" *Consul of the Republic of France, at New York.*"

Next in order is the *Cabinet Opinion* of President Washington's three principal Secretaries, justifying the arrest and further detention of the Republican. The latter part of the document embraces another case of seizure, which is so much to the purpose of our general argument, that we do not feel at liberty to omit it. We copy from 4 Hamilton's Works, p. 424:

"CABINET OPINION.

"June 12, 1793.

" The President having required the opinions of the heads of the three departments, on a letter from Governor Clinton of the 9th instant, stating that he had taken possession of the sloop Polly, now called the Republican, which was arming and equipping, and manning by French and other citizens to cruise against some of the belligerent powers, and they having met and deliberated thereon, are unanimously of opinion, that Governor Clinton be desired to deliver over to the civil power the said vessel and her appurtenances to be dealt with according to law ; and that the Attorney of the United States for the District of New York be desired to have such proceedings at law instituted, as well concerning the said vessel and her appurtenances, as against all the persons, citizens, or aliens, participating in the armament or object thereof, as he shall think will be most effectual for punishing the said offenders, and preventing the said vessel and appurtenances from being applied to the destined purpose; and that, if he shall be of opinion that no judiciary process will be sufficient to prevent such application of the vessel to the hostile purpose intended, that then the Governor be desired to detain her by force till the further advice of the General Government can be taken.

The President having also required the same opinion on the memorial of the British Minister of the 11th inst., on the subject of the British brigantine Catharine, captured by the French frigate, the Embuscade, within the limits of the protection of the United States, as is said, and carried into the harbor of New York, they are of opinion unanimously, that the Governor of New York be desired to seize the said vessel in the first instance, and then deliver her over to the civil power, and that the Attorney of the United States for the District of New York be instructed to institute proceedings at law in the proper court, for deciding whether the said capture was made within the limits of the protection of the United States, and for delivering her up to her owners, if it be so decided; but that if it shall be found that no court may take cognizance of the said question, then the said vessel to be detained by the Governor, until the further orders of the General Government can be had thereon.

"TH. JEFFERSON, *Sec'y of State.*
"H. KNOX, *Sec'y of War.*
"ALEXANDER HAMILTON, *Sec'y of Treasury.*"

We give, next, Mr. Genet's official demand for restitution, which for once observed a show of respectfulness. We suppose that he had been apprised of the energetic advice given to the President by his Cabinet: (1 *Am. State Papers*, 152.)

"*The Citizen Genet, Minister of the Republic of France, to Mr. Jefferson, Secretary of State.*

"PHILADELPHIA, June 14, 1793.

"SIR,— You will see by the papers hereto annexed, that, in contempt of the treaties which unite the French and Americans, that, in contempt of the law of nations, civil and judiciary officers of the United States have permitted themselves to stop, at Philadelphia, the sale of vessels taken by an armed French galliot, and, at New York, have opposed the sailing of a French vessel [The Republic] commissioned by the Executive Council of the Republic of France. I request you Sir, to inform the President of the United States of these facts; to let him know that they have used his name in committing those infractions of the laws and treaties of the United States; and engage him to develope, in the present circumstances, all the authority which the people of the United States have confided to him to enforce the execution of the laws and treaties.

"Not doubting, Sir, the purity of the President's sentiments, I hope to obtain immediately, from the aid of his good offices and energy, restitution, with damages and interest, of the French prizes arrested and seized at Philadelphia, by an incompetent judge, under an order which I ought to believe not genuine; and the like restitution, with damages and interest, of the vessels stopped and seized at New York.

"It is through the intervention of the public ministers, that affairs of the nature which produce my present complaints and reclamations, ought to be treated. As the representative of a people, generous and confident in their friends, I have already given proofs of the sentiments with which they are animated, in causing to be restored, without examination, on the requisition of the Federal Government, the English ship Grange, taken by a vessel of the Republic. I shall, in all my conduct, show an equal deference; but at the same time, Sir, I should expect from your Government, all the support, which I at present stand in need of, to defend, in the bosom of the United States, the interests, the rights, and the dignity of the French nation, which persons, on whom time will do us justice, are laboring secretly to misrepresent. "GENET."

To this Mr. Jefferson replied, three days later, in one of his most emphatic and memorable letters. Considering the circumstances under which this reply was made, — that it was written by the acknowledged head of the French party in our political divisions, and the former representative of the American Confederation to the court of Louis XVI, — that it was written to favor the British with whom we had so shortly before been at war, and to thwart and oppose the French who had so recently sided with us in the struggle for Independence, — but, more especially, that it was written to throw down the gauntlet of defiance to one of the great powers of Europe, at a time when we had not a sailor nor a ship to back up our pretensions, — we submit that it is one of the most creditable specimens of national assertion of an honest neutrality on record. Certainly it is quite in contrast with the balancing of the *pros* and *cons* which belong to the Attorney-General's statement of reasons for admitting the Georgia : (1 *Am. State Papers*, 154.)

"*Mr. Jefferson, Secretary of State, to M. Genet, Minister Plenipotentiary of France.*

"PHILADELPHIA, June 17, 1793.

"SIR, — I shall now have the honor of answering your letter of the 8th instant, and so much of that of the 14th (both of which have been laid before the President) as relates to a vessel armed in the port of New York, and about to depart from thence, but stopped by order of the Government. And here I beg leave to premise, that the case supposed in your letter, of a vessel arming merely for her own defence, and to repel unjust aggressions, is not that in question, nor that on which I mean to answer; because not having yet happened, as far as is known to the Government, I have no instructions on the subject. The case in question, is that of a vessel armed, equipped, and manned, in a port of the United States, for the purpose of committing hostilities on nations at peace with the United States.

"As soon as it was perceived that such enterprises would be attempted, orders to prevent them were despatched to all the States and ports of the Union. In consequence of these, the Governor of New York, receiving information that a sloop called the Republican, was fitting out, arming and manning in the port of New York, for the express and sole purpose of cruising against certain nations with whom we are at peace, that she had taken her guns and ammunition aboard, and was on the point of departure, seized the vessel. That the Governor was not mistaken in the previous indications of her object, appears by the subsequent avowal of Citizen Hauterive, consul of France at that port, who in a letter to the Governor reclaims her as a vessel armed for war, &c., [in the terms above given].

"This transaction being reported to the President, orders were immediately sent to deliver over the vessel and the persons concerned in the enterprise, to the tribunals of the country; that if the act was of those forbidden by the law, it might be punished; if it was not forbidden, it might be so declared; and all persons apprised of what they might or might not do.

"This, we have reason to believe, is the true state of the case, and it is a repetition of that which was the subject of my letter of the 5th instant, which animadverted not merely on the single fact of the granting commissions of war by one nation within the territory of another, but on the aggregate of facts; for it states the opinion of the President to be, that "The arming and equipping vessels in the ports of the United States, to cruise against nations with whom they are at peace, was incompatible with the sovereignty of the United States; that it made them instrumental to the annoyance of those nations, and thereby tended to commit their peace." And this opinion is still conceived to be not contrary to the principles of natural law, the usage of nations, the engagements which unite the two people, nor the proclamation of the President, as 'you seem to think. . . . You think, Sir, that this opinion is also contrary to the law of nature and usage of nations. We are of opinion, it is dictated by that law and usage; and this had been very maturely inquired into before it was adopted as a principle of conduct. But we will not assume the exclusive right of saying what that law and usage is. Let us appeal to enlightened and disinterested judges. None is more so than Vattel. He says, &c. . . . The testimony of these and others writers on the law and usage of nations, with your own just reflections on them, will satisfy you that the United States, in prohibiting all the belligerent Powers from equipping, arming, and manning vessels of war in their ports, have exercised a right and a duty, with justice and with great moderation. By our treaties with several of the belligerent powers, which are a part of the laws of our land, we have established a style of peace with them. But without appealing to treaties, we are at peace with them all by the law of nature; for, by nature's law, man is at peace with man, till some aggression is committed, which, by the same law, authorizes one to destroy another, as his enemy. For our citizens, then, to commit murders and depredations on the members of nations at peace with us, or to combine to do it, appeared to the Executive and those whom they consulted, as much against the laws of the land, as to murder or rob, or combine to murder or rob, its own citizens; and as much to require punishment, if done within their limits, where they have a territorial jurisdiction, or on the high seas where they have a personal jurisdiction, that is to say, one which reaches their own citizens only; this being an appropriate part of each nation, or an element where all have a common jurisdiction.

" So say our laws, as we understand them, ourselves. To them the appeal is made; and whether we have construed them well or ill, the constitutional judges will decide. Till that decision shall be obtained, the Government of the United States must pursue what they think right, as is their duty.

" On the first attempt that was made, the President was desirous of involving in the censures of the law, as few as might be. Such of the individuals only, therefore, as were citizens of the United States, were singled out for prosecution. But this second attempt being after full knowledge of what was done on the first, and indicating a disposition to go on in opposition to the laws, they are to take their course against all persons concerned, whether citizens or aliens; the latter, while within our jurisdiction, and enjoying the protection of the laws, being bound to obedience, and to them to avoid distubances of our peace within, or acts which would commit it without, equally as our citizens are.

"I have the honor to be, &c.,
"TH. JEFFERSON."

We next give an extract from the British Minister, Mr. Hammond, thanking the Federal Government for their firmness in this matter. It is contained in a letter from him to Mr. Jefferson, under date of June 14, 1793. We copy from unpublished documents in the State department at Washington, to which access is permitted to the public at large, as stated above:

. . . . "I beg to acknowledge my sense of the very dignified conduct of the Governor of the State of New York, in the transaction which you have been so obliging as to communicate to me [the seizure of the Republican], and from which I derive the firmest confidence that the measures taken by the Executive Government of the United States to prevent a repetition of enterprises similar to that which has thus been pressed at New York, will be equally efficacious in other ports of the Union.

GEORGE HAMMOND."

The final termination of this seizure of the Republican, was, that she was discharged from custody on the fifth of July 1794, upwards of a year after her arrest; "the object of that arrest"— (stated to be the prevention of her cruising against friendly powers) — "having been attained" (probably by dismantling), and upon the condition of the owners discharging their suit against the Governor of New York. (*Opinions of Attorney-Generals*, vol. 1, p. 48.)

The next precedent which we shall cite, relates to the general principle underlying both the cases of the Georgia and the Alabama, that no neutral nation has a right to make its ports a *base of hostile operations* against a belligerent. If, by chance, the Georgia, instead of being dismantled should *happen* to renew her warlike equipment in the port of Liverpool, and take to the sea again as a Confederate cruiser, we suppose that there could not be much doubt that it would afford the American Government just ground of complaint that England would thereby have afforded its ports, in this instance, for a base of hostile operations. In regard to the Alabama, " Historicus " has already virtually admitted, in that same letter which Mr. Baring quoted, but in a part not included in his quotation, that the doings of the Alabama at the Cape of Good Hope show that England has allowed that portion of her territory to be made a base of hostile operations. In Historicus's view, her concession seems to have tolerated an *habitual*, rather than an *accidental* use of those ports, by the Alabama, within Lord Stowell's distinction in the *Twee Gebræders*.

As showing how carefully the United States guarded their neutrality under this head, we copy the following Circular to the Governors of the States, issued about the time of the first Foreign Enlistment Act, and which we have never seen noticed before. We find it in 1 *Am. State Papers*, p. 608:

" CIRCULAR.

" *The Secretary of State, to the Governors of the several States.*

" DEPARTMENT OF STATE, April 16, 1795.

" SIR, — As it is contrary to the law of nations that any of the belligerent powers should commit hostility on the waters which are subject to the exclusive jurisdiction of the United States, so ought not the ships of war, belonging to any belligerent power, to take *a station in these waters in order to carry on hostile expeditions from thence*. I do myself the honor, therefore, of requesting of your Excellency, in the name of the President of the United States, that as often as a fleet, squadron, or ship, of any belligerent nation, shall clearly and unequivocally use the rivers or other waters of ———, *as a station, in order to carry on hostile expeditions from thence*, you will cause to be notified to the commander thereof, that the President deems such conduct to be contrary to the rights of our neutrality; and that *a demand of retribution will be urged upon their Government for prizes which may be made in consequence thereof.*

" A standing order to this effect may probably be advantageously placed in the hands of some confidential officer of the militia; and I must entreat you to instruct him to write by the mail to this Department, immediately upon the happening of any case of the kind.

"I have the honor to be, &c.,

"EDM. RANDOLPH."

We commend this Circular to the attention of those candid Englishmen, who believe, in common with all American writers who have treated of the subject, that England's toleration of the home-ports for the equipment of the Alabama, the Florida, &c., constitutes the making of England herself a base of hostile operations. It will be seen that a single "ship" was treated by the American precedent as amounting to a hostile "expedition " (of the-text-writers), and that, at that early day, the Americans gave notice, that they should demand reparation for captures which followed in consequence of such infringement of their neutrality, and that, too, without any limitation whether such prizes were brought back again into their ports, or not.

The next and last precedent which we shall cite, is chiefly important, because it relates to an *English* infringement of our neutrality; not the only one, by any means, of that period, but the only one which we happen to have at hand, where the American Government fulfilled its duty of *prevention*, by seizing the offending vessel before it got away from the port of its illegal equipment. The seizure in this case was also made before the passage of any Foreign Enlistment Act. We quote our precedent on the authority of the statement of Mr. Jefferson, the American Secretary of State, who seems to have communicated the fact of the seizure to the French minister as a proof of our impartiality, and by way of answering his loud complaints of our indulgence towards the English: (1 *Am. State Papers*, p. 159.)

"*Mr. Jefferson, Secretary of State, to Citizen Genet, Minister Plenipotentiary of France.*

"PHILADELPHIA, June 23, 1793.

"SIR, — I have the honor to inform you, that, in consequence of the general orders given by the President, a privateer, fitted out by English subjects within the State of Georgia, to cruise against the citizens of France, has been seized by the Governor of Georgia, and such legal prosecutions are ordered as the case will justify. I beg you to be assured, that the Government will use the utmost vigilance to see that the laws which forbid these enterprises, are carried into execution.

"I have the honor to be, &c.,

"TH. JEFFERSON."

We have not the means of tracing the issue of this case. We suppose that dismantling of the vessel followed, and a dismissal of the prosecution on an abandonment of the undertaking and giving security for future good behavior.

The French minister seems to have been highly delighted at seeing American justice administered in this instance upon English offenders; and by way of returning the compliment, furnishes the American Secretary of State with quite a catalogue of other British privateers, which he says he is informed are fitting out in Charleston, Baltimore, &c., in violation of American neutrality. (See 1 *Am. State Papers*, 159.)

Without stopping to give the French minister's list, or the measures taken by the American Government in consequence of the information, we deem the precedent cited sufficient proof that the English infringed upon our neutrality as well — if not as much — as the French. And this leads us to notice the statement of the Attorney-General's, upon which he lays so much stress, that the Americans, under their precedents of neutrality of Washington's day, confined their restitution of prizes restored, or for which they indemnified, *to prizes brought within American ports;* not extending it to captures made on the high seas, such as are mainly the captures made by the Alabama, and for which the Americans are urging their present claim for indemnity.

The precedent which we have last cited, leads to one sufficient answer, at least, which may be made to Sir Roundell Palmer's point; and that is, that the British would be hardly likely to have insisted on a large rule of indemnity at a time when they were themselves infringing upon American neutrality, and, perhaps, reserved the intention to infringe still further; and so might be shortly held to that measure of justice which they were exacting from others. Thus, to take this last case of equipment in the State of Georgia:—Would it have been worth while to establish a rule of exacting satisfaction from the United States, for all damages done by illegally-equipped French privateers—as well where the prizes were not brought back into American ports, as where they were so brought back—when England herself would have to answer to the United States, after the same measure, for the possible future captures of this Georgia adventurer?

We presume that the Attorney-General has not overlooked the fact, that following the force of this reasoning, or from some inducement or other, the British minister himself, Mr. Hammond, at the very earliest outset of the American neutral era, contended for no broader rule of compensation than that ultimately conceded by the Americans, and now brought forward by the Attorney-General to their prejudice. As this important starting-point of the Alabama contention does not seem to have been at all noticed, as yet, we give Mr. Hammond's letter of the 8th of May, 1793, dated just one month after Genet landed at Charleston, and after he first began his series of hostile equipments, of which that letter was to complain. By way of preface, however, we will first quote three lines from a private letter of Mr. Jefferson's to Colonel (afterwards President) Monroe, written three days before Mr. Hammond's letter, as showing the self-sufficient and arrogant attitude which Great Britain up to this time had manifested towards us.

Mr. Jefferson, writing then to Colonel Monroe, May 5th (3 Jeff. Works, 9–vol., ed. 1861), says:

"Great Britain has as yet not condescended to notice us in any way. No wish expressed of her [our?] neutrality, no answer of any kind to a single complaint for the daily violations committed on our sailors and ships. Indeed, we promise beforehand so fast, that she has not time to ask any thing. We expect Genet daily [at Philadelphia, then the seat of government], &c."

Now Mr. Hammond breaks this dignified and self-sufficient

silence, by the following: [we quote from Wharton's State Trials, p. 50, *note*.]

"*Mr. Hammond to Mr. Jefferson.*

"The undersigned, His Britannic Majesty's Minister Plenipotentiary to the United States of America, has the honor of informing the Secretary of State, that he has received intelligence from His Majesty's Consul at Charleston, South Carolina, that two privateers have been fitted out from that port, under French commissions. They carry six small guns, and are navigated by forty or fifty men, who are for the most part citizens of the United States. One of these privateers left the harbor of Charleston on the 18th ult., and the other was, on the 22d, ready to depart.

"The undersigned does not deem it necessary to enter into any reasoning upon these facts, as he conceives them to be breaches of that neutrality which the United States profess to observe, and direct contraventions of the Proclamation which the President issued upon the 22d of last month. Under this impression, he doubts not that the Executive Government of the United States will pursue such measures as to its wisdom may appear best calculated for repressing such practices in future, and *for restoring to their rightful owners any captures which these particular privateers may attempt to bring into any of the ports of the United States.*

"GEO. HAMMOND.

"The Secretary of State,
"*Philadelphia*, 8th May, 1793."

It will be seen by the last two lines, which we take the liberty of italicizing, that Mr. Hammond demands just the measure of compensation which the Attorney-General objects, afterwards became the measure that was acted upon. This was Mr. Hammond's first starting-point: — *to demand restitution, only, of prizes brought into American ports;* and if he shifted his ground from this, down to September 5th, 1793 (the date of Mr. Jefferson's letter, which became a part of the treaty of 1794), we have yet to learn it from any thing disclosed by the State documents published this side of the water. There was, to be sure, one unimportant particular in which the British minister suggested a modification of his proposal, in his letter of August 30th; and that was, in regard to damages for detention, wastes, &c., of the prize *when actually brought into port*, — a demand, which Mr. Jefferson cheerfully acceded to, in his letter of September 5th (made the basis of article seven of the treaty, as just referred to), and the compliance with which elicited from Mr. Hammond, in his reply of next day, an acknowledgment of its being " perfectly just and satisfactory."

If, then, under the treaty of 1794, no compensation was made by the Americans for prizes illegally captured, unless when brought into their ports, as Sir Roundell Palmer asserts, is it to be taken as any precedent against them, that, at that period, they yielded all that the British, from motives of their own, saw fit to demand?

But there are other important considerations, which, we would suggest, might have operated on the British Government in entering into an arrangement for this limited measure of compensation. Would it not have been below the dignity of the British crown, to expect American public ships of war (of which there were, in fact, none at that day) to do the duty of patrolling the ocean for British protection, and catch these illegally-equipped privateers after they had got out upon the open sea? Would not British pride have revolted at the idea, that her own navy was not sufficient to look after that of the French, or of any other nation that could be named?

Again, would it have been *the fair thing*, at that early day of American nationality, when she had no navy and no marine police of any kind, to ask her to do any thing more than use her best and fairest efforts at compelling neutrality by a *land force?* She did that, time and again, in Virginia, in New York, in Pennsylvania, and in Georgia, as we have already seen; and France, at least, thought her over-zealous in defending neutral sanctities, even with that kind of force. It is, no doubt, with reference to this admitted national weakness, in the time of Washington's administration, that the phrase was so constantly in use in the American State papers of that day, of — " *all the means in our power* " — " to enforce neutrality," " to defend friendly ships in our waters," &c.

But a still more decisive consideration, and one which we hope the Attorney-General will not lose out of sight, in estimating the importance of this ratio of adjustment which he cites, is, that the American vindication of neutrality at that period, was so honest and thorough, that we do not believe it could have entered into the heart even of a diplomatist to make a greater demand for compensation, in the instance of the privateers which got to sea in spite of American watchfulness, than restitution of the specific prizes which those privateers might happen to bring again into American ports. There was, in other words, such a total absence, on their part, of all complicity with the offenders, and of culpable slackness (to use a phrase already quoted) in repressing such enterprizes, that moral justice forbade the notion of exacting from them more than what was within their reach to give back.

We venture to predict, therefore, — without touching on more than the outside merits of this restitution-of-prize question, brought forward so imposingly by Historicus and the Attorney-General — that, if it shall turn out, as they suppose, that no compensation was made under the seventh article of the treaty of 1794, for captures on the high seas, — it will be found that such refusal of compensation was based, either upon the idea, that Mr. Jefferson's letter of September 5th limited the power of the Commissioners to Mr. Hammond's claim of May 8th, or upon the admitted fact, that there was such a total want of complicity or negligence on the part of the United States, in regard to permitting the equipment of these privateers, that natural equity forbade the exaction of any greater indemnity than restitution in specie.

If this latter consideration decided the action of the Commissioners, who passed upon that question of compensation, then, all we have to say, is, that their decision, so far from establishing the American rule of 1793 as a precedent to govern the Alabama claim, is an express decision the other way; — on the footing, that, where there *is* neutral complicity or neutral negligence, there, there *should be* liability over to the belligerent for captures on the high seas, equally as when such captures are brought into the home ports; in other words, there should be liability *for all the injury sustained.*[1]

Having thus digressed entirely beyond what we intended, in commenting on the precedent of the American seizure of the British privateer, engaged in violating our neutrality in 1793 (another *Georgia* case, though not the English " Geor-

---

[1] We should be glad to meet and fully expose, if our limits and the occasion permitted, another mistake of the Attorney-General's, which he has fallen into at pp. 323-4 of his otherwise admirable argument at the law-hearing in the Alexandra case, in regard to the *bona-fide* and complete character of our neutrality in 1793, where he supposes that we made restitution on account of the Lovely Lass, the Prince William Henry, and the Jane of Dublin (mentioned in Mr. Jefferson's letter of September 5th), because we did not use all the means in our power to prevent the cruising of Genet's privateers for a time, for reasons of public policy. Sir Roundell, or his junior, is entirely at fault here. The reason why we abstained from restoring those vessels *in specie,* and instead of it made pecuniary indemnity to Great Britian, was, that we preferred to pay for those vessels to risking a war with France by taking forcible possession of them. Such was the well-established version of the affair, given not only by Mr. Jefferson, but by all the contemporary accounts of the matter. We suppose Sir Roundell will, of course, accept Mr. Hammond's own statement to this effect. Here is what the British minister says, writing to Mr. Jefferson, December 29, 1793, just before the latter retired from the Secretaryship of State:

After acknowledging that he considered the satisfaction offered by the United States, under the terms of the letter of September 5th, "as not dictated more by a sense of avenging its own insulted dignity, than by the desire of compensating individual loss from unauthorized depredations, and from annoyance originally created in, and issuing from, American ports " — he adds, " considering the latter as just as the former, I also concluded, that, as this Government preferred the prohibition of future asylum, and the restitution of, or compensation for, any prizes they might make, *to the suppression of those privateers whilst on their first return to its ports, they were in its power,* &c." — that is, that the United States preferred to pay rather than to suppress or seize by violence certain of those privateers which, by coming back to its ports without warning, seemed to have put themselves in its power, under a guaranty, in honor, of safe anchorage.

It is the first time we ever heard this forbearance, through motives of honor, treated as a charge of complicity against the Federal Government, of purposely letting those privateers continue their depredations, in order to compass certain ends of State policy of their own. The Attorney-General will find that the United States kept up their demand, *as against France,* for the restitution of the Lovely Lass, &c., to the end of the chapter. *See (inter alia),* Am. State Papers, p. 185.

Possibly this error of the Attorney-General may have clouded with suspicion throughout, his estimate of American neutrality in 1793. If so, we shall not regret to have said thus much.

gia" of 1864), and the supposed bearing of the American practice to only restore prizes *in specie*, we have only to say, — in concluding our comments on the Attorney-General's late speech, — that we hope that both he and all his impartial fellow countrymen will bear in mind, that this question of the Georgia and the Alabama is not one of theoretical discussion, as of a dead and buried past, but one which connects itself immediately with passing events and future responsibilities.

As we write, news comes of the continued devastations of the Alabama, coaled, provisioned, and harbored, for the most part, through British friendliness. In view of this and the probable future career of the other Alexandras and Georgias and Rappahannocks, which our allies and kin by blood have in store for us, we are tempted to ask Sir Roundell Palmer, and any other justifiers of these exponents of British neutrality and British civilization, — If so thorough an Englishman as Mr. Harcourt [for once we will take the liberty of dispensing with his *alias*] can so far cast off his class-prejudice as to acknowledge that the Alabama ought to be excluded from British ports, her prizes taken from her when brought into British waters, and the Confederate Government called to account for her repeated violation of British neutrality; — if the British Secretary of State for Foreign Affairs, — occupying a position second to none, perhaps, in the civilized world for influence and importance, and who with political nonchalance can say, in the face of humanity and before high heaven, that " he has no particular sympathy with either party in the American controversy " — can yet deliberately put on record, that the connection of the English nation with the Alabama is " a scandal and a reproach " to it; — if the same prominent statesman can virtually admit (as he did in the House of Lords on the 29th of April last), that the escape of the Laird iron-clad rams would have been a just cause for war on the part of the United States; — can the Attorney-General and the British nation suppose, that the Americans have so poor an estimate of the justice of their claims, both for an honester neutrality for the future and a substantial indemnity for the past, that they are going to be put aside by being told that their pretensions are extravagant and extraordinary, and that they show too much irritation at imaginary wrongs?

Added to this, if they are to be told that their claims are extravagant and extraordinary *on American principles*, may they not justly conclude — in view even of a few such specimens of those principles as we have re-produced — that the consummate English lawyer, who speaks for the Government in this debate of May 13th, supposes that he can mould facts as well as arguments to suit his purpose, and that, having attempted to prove that the escape of the Alabama was all right, and having succeeded in convincing his countrymen of it, he now thinks he may, with equal success, attempt to convince Americans that their neutrality, in Washington's day, was all wrong, and that they know nothing about their own history or jurisprudence?

POSTSCRIPT.

Since the preparation of most of our matter, as above, for the press, the Atlantic steamer brings intelligence of the termination of the Laird iron-clad prosecution by compromise; and though the matter does not strictly fall within the scope of our undertaking, we feel impelled to give it a word of passing comment.

Of course, as a matter of practical preservation of the peace between two nations, and of the removal of a ground of quarrel, — purposely started, perhaps, to bring on a war between them, — we rejoice in the settlement, and deem it of the highest mutual advantage. But looking at the compromise in the light of its moral bearing, and of its importance as an international precedent, we are tempted to ask our English friends, if they feel entirely contented with their own transaction? Does it not strike them a little like compassing justice through the medium of — what is usually considered a Yankee device — a trade? Shakspeare says:

> " And oft 'tis seen the wicked prize itself
> Buys out the law."

But here, we would suggest, is it not the *law itself* that " buys out" *the wicked prize?*

Perhaps it was their experience of English justice in the Alexandra case that determined the Cabinet to end the iron-clad controversy by process of bargain and sale. And considering the Attorney-General's experience in the "*smooth running*" of English law in the Alexandra instance, we do not wonder at his heartily coöperating in any expedient to get rid of the agency of the courts in this case. Certainly, it was better to bargain for a decision beforehand, at almost any price, than to take the chance again of having the judge borrow his law from Webster's Dictionary, then deny that he had instructed the jury at all, and then (*mistakenly*, we concede) recommend the Crown to go up on appeal, to be finally answered at the end of a year, that there was nothing before the court above, and no law to be gathered from the court below.

Now, if it be added to this keeping back from the courts, that a settlement (*a trade*, in effect) has to be made with a set of legal opponents whom Earl Russell likens to a parcel of housebreakers, stealing out of a mansion-house at three o'clock in the morning with a sackful of plate on their backs, we confess that the attitude of the imperial government is, to our eyes, neither dignified nor creditable.

By way of contrast, we would ask the candid Englishman, If the rustic republic across the water — seizing the Republican and the Cassius at a time when it could hardly reckon eight years of national existence — telling the French ministers that the matter was in the hands of the law, and " till that decision was had, the Government of the United States should pursue what they think right, with firmness, as is their duty," and that France must wait till the courts had spoken — and keeping hold of " the wicked prize" with a strong hand, till, in the one case, it rots at the wharf, and in the other, has to ask for mercy and dismantle itself — then, when the courts had dealt with these vessels and found their powers defective, this same rustic (and, so-called, *lawless*) republic, voluntarily amending its statutes so as to clothe its judiciary with the required powers, and convicting and punishing the equipper of the Cassius, and compelling the recal of the French minister for participating in these infractions of its neutrality — we ask the candid Englishman, If this same rustic republic — in all these transactions, forced upon it in the performance of its neutral obligations — does not appear to better advantage, than his own imperial government, in this Laird compromise?

We know that comparisons are so odious, that we can hardly expect an affirmative answer to our question. But we feel entire confidence in asking our English friend another interrogatory, the counterpart of that just put: — Would he have commended a settlement of the iron-clad question on the part of the United States, if made by them under circumstances parallel to those in which his own country has just made it?

APPENDIX.

EXTRACT FROM THE SPEECH OF MR. THOMAS BARING, AND THE SPEECH OF THE ATTORNEY-GENERAL, IN FULL.

WE give a portion of the very candid and honorable speech of Mr. Thomas Baring, and the entire speech of the Attorney-General, as reported in the London Times of May 14th. We regret that our limits do not permit us to add also the able and high-toned speeches of Messrs. Forster, Cobden, and Shaw-Lefevre, in the same debate. Our American readers, however, will feel less regret at the omission, as they have had a very general opportunity of seeing them (certainly Mr. Cobden's) through the extensive reprints of the New York journals, and as a pamphlet edition of them has just appeared in this city, on the eve of our going to press with this note:

THE GEORGIA.

Mr. T. BARING, in rising to call attention to the circumstances under which this vessel has been allowed to enter the port of Liverpool, and to put a question on the subject, said, that as he brought this matter before the House simply as one of English interest, he should not refer to the feelings or prospects of either of the contending parties, nor should he endeavor to provoke an expression of sympathy with either side. He wished to make no charge against the Government, and, if he referred at all to the past, it would be to illustrate the position in which the country was placed as to its international engagements. An incident had recently occurred which was of a most extraordinary character. A vessel of war carrying, as they were told, the flag and commission of the Confederate Government, had recently entered the port of Liverpool. She was still there, and when the House heard her history, it would be somewhat surprised at the course which had been pursued. This was her history : — The Japan, otherwise the Virginia, commonly known as the Georgia, was built at Dumbarton on the Clyde. She was equipped by a Liverpool firm. Her crew was shipped by the same Liverpool firm for Shanghai, and sent round to Greenock by steamer. She was entered on the 31st of March, 1863, as for Point de Galle and Hongkong, with a crew of forty-eight men. She cleared on the first of April. She left her anchorage on the morning of the 2nd of April, ostensibly to try her engines, but did not return. She had no armament on leaving Greenock, but a few days after her departure, a small steamer called the Allar, freighted with guns, shot, shell, &c., and having on board a partner of the Liverpool firm who had equipped her and shipped her crew, left New Haven and met the Georgia off the coast of France, near Ushant. The cargo of the Allar was successfully transferred to the Georgia on the 8th or 9th of April; her crew consisted of British subjects. The Allar put into Plymouth on the 11th of April, bringing the Liverpool merchant who had directed the proceedings throughout, and bringing also fifteen seamen who had refused to proceed in the Georgia on learning her real character. The rest of the crew remained. At the time of her departure, the Georgia was registered as the property of a Liverpool merchant, a partner of the firm which shipped the crew. She remained the property of this person until the 23d of June, when the register was cancelled, he notifying the collector of her sale to foreign owners. During this period — namely, from the 1st of April to the 23d of June, — the Georgia, being still registered in the name of a Liverpool merchant, and thus his property, was carrying on war against the United States, with whom we were in alliance. It was while still a British vessel, that she captured and burnt the Dictator, and captured and released under bond the Griswold, the same vessel which had brought corn to the Lancashire sufferers. The crew of the Georgia was paid through the same Liverpool firm. A copy of an advance-note used was to be found in the diplomatic correspondence. The same firm continued to act in this capacity throughout the cruise of the Georgia. After cruising in the Atlantic, and burning and bonding a number of vessels, the Georgia made for Cherbourg, where she arrived on the 28th of October. There was at the time much discontent among the crew. Many deserted, leave of absence was given to others, and their wages were paid all along by the same Liverpool firm. In order to get the Georgia to sea again, the Liverpool firm enlisted, in Liverpool, some twenty seamen, and sent them to Brest. The Georgia left Cherbourg on a second cruise, but having no success she returned to that port, and thence to Liverpool, where her crew have been paid off without any concealment, and the vessel is now laid up. Here, then, was the case of a vessel clandestinely built, fraudulently leaving the port of her construction, taking Englishmen on board as her crew, and waging war against the United States, an ally of ours, without having once entered a port of the Power the commission of which she bore, but being for some time the property of an English subject. We heard nothing of the steps which under those circumstances were taken by the Government, but he felt assured they had done all that lay in their power, and was consistent with their duty under the existing law. It was, therefore, not their conduct in the matter, but the impotency and insufficiency of the Foreign Enlistment Act, which our Courts of justice found it impossible to interpret, that he wished to bring under the notice of the House. The vessels to which he alluded were vessels which would undoubtedly have been arrested if time had been given, and if their purpose had been known. The question was, in fact, could we be said to be carrying out our obligations as a neutral Power towards a belligerent which was an ally, in a manner consistent with international law, though it might be in harmony with our municipal law, while such a state of things was permitted to exist? For his own part, he had no wish to lose himself in the mazes of a legal discussion on the subject, but common sense, as well as international law, he believed, prescribed that a neutral should act towards a belligerent who was an ally as she would like to be done by. (Hear). It was in order to prevent a war between neutrals and belligerents that the Foreign Enlistment Act was passed, and if vessels were allowed to proceed on a course of devastation, if they were admitted into the ports of our dependencies and colonies, and not only that but to put into ports in this country, was it not, he would ask, time to consider whether we should not do our duty towards others, and whether the existing law afforded us the means of protecting the interests of our ally as well as our own? The question as to the extent to which those vessels ought to be admitted to the ports of our colonies and dependencies was, he contended, one of serious importance; but it was, at the same time, one as to which he thought there could be no doubt what course the Government should adopt. When a vessel left our ports, which would have been arrested here had her objects been ascertained and her construction certified, and proceeded to carry into effect proceedings of hostility against an ally to the endangering of the peace of this country, it seemed to him that it was the duty of the Government to avail themselves in her case of the powers which they possessed, and to shut our ports against her. (Hear, hear.) If the House would permit him, he would read on the subject a passage from a writer on international law, who signed himself "Historicus," and who said, speaking of the Alabama:

"First of all, the English Government must decide on the best information at their disposal, whether she was or was not unlawfully equipped in this country in breach of our neutrality. Their decision on this point ought to be final, for they are the sole judges of it, and the Federal authorities may inform their judgment, but cannot question their determination. If the English Government determine that the Alabama was not unlawfully equipped within the realm, she will, of course, enjoy the privileges and immunities of any other lawful belligerent cruiser. If, on the other hand, she is decided to have been unlawfully equipped, then she ought to be forbidden access to any port within the jurisdiction of Great Britian. If she comes within our ports with a prize, her prize should be taken from her and restored to the original owner, and she herself compelled to depart."

There was another extract from the same writer to which he wished also to invite the attention of honorable members. It was as follows:

"Now, it is a sound and salutary rule of international practice, established by the Americans themselves in 1794, that vessels which have been equipped in violation of the laws of a neutral State, shall be excluded from that hospitality which is extended to other belligerent cruisers, on whose origin there is no such taint. Accordingly, the Cabinet of Washington compelled all the French privateers which had been illegally fitted out in America against England, to leave the ports of the United States, and orders were issued to the Custom-house officers to prevent their return. This course of proceeding appears equally consonant to the principles of law and the dictates of policy. The question then remains, — Was the Alabama unlawfully equipped and manned within the jurisdiction of Great Britain? Now, setting aside the vexed question of equipment, I think there can be very little doubt on that of enlistment. The question is one which, from its very nature, is not and cannot become the subject of judicial determination, because a neutral Government cannot exercise a jurisdiction over such a vessel. It is a matter on which the Executive of the neutral Government must, according to the best information it can obtain, form its own judgment, and that judgment is final and conclusive on all parties. Now, I observe that in a despatch dated March 27, 1863 (Parliamentary Paper, p. 2), Lord Russell writes, 'The British Government has done every thing in its power to execute the law; but I admitted the cases of the Alabama and the Oréto were a scandal, and in some degree a reproach to our law.' Now, with the greatest deference to those persons who may be of an opposite opinion, I submit that vessels of which such a statement can be properly made — and that it was properly made, no one acquainted with the circumstances of their outfit and manning can honestly doubt — are not entitled to the hospitality of the country whose laws they have eluded and abused. I think that to deny to the Florida and Alabama access to our ports, would be the legitimate and dignified manner of expressing our disapproval of the fraud which has been practised upon our neutrality. If we abstain from taking such a course, I fear we may justly lie under the imputation of having done less to vindicate our good faith than the American Government consented at our instance on former occasions to do."

Now, these were vessels which avowedly ought to have been stopped if their purpose had been known. They were vessels whose destination was to roam about, never getting home, and which were tainted with the offence of having violated our neutrality. They were vessels, therefore, which on every ground had no claim to the hospitality of the country, and he was bound to say that both our international obligations and a due regard for our own interests ought to have led us to exclude them from our ports. The Georgia had arrived in Liverpool and there discharged her crew, and what guarantee had we that other vessels might not do the same; that our neutrality might not be violated, and that we might not hereafter have to deal with a state of things in which our position would be reversed. (Hear, hear.)

The ATTORNEY-GENERAL. — With many things which have been said by my honorable friend in the course of his able and temperate speech I entirely agree. (Hear, hear.) No one who has observed the conduct which the Government have endeavored to pursue with regard to this most important political subject during the past two years, can doubt, that, whether successfully or otherwise, they have endeavored, to the best of their power, to vindicate the laws of this country, and at the same time to fulfil the obligations of a sincere and impartial neutrality. I know that these professions will not meet with the assent of those who, in their own minds, have no sympathy with the neutrality itself, who have given themselves, doubtless under the impulse of generous motives, to entire, unqualified, and enthusiastic sympathy with one or the other of the belligerents. Nevertheless, I have great confidence that the country generally will perceive that the Government, in the course which they have pursued in circumstances of some slight difficulty, have really desired to maintain the law and preserve the honor of the country, and at the same time not to deviate from the path of a real and impartial neutrality. (Hear, hear.) Addressing myself first to the last and most generally important of the topics of my honorable friend's speech, I need hardly say that we are quite sensible of the gravity of the public evil which exists when merchants, or any other persons in this country, hold themselves at liberty, by all kinds of shifts and evasions (hear, hear), to treat with contempt Her Majesty's proclamation of neutrality, to make themselves parties in a war in which Her Majesty has proposed to be neutral; to shelter themselves under all those opportunities of escape which the just regard of the law of our country for persons accused of any offence invariably offers; and to do acts which in their immediate effects place in peril the friendly relations of this and another great nation (hear, hear), and which in their ultimate consequences may possibly recoil with the most disastrous and destructive effect upon the trade and commerce of their own country. (Hear, hear.) The Government had some right to hope that in the circumstances of such a war as this, English merchants, occupying eminent positions, would not spell out the law under the advice of lawyers, saying, "I cannot find it in the bond" (hear, hear), and, availing themselves of every means of escape which ingenuity can suggest, bring this country into peril, and create a precedent for future mischiefs and danger, against which the law of this country seeks to provide. (Hear.) I hope the time will soon come — indeed, I think I may infer from the memorial to which my honorable friend has referred, that the time has come — when the voice of the mercantile community will be raised, so that those who may be unwilling to hold themselves bound by Her Majesty's proclamation of neutrality, shall see that they cannot expect the support of the great body of their fellow-countrymen. (Hear, hear.) I must endeavor to show that the conduct which has been pursued by Her Majesty's Government has been that which the country had a right to expect. The House is aware that there are only three vessels which are alleged, — and in those cases I do not say the allegations are well founded, as they have never been brought to the test of judicial proceedings, but there are only three vessels which are alleged — to have been fitted out in this country in violation of the law, and with the practical effect of placing this country in the situation of ministering, in a most important and formidable manner, to the warlike requirements of one of two belligerents. (Hear.) The Government believe that the law was intended to strike, and does strike, at such acts. With regard to these three ships, the House will recollect that the first which left the shores of this country, the Oreto, afterwards the Florida, left before any information upon which the Government could act had been imparted to them. That vessel was afterwards arrested at Nassau, was tried there and acquitted, but it was found that there was reasonable cause for the arrest. So far the Government was not to blame. As to the next ship, the Alabama, I need not repeat what was said upon a former occasion as to the steps which were taken by the Government, after full consideration of the evidence laid before them, with a view to arrest that vessel. It is well known to the House and to the country that orders to that effect were given, but the ship in the mean time made her escape. Then, lastly, there was this vessel, the Georgia, as to which no information whatever reached Her Majesty's Government; no evidence upon which we could act until she was actually gone. So successfully disguised were the real designs of those connected with that ship, that, as my honorable friend has stated, the crew were actually engaged for a voyage to Shanghai, and all other arrangements were made with a view to concealment and disguise, and it was only off the coast of France, that, meeting another vessel, she received her armament and re-enlisted her crew. The Government had no opportunity of interfering so as to stop that vessel. If there be those who think that all those proceedings, connected with these ships, were perfectly lawful, they will, I am sure, join with me in regretting, that, being lawful, they were not also open, avowed, and above-board. (Hear.) It does not seem favorable to the conclusions of the persons engaged on these proceedings, that, believing in their lawfulness, they should have taken all possible pains to disguise their real character. (Hear.) Afterwards, as the House is aware, Her Majesty's Government took action in the case of the Alexandra, and since then with regard to other vessels, concerning which I will say nothing, as they will soon be the subject of judicial trial. I may also mention, that in Scotland, the Government directed the seizure of the vessel, Pampero, under the Foreign Enlistment Act, and the result of that proceeding has been that a verdict has been given by consent for the Crown, and that, while great liberality has been shown in the waiving of the forfeiture to the Crown, security has been taken against the employment of the vessel for any belligerent service, and the authority of the law has been successfully vindicated. (Hear.) I am happy to be able to say that, whatever may happen in these cases in point of law or evidence, the interference of the Government does appear to have been productive of good effect, as it has impeded the progress of the system of fitting out of naval armaments for a belligerent State. We have no reason to believe that the efforts of the Government have been unsuccessful in the practical object, nor even so far as regards the elucidation of the law, although it would, perhaps, be premature to express a confident opinion upon a subject concerning which high authorities have differed. But I cannot avoid expressing a sanguine hope, that the result of the measures taken by the Government will be to clear up much of the difficulty attaching to the construction of the law, and to lead in future to a better observance of it. I am encouraged in that hope by the fact, that in the Court of Exchequer two learned Judges adopted the construction of the Act upon which the Crown had been advised to proceed. Their construction has since received the endorsement of a learned Judge in the Queen's Bench, under circumstances which make it probable that other Judges of that Court may concur in his opinion; and in the case of the Pampero, in Scotland, the Judges of the Court of Session pronounced opinions, tending, to a great extent, to confirm the construction of the Act contended for by the Crown. (Hear, hear.) The result of all this is to leave the Government in a situation in which they have a right to hope that the law, as it is, may be capable of being vindicated, and that the steps taken to vindicate it will not fail in their object, and therefore the House will probably think that it will not be improper, in the event of any suggested change of the law, for the Government to act upon that view; but if it should prove to be otherwise, and that the present law is not sufficient, that then they may look for that support and encouragement from this House and the country, which, upon a subject so important, it is essential to obtain. If, in the absence of such support and encouragement, proposals for a change of the law were ineffectually made, it would commit those, who ought to have the common interest of the country at heart, to a premature expression of opinion, which might have disastrous effects upon the future of this country. We think, therefore, that if it should ever become necessary to consider the subject, it should be considered at a time when no party feelings nor temporary sympathies may exist to induce the House to take a course which it will be difficult afterwards to retract, and which, if persevered with, might be attended with serious consequences to the welfare of the country. Under these circumstances, the House will, no doubt, consider that Government are doing right in adhering to their original hope that the law as it is, may be found sufficient for its purpose, and, at all events, that they ought not to propose any change in the law until they are convinced that there is absolute necessity for it, and that such proposals will receive the encouragement and support of the House and the country, without which they could not be carried into effect. Having said that, I will address myself to the particular subject of the motion of my honorable friend. I have shown that with regard to the former history of the Georgia, the Government have omitted nothing which they could do under the circumstances. That ship has now returned as a Confederate ship — a public ship of war, with a regular commission as such. I must here notice one observation of my honorable friend. He says, that from the 1st of April, 1863, until the following 23d of June, this ship — the Georgia — was registered in this country in the name of a British owner, a merchant of Liverpool, and that, therefore, she was cruising, burning, and destroying vessels at a time when she was a British ship. I must demur altogether to the law of my honorable friend in that respect. The register is nothing but the title of a British owner for a municipal purpose in this country. A ship which has a British register, and which is afterwards transferred to a foreign belligerent Power, cannot, by the mere fact of her still remaining registered in England as the property of a British owner, in any way be justly styled a British ship. (Hear, hear.) Nor can it be said that she has not become what this vessel really is — a public vessel of war. I regret that my honorable friend should have used an argument that may seem to give countenance to assertions which have repeatedly been made, but which are quite destitute of foundation, that these ships are British pirates. (Hear, hear.) That expression is untrue in fact — dishonorable to this country; and I trust that all those who have the honor of this country at heart, whatever they may see to condemn in the conduct of persons concerned in fitting out and navigating such vessels as those referred to, will not give encouragement to a proposition so extravagant, and so completely without foundation. I now come to the point suggested by the motion of my honorable friend. He points to the fact that the Georgia is now at Liverpool. The ship came in, being at the time a regular commissioned public ship of war. There is no doubt she was entitled to come in in that character by license of the Crown as long as the rules issued by Her Majesty in January, 1862, remain unaltered, because those rules permit ships of war belonging to the belligerents to come into our ports under certain restrictions. They must not remain more than twenty-four hours, except for repairs, they must not receive repairs in the nature of warlike equipment, and there are strict limits as to leaving as soon as the repairs are completed. This ship being a public ship of war, is permitted to come into our ports, and so comes in lawfully as a ship of war. The Government desired to have information regarding the circumstances under which she had entered our port, and as to the length of time she was likely to remain. They understood she had been brought into dock, it was presumed, for the purpose of repair, and it was afterwards stated that she was likely to be dismantled and sold. If the latter were the case, there would be no harm done to the other belligerent Power by relieving her from all fear of opposition on the part of the dismantled vessel. My honorable friend has asked whether the Government think the admission of such ships as he describes that ship to be, consistent with their international obligations, their profession of neutrality, and the preservation of British interests. The Government certainly has not considered the limited and qualified admission of ships of this kind into British ports to be at all inconsistent with their duty in any respect. But for the first element in the case to which the honorable gentleman has called attention, that the vessel was originally manned and equipped from British ports, I think that every one would grant her right to admission into our ports. I must, however, notice that my friend has imported into the case a consideration which has been frequently dwelt upon in the various publications issued upon this subject — namely, that this ship has never been in any of the ports of the belligerent Power under whose flag she sails. It is argued from this fact that this is a circumstance which prevents a ship from acquiring the character of a belligerent ship of war. It has been said that there is some rule or other, some settled principle of international law, which will bear out this conclusion. It should not be our practice to invent new rules of international law to suit particular cases, and such a rule as this was never heard of. (Hear, hear.) To say that a country whose ports are blockaded is not at liberty to avail herself of the resources which are at her command in other parts of the world, that she may not buy ships in neutral territory and commission them as ships of war without bringing them to her own country first, is a doctrine which is quite preposterous (hear, hear), and all the arguments founded upon such a doctrine only tend to throw dust into men's eyes and to mislead them. We cannot, therefore, upon those grounds make this ship an exception in our ordinary rules. And now I come to the real question. I have not the least doubt that we have a right, if we thought fit, to exclude any particular ship or class of ships, if we consider that they have violated our neutrality; but such power is simply discretionary on the part of the Government, and should be exercised with a due regard to all the circumstances of the case. Does the circumstance of a ship happening to have been fitted out in violation of the neutrality of a neutral nation entitle her to be refused recognition as a public ship of war? Happily, we find an answer to this question in the history of the jurisprudence of the United States, and I do not find that the United States, which have really settled all the doctrines of law applicable to this kind of neutrality, by fitting out vessels in their ports for belligerent nations, ever adopted the practice of inquiring into the previous history of public ships of war which labored under the suspicion or allegation of having been fitted out in their ports in violation of their neutrality. In the cases of the Santissima Trinidad and the Cassius, the particulars of which were similar to those of the Georgia, Mr. Justice Story said:

"In general, the commission of a public ship, signed by the proper authorities of the nation to which she belongs, is complete proof of her national character. A bill of sale is not necessary to be produced, nor will the courts of a foreign country inquire into the means by which the title to property has been acquired. It would be to exert the right of examining into the validity of the acts of the foreign Sovereign, and to sit in judgment upon them in cases where he has not conceded the jurisdiction, and where it would be inconsistent with his own supremacy. The commission, therefore, of a public ship, when duly authenticated, so far at least as foreign courts are concerned, imports absolute verity, and the title is not examinable. The property must be taken to be duly acquired, and cannot be controverted. This has been the settled practice between nations, and it is a rule founded in public convenience and policy, and cannot be broken in upon without endangering the peace and repose as well of neutral as of belligerent Sovereigns. The commission, in the present case, is not expressed in the most unequivocal terms, but its fair purport and interpretation must be deemed to apply to a public ship of the Government. If we add to this the corroborative testimony of our own and the British Consul at Buenos Ayres, as well as that of private citizens, to the notoriety of her claim of a public character, and her admission into our own ports as a public ship, with the immunities and privileges belonging to such a ship, with the express approbation of our own Government, it does not seem too much to assert, whatever may be the private suspicion of a lurking American interest, that she must be judicially held to be a public ship of the country whose commission she bears."

That decision referred to a case in which the United States Foreign Enlistment Act had been violated over and over again. The other belligerent has no concern whatever in the course which the Government may think fit to adopt with reference to this vessel; and if the Government refused her admission to the ports of the United Kingdom, it would only be done for the purpose of vindicating our authority. I cannot find, however, that the United States ever followed such a course. The Santissima Trinidad and the Cassius were both received into the ports of the United States, held not to be amenable to courts of law, and never ordered by the Government to leave any port. There are, also, a very considerable number of cases reported in which prizes brought into the ports of the United States were either restored, or questions raised in courts of law as to their restoration; but I can find no instance of any prohibition or exclusion from any port of any prize after her conversion into a ship-of-war. We are not therefore warranted, upon the authority of the United States, in excluding this vessel from our ports. The honorable member for Huntingdon has asked if the Government think the admission of such vessels to British harbors consistent with our international obligations. This question renders it necessary to determine the right of the other belligerent in this matter. Now, upon this question, I will quote from the judgment of Mr. Justice Story in reference to the case of the Amistad de Rues. I hope not to utter a single word in the slightest degree offensive to any one in the United States, and least of all to their Government; but I cannot help wishing that the authority I have mentioned had been more recognized, when, over and over again, those extraordinary and extravagant demands were made upon our Government to pay the value of all the ships taken on the high seas by the Alabama and similar vessels. (Hear, hear.) I need hardly remind the House that in 1793, when the United States did give us compensation for certain prizes not restored, that compensation was strictly limited to ships when brought into their ports fitted out in violation of their laws, and was not extended to any prizes taken upon the high seas. All they did was to name a particular date, and to prohibit the French from bringing in any more of their prizes after that date. Mr. Justice Story thus lays down what is the limit of the obligation which the neutral owes to the belligerent in this matter:

"When called upon by either of the belligerents to act in such cases, all that justice seems to require, is, that the neutral nation should fairly execute its own laws, and give no asylum to the property unjustly captured. It is bound, therefore, to restore the property if found within its own ports; but, beyond this, it is not obliged to interfere between the belligerents."

So that he distinctly says that we are to execute our laws fairly, we are to give no asylum to prizes captured by ships fitted out in violation of our neutrality, and to property unjustly captured; but he does not say, that an asylum may not be given to public ships of war, whatever their previous history; and he adds, that, beyond the limits which he mentions, we are not obliged to interfere between the belligerents. The authority of Mr. Justice Story, therefore, distinctly excludes the proposition that belligerents have any rights entitling them to require interference by the neutral, to the extent of excluding absolutely from her ports ships of this description, if it does not seem to the neutral herself necessary so to do. (Hear, hear.) I say, then, we have done all that authority requires us to do. And now I will ask what reasons there are for the ltesitation of the Government to take the extreme step of absolutely excluding these particular ships from our ports, when, at the same time, all the ships of the United States Government were (are) admitted. (Hear.) Some reasons can be given; the House will judge of them; I believe they have had considerable influence upon the determination of the Government upon this question, and I think they are such as are consistent with an honest desire to maintain our neutrality and fulfil our international obligations. In the first place, the maintenance of neutrality is plainly consistent with the maintenance of our own rights, and I entirely repudiate the argument sometimes used that you are not to enforce your own laws, because the effect of doing so may possibly be to put one of the parties to greater disadvantage than the other. Neutrality does not require that. On the other hand, where you have no law to enforce, then it becomes worthy of consideration, whether you may not be weighing down the balance in a manner not entirely consistent with neutrality, if you adopt voluntarily a rule which would practically exclude from the asylum you allow in your ports the whole of the navy of one belligerent and no part of the other belligerent. (Hear, hear.) That is one principle. And then there is another. The whole of the honorable gentleman's argument assumes, that the facts, and the law applicable to the facts, are substantiated, that we are in a position as between ourselves and the Confederate States to treat the matter as beyond controversy, and that the Georgia was, in fact, fitted out in violation of our neutrality. Now, we may have strong reason to suspect this, and may even believe it to be true; but to say that we are to act upon mere suspicion or belief against another State, upon certain facts which have never been judicially established, and which it is not easy to bring to the test as between Government and Government — that is a proposition which is not without grave consideration to be accepted. (Hear, hear.) The difficulty of that view is increased by the fact that we have no diplomatic relations with the Confederate States, and cannot communicate with them in the ordinary way. We have not recognized them, and, what is more, the Government of the United States, by its ships, bar us from the means of communication. (Hear, hear.) Only the other day, Her Majesty's Government were anxious to communicate and remonstrate with the Government of the Confederate States, and actually gave a commission to one of our diplomatic servants, a consul, to do so; and then it was announced, that the blockading squadron, under the orders of the United States' Government, could not permit even a ship of war of this country to enter into a blockaded port for the purpose of this communication. (Hear, hear.) These circumstances greatly enhance the difficulty of bringing to a practical test the question whether there has been in this case a violation of our neutrality. Upon that allegation the whole thing depends; and here, again, American authority by no means warrants the notion that you ought to act lightly or without cogent proof. In the case of the Santissima Trinidad, to which I have before referred, Mr. Justice Story says, as to the kind of proof which ought to be insisted on in these cases:

"In a case of the description of that before the Court, where the sovereignty and rights of a foreign belligerent nation are in question, and where the exercise of jurisdiction over captures made under its flag can be justified only by clear proof of the violation of our neutrality, there are still stronger reasons for abstaining from interference, if the testimony is clouded with doubt and suspicion. We adhere to the rule which has been already adopted by this Court, that restitution ought not to be decreed upon the ground of capture in violation of our neutrality, unless the fact be established beyond all reasonable doubts."

There, again, is a principle which the Confederate Government are entitled to have the benefit of, and which makes it matter of serious difficulty to say, that, because we have very strong moral presumptions and very strong reason to believe that a certain ship of war was fitted out in violation of our neutrality, we are, therefore, to act summarily upon the supposition. (Hear, hear.) You have here a mixed question of facts and of law — the facts to be established by evidence, the law to be decided with reference to the facts; and, considering the controversy which has gone on as to the bearing and effect of our law, it is not impossible that in some of these cases the Confederate States may have believed they were acting within that law. (Hear.) All this increases the difficulty; and now I want to suggest other reasons. Of course, if we act according to the suggestions made to us in this case, we must act on the same principles, and deal out the same measure to the other belligerent. And, if we are to proceed on grounds of moral belief, and do not stop to ask whether they constitute proper legal grounds of action — if we are to proceed upon information of the kind which carries conviction to the mind — it is impossible to acquit the agents of the United States, although we may acquit the Government, of acts which are inconsistent with our neutrality. The case of the Kearsage was a case of this character. Beyond all question a considerable amount of recruiting was carried on at Cork for the purpose of that ship, she being employed at the time in our own waters, or very near them, in looking out for her enemy; and she was furnished with a large addition to her crew from Ireland. (Hear, hear.) Upon that being represented to Mr. Adams, he said, as might have been expected, that it was entirely contrary to the wishes of his Government, and that there must be some mistake. The men were afterwards relanded, and there can be no doubt that there had been a violation of our neutrality. (Hear, hear.) Nevertheless, we admitted the Kearsage afterwards into English waters. We have not excluded her from our ports, and if we had, I think the United States' Government would have considered that they had some cause of offence. (Hear, hear.) But it does not rest there. I see from the paper that the honorable member for Horsham wants information respecting the enlistment of British subjects for the Federal army. Now, from all quarters reports reach us which we cannot doubt to be substantially true, that agents for recruiting for the Federal army, with or without the concurrence of the Government, are in Ireland, and engage men under the pretext of employing them on railways and public works, but really with the intention of enlisting them, and that many of these men are so enlisted. (Hear, hear.) In Canada and New Brunswick the same practices prevail. Representations have been made to the United States' Government respecting particular cases of persons who have been kidnapped into the service, and I feel bound to say that those representations have not met with that prompt and satisfactory attention we might have expected. (Hear, hear.) How are we to act in this case? Are we to exclude from our ports all the ships of the belligerent, whose agents are believed to have engaged in these practices? — practices, which, whatever may be the intention of the United States' Government, operate to supply their ranks with British subjects in violation of British law. (Hear, hear.) If we are to act in the one case upon suspicion, or upon moral belief going beyond suspicion, it would be difficult to say that we ought not to act so in the other. But in what difficulties we should entangle ourselves were we so to act, not being bound to act by any international obligation? What may fairly be asked, is, that we should do all we can to enforce our own laws within our own jurisdiction. That is the course which the Government have taken; that is the course to which they will adhere; and, in view of the difficulties I have mentioned, I think it is a course which is fully justified. (Hear.) There is one other consideration of importance which I wish to mention; and here again, I hope that what I say will not cause offence in the United States, for I state it because it is true, and because it is important that the matter should be understood. The British Government are not assisted by the Government of the United States in matters of this description. The demands which the United States' Government make upon us go so far beyond the limits of any thing they can be entitled to ask, according to any recognized rules and privileges of international law, that it becomes absolutely necessary that this Government should exercise great caution indeed, before they do acts which might possibly be misunderstood, and might give foundation to the idea that they do them under the supposed necessity of complying with demands of this kind. (Hear, hear.) The House well knows that I refer to the extraordinary demands arising out of the case of the Alabama. (Hear, hear.) I have no hesitation in saying, that the United States' Government, by advancing such demands, and by seeking to make our Government responsible for pecuniary compensation for prizes taken by the Alabama upon the high seas, and never brought within our ports or in any way whatever under our control, are making demands directly contrary to the principles of international law laid down by their own jurists, and thereby render it infinitely more difficult for us, at their request, to do any thing resting on our own discretion, and which we are not bound to do in law. (Hear, hear.) What we may fairly say is this: — "We will adhere to the rules laid down by your own authorities. We will execute our own law. We will allow no asylum to prizes or to property unjustly captured. If any such are brought in, any demand for their reclamation shall be investigated. But we will not undertake to recognize claims going beyond these limits. We will not undertake to interfere between belligerents in any other way than that in which by the rules of international law we can fairly be called upon to interfere." (General cheering.)

AMERICAN NEUTRALITY:

ITS HONORABLE PAST, ITS EXPEDIENT FUTURE.

A PROTEST AGAINST THE PROPOSED REPEAL OF THE NEUTRALITY LAWS, AND A PLEA FOR THEIR IMPROVEMENT AND CONSOLIDATION.

By GEORGE BEMIS.

BOSTON:
LITTLE, BROWN, AND COMPANY.
1866.

Entered according to Act of Congress, in the year 1866, by
GEORGE BEMIS,
In the Clerk's Office of the District Court of the District of Massachusetts.

CAMBRIDGE:
PRESS OF JOHN WILSON AND SON.

PREFACE.

BEYOND the information conveyed by its title-page as to the contents of the somewhat thick and perhaps *heavy* pamphlet which the reader now holds in his hands, the writer would state, that, while his main purpose has been to discuss the American question, — whether it is best for the United States, at the present juncture, to repeal all its neutrality laws, or "scale" them down (in General Banks's phrase) to an indefinitely low level, — he has at the same time undertaken to treat the general and scientifically important topic, of what constitutes the true duty of a neutral nation towards its belligerent neighbors and allies. As a supplementary branch of the first inquiry, and as a practical illustration of the second, he has further touched upon some general considerations of what ought to be the true future neutral policy of the people of the United States. These divisions of his subject-matter constitute, in fact, his "Honorable Past and Expedient Future of American Neutrality."

Beyond thus much of primary intent, the writer takes advantage of the present opportunity, to further discuss, incidentally and secondarily, various great questions of the day, now pressing upon public attention, and which may, at any moment, demand the political action of the American voter or his congressional representatives. Such are the settlement of the "Alabama" and similar claims upon England for the devastations of

PREFACE.

Confederate cruisers; the proposition of the British Government, that the United States should co-operate with it in a Mutual Reform of the Neutrality Laws of the two nations; what is our just Duty in regard to Fenianism; and whether we are called upon to put forth some New (Monroe) Declaration of Foreign Policy.

To the American general reader, the writer would especially commend the first and last parts of his pamphlet, — those in which he treats of the past and the future of the country's history. On *all* of the subjects above named, however, every American, according to the theory of his free government, is bound to have an intelligent and decided opinion; but, as to his country's honorable record in the past, the writer believes that every fellow-countryman ought to share with him in a feeling of just pride at being a member of a nation so honorably distinguished as our own. Now that we have fought three wars of national independence or existence, and, with God's blessing, have come out of the last and worst struggle a great and free, if not a united, people, it is not for us to feel any longer that we have not an established nationality. We are no longer — I affirm it — *new men*, " novi homines," in the family of nations. But we have an ancestry and an inherited reputation from the Washingtons, the Adamses, the Hamiltons, the Marshalls, the Jeffersons, the Madisons, &c., such as hardly belongs to any other nation of the globe. My just deduction from this premise, however, is, that we are called upon all the more to see to it that the sons do not degenerate from their fathers' noble example.

Of the past of our national record, so far as the writer has undertaken to make *a study*, or historical sketch, — not paint the historical picture, for which he hopes his sketch may serve as a hint, — he confidently trusts that its perusal will give pleasure to his American readers. He ventures to believe that he has brought to light new facts in our Neutral History before unknown or forgotten, and that his combination of materials to fairly bring out our national transactions of that day is quite his own; at least, he is quite unconscious of its existence elsewhere. His only wonder is that publicists and jurists like Marshall, Kent, and Wheaton, who were born and brought up with American Neutrality, — nay, who may be said themselves to compose a great and an honorable part of our neutral renown, — should have had so little to say on this topic. It only begets, in the writer's mind, a distrust lest he may himself have exaggerated the importance of his study. He submits his delineation, however, to the candor of his readers, conscious of having been actuated by a sincere desire of stating only the truth; and perfectly sure, that, if he *is* accurate in his delineatory outline, that portion of American history which he only sketches in pencil ought forthwith to be painted in full by some more competent artist, and put into the hands of every voter in the United States, to inform him what it is to be invested with the birthright of an American citizen.

The writer forbears comment on other portions of his pamphlet, particularly on the discussion of our relations with England, now so important and interesting, and which have grown almost every day more and more so, since he first took up his pen, several weeks since. He must, however, make an exception so far as to say a word upon its concluding division, in which he ventures in some degree to cast the horoscope of the American future. Perhaps in this portion of the work, as a discussion of the scientific and yet practical principles of neutrality, the professed student of public law may find most to interest him. The writer's views may seem rather those of the moralist than the publicist; yet he ventures to put them forth, in the belief that national actions, like private morals, are growing more and more subject to the domain of moral justice; and that, whether the statesman will or no, he must inquire of the enlightened public sense of mankind — another name for the progress of civilization — whether his measures are worthy of national approbation and adoption.

Boston, December, 1866.

CONTENTS

PART I.

VINDICATION OF THE NATIONAL FAME FOR PAST NEUTRALITY . 1

PART II.

THE TRUE ESTIMATE OF BRITISH NEUTRAL LAWS AND BRITISH NEUTRALITY 63

PART III.

UNWORTHY PROMOTION OF FENIAN BELLIGERENCY 89

PART IV.

DEFECTIVE EXECUTION OF THE ATTEMPT TO DETERIORATE ("SCALE") THE NEUTRALITY LAWS OF THE UNITED STATES 103

PART V.

THE EXPEDIENT FUTURE OF AMERICAN NEUTRALITY 123

VINDICATION OF THE NATIONAL FAME FOR PAST NEUTRALITY.

CHAPTER I.

Preliminary. — The unanimous adoption of General Banks's Report and Bill by the House of Representatives, and the pressure upon the Senate to concur, demand serious inquiry. — The scheme believed to be a crude and hasty one, from which the writer strongly dissents, and which was well checked by Senator Sumner. — It is still pending, however, and likely to come up again for discussion shortly. — The writer protests against it on five grounds, corresponding to the general divisions of his subject. — Preliminary suggestion of the Report's being written in haste, and with conflicting expressions of sentiment in different parts. — General Banks shares its faults in common with the able and patriotic House who have adopted it; and therefore any criticism on it cannot be thought personal or unfriendly towards him. — Further preliminary approbation of the views of the Report as to the Alabama Indemnity; Hasty Recognition of Rebel Belligerency; and Free Trade in Ships of War as Articles of Commerce. — Summary of General Banks's Report.

THE late movement in Congress towards the fundamental repeal of the neutral code of the United States seems to demand the gravest attention of the nation. When such an important measure as that proposed by General Banks, as Chairman of the Committee on Foreign Affairs, a few days before the close of the late session at the end of last July, — having for its object a new departure in the line of conduct of our foreign relations with the rest of the world, and based on an avowed hostility to the spirit and letter of our present neutral system as its starting-point, — passes the House of Representatives of the

United States *by a unanimous vote*, and is only arrested in the Senate by a persistent enforcement of the usual routine of reference to a committee for consideration, it seems high time to inquire what motives can have prompted such an attempted overthrow of our traditional policy, and whether the country should not arouse itself to prevent the consummation of the proposed *coup d'état*.

Believing, as an humble citizen, that the new scheme is fraught with untold dangers to our present peace and our permanent welfare as an industrial, peace-loving, and simply governed republic, I feel called upon to protest against its further progress, and to challenge the soundness of the reasons and the justice of the motives held out for its adoption by its chief promoters.

As one of General Banks's constituents, (though not indeed of his congressional district,) I desire to express my entire dissent from the general scope and spirit of the new project, as well as from the tenor and effect of most of its details. I conceive, that the Report, Bill, and accompanying debate, so far as they bespeak the moving spirit of that project, all misrepresent the true feeling and love of justice of the American people; and that, when the matter shall again be more candidly considered and more carefully weighed by the House of Representatives themselves, — if it shall ever come back to them for reconsideration, — both they and the gallant chairman will be ready to acknowledge that they have acted with undue haste and that they were tempted to put to hazard important public interests, under the excitement of a temporary gust of national passion, or from motives of temporary party policy.

Viewed as a measure of legislative enactment, I feel quite sure that the honorable chairman could not have given sufficient study to the framework or to the details of his new law, amidst his other numerous and pressing legislative duties; and that the House were quite unaware of its crudeness and want of scientific accuracy, when they so hastily voted its adoption. Meanwhile, I conceive that the country are under great obligations to Senator Sumner for sturdily standing in the way of this ill-digested and revolutionary legislation, and preventing its passage through the Senate by storm, amid the excitement of the closing hours of the session.

As it is, a breathing-time has been given for reflection. Yet, as the new session of Congress is about opening, and as the Bill will shortly be up again for discussion, it is to be hoped that wiser and better counsels will take possession of the minds of Senators, and that they will hear reflected from their constituents a juster and a cooler voice of public opinion than that which seems to have filled the ears and mastered the judgment of the House of Representatives.

Hoping to contribute my part, as a lover of international justice, towards awakening the public mind to the importance of the new stroke of state policy, and towards creating a public sentiment which shall make itself felt at the Capitol in its reprobation, I desire to urge some considerations upon the character and probable effects of the new policy, which I hope will tend to convince our legislators and their constituents, that, so far from its being progress and a movement forward, as its friends contend, it is rather retrogression towards barbarism and bruteforce, wholly unchristian and unrepublican, and therefore altogether inexpedient and inadmissible for adoption by the American people. I have to protest, then, against the new movement, upon these five grounds : —

(I.) That it begins its work with an unjust and unjustifiable disparagement of the country's historic good name and fame.

(II.) That it untruly and unfairly characterizes British neutral legislation, which it professes to adopt for its standard of comparison and imitation.

(III.) That it virtually amounts to protective legislation in favor of filibusterism and Fenianism.

(IV.) That the present legislative embodiment of the scheme is so imperfect and defective a piece of law-making, that it fails of any legal validity and effect, except to express the ultimate and objectionable designs of its originators.

(V.) That the whole movement is antagonistic to our truest and best future neutral policy.

Before developing these specifications of protest in detail, I dare say my readers will deem it desirable to be first possessed of some little summary of General Banks's Report, now some three months old, and of the general topics covered by that and the accompanying Bill, in order to start fairly in the proposed discussion. I regret that my limits forbid my appending the Report in full to the end of this pamphlet, as I do the Bill which passed the House, and which embodies, more significantly and potentially than the Report itself, the ideas of the chairman and the majority of his committee, and the unanimous sense of the House of Representatives.

In making this abstract, I feel bound to notice that the honorable chairman's Report seems to have been prepared in haste, — doubtless under the pressure of other heavy duties, — and to have been written at different intervals, and perhaps at odd snatches of time, and contains a good many conflicting passages, sometimes almost self-contradictory of each other. Indeed, the divergence of sentiment and expression is so great, in different parts of the document, that the reader would almost think that different minds had been concerned in its composition, or else that amendments and corrections had been inserted into the text after the whole was completed, without regard to the consistency and compatibility of other portions going before or following after.

I feel quite sensibly, therefore, in quoting particular passages as illustrative of the chairman's ideas, that I may seem to do injustice to what he says elsewhere, inasmuch as some other portion of the Report may read quite at variance with those parts which I select. Yet, as a whole, I have endeavored to seek out the *general drift* of the honorable chairman's meaning and direction; and, when I have obtained that, to estimate the seeming qualifications or contradictions elsewhere stated (especially if dissevered, and standing in no appropriate connection), as something exceptional and deserving of less consideration.

Perhaps, too, the sharp criticism which I may feel it necessary to make upon the reported Bill, and the subsequent congressional ratification of its crudities by the House, deserves some qualifying word of apology, on the score of haste and the pressure of the closing business of the session. I hardly think, however, that much extenuation is fairly admissible on this ground, considering the peremptory voting-down by the House of the urgent appeals of Messrs. Raymond and Patterson, from the minority of the committee, for further deliberation, and opportunity for examination; and, as General Banks himself took the leading part in forcing the measure through all its preliminary stages to its final passage at one sitting, he ought also to be precluded, for the same reason, from the benefit of the apology suggested. As the House, nevertheless, put themselves upon the same platform with the Chairman of their Committee of Foreign Affairs, by unanimously sanctioning and approving of his measures, I have the satisfaction of feeling, that whatever strictures I may have to make upon his Report, Bill, and congressional defence of it, are shared by him in common with that able, intelligent, and patriotic representative body; and that my remarks cannot therefore be construed into having any personal or unfriendly application.

To premise one word more, before proceeding to my discussion, I feel bound also to appreciatively acknowledge, in General Banks's Report, a just recognition of several of the great doctrines of American Neutral Law, for which, in common with many others, or else in some independent discussions on my own responsibility, I have had the honor of contending: such as the unneutral and unwarranted toleration by England of the outfit and subsequent keeping-afloat, of the "Alabama;" the precipitate and unprecedented recognition of a state of belligerency extended by that same Government to our Confederate rebels; and the clearly settled declaration of American law, that ships of war constitute a justifiable article of traffic when built and sold with a purely commercial intent. On these points, at least, it does not become me to censure the Report of the Chairman of the Committee on Foreign Affairs, nor to question the sanction lent to its sentiments by the unanimous action of the House of Representatives.

There are other issues, however, besides these which come up for discussion; and I cannot allow myself to be blinded to the more objectionable character of the measures in question by these favorable features referred to.

To give a brief summary, then, of General Banks's Report, and afford a clue to his leading motives in setting on foot the new scheme of neutral policy, I believe his general drift may be fairly stated to be about as follows: —

That our early neutrality — that of Washington's day and the era of the law of 1794 — was well enough, but not deserving of praise. —

"It was the result of the situation of the country; and the deficiency in armies, navies, fortifications, and the implements of war, had as much to do with it as the opinions of legislators, executive officers, or the people." ("House Report, No. 100," p. 5.) It was a policy of isolation and estrangement from foreign nations, rather than of mere neutrality." (*Ib.*, p. 6.) "The government accepted it, not because it was just, but necessary." (*Ib.*) "For a time it answered the demands of other governments." (*Ib.*, p. 2.)

The law of 1794 having received its first amendment three years later, — viz., in 1797, — General Banks says of the amendment, and of the combined effect of the two laws: —

"In 1797 the statute was amended by further restrictions upon commerce and the people. Neither the interests of France nor public sentiment prompted this change in the existing law. It could have been suggested only by the power that prompted the original enactment." (*Ib.*, p. 2.)

"Public opinion . . . enabled the Administration . . . to gratify England by the enactment of statutes for its protection, more explicit and stringent than those imposed by the law of nations." (*Ib.*, p. 2.)

"The statutes of 1794 and 1797 . . . were sufficiently stringent in their prohibitions upon American commerce and the American people, to satisfy and silence the claims of the nation most ambitious for supremacy upon the land and sea." (*Ib.*, p. 3.)

Passing to the next and concluding period of neutral legislative history, — the acts of 1817 and 1818, — the General says of the former (p. 4), —

"It was not legislation to punish crime against the law of nations, but to prevent offences against Spain." The law of 1818, the existing statute, "was enacted upon the pressing claims of Spain and Portugal, backed by the representations of Great Britain."

After going into an analysis of its provisions (as if new legislation, when in fact it was substantially a re-enactment of the law of 1794, made perpetual in 1800, as I shall presently show), General Banks proceeds to say of it: —

"It is impossible to suppose that provisions so repressive upon American commerce, so hostile to the cause of liberty in the colonies, and so strongly in favor of a government whose principles were so repugnant to the people as those of Spain, were voluntarily adopted. They had their origin in the interests of European governments, hostile to the cause of the colonies." (p. 4.)

And again, three pages later (p. 7) : —

"In reviewing the statute of 1818, we cannot escape the conclusion, . . . that it disregards the inalienable rights of the people of all nations; that it was imposed upon the country by considerations affecting exclusively the political interests of other nations; that it criminally restrains the rights of nations at peace, for the benefit of those at war; that it was intended to perpetuate the supremacy of favored nations on the sea. It properly belongs to another age, and is not of us nor for us."

Following up these disparaging views of our past neutral legislation, as one reflecting no credit upon the country, but as at all times imposed upon us by foreign dictation, and to which we yielded through maritime weakness and a disposition to favor England, General Banks goes on to recommend a thorough revision of the neutrality laws hereafter; and, in the mean time, to repeal so much of the provisions now in force as "to scale" our own code down to the level of English legislation. Accordingly, his *project*, as ultimately amended and voted by the House, contains various modifications of the law of 1818 designed to that end; the "scaling" down, as the chairman explains, being motived upon the idea —

"That we can no longer stand bail for the peace of the world, and that we have stood guard for other nations long enough;" and that, "when the maintenance of national honor is identified with the defence of principles essential to the independence of States and the progress of civilization, we cannot falter on a course marked out for us by duty and destiny." (Report, p. 10.)

The Report concludes with a special arraignment of the conduct of Great Britain towards the United States during the late civil struggle, in permitting the equipment and outfit of rebel cruisers from British territory, and afterwards receiving them with friendly hospitality into British outports; and, having shown that the proposed reduction of the tone of our neutrality laws will not prejudice our claims against England for indemnity for those grievances, it then closes with a strong denunciation of Irish wrongs, and an expression of opinion that the voice of the Government should be heard in aid of the cause of Irish independence against British oppression.

Now, to this proposed step forward in the course of manifest destiny, so far as its expediency is sought to be justified by the *exposé* of our neutral history above abbreviated from General Banks, I have to object, in the first place, that it unjustly and unjustifiably disparages the country's historic good name and fame.

CHAPTER II.

The fame of the United States for neutrality only second to its being the country of Washington. — This especially true of its neutrality in Washington's day. — General Banks's sentiment contested, that we only observed neutrality from necessity and national weakness. — On the contrary, it is a special glory that we were so bravely and honestly neutral when so weak. — Statement of the characteristics of early American neutrality. — Proof of the position by historical instances. — The case of the " Grange," prize to the " L'Embuscade," the French war-frigate which brought Genet to the United States. — The prize given back to England, and the surroundings of the case. — The case of the " William," a prize under charge of Gideon Henfield. — The sale of the prize stopped, the prize seized, a libel filed for its restitution, and Henfield arrested and tried for a violation of the law of nations. — Letters between Genet and Jefferson. — Henfield acquitted; but his case made the occasion for the passage of the law of 1794, June 5. — Note to this case, showing its bearing on the method of restoring prizes taken in violation of neutrality. — Case of the seizure of the French privateer " The Republican," with an armed force. — The recall of Genet demanded in one of the boldest and ablest of American State papers. — Mr. Pickering's despatches also commended for their able assertion of neutral independence. — As to subservience to England, at this time we were almost at swords'-points with her, and therefore could not have been over-complaisant. — Jay's instructions and Mr. Randolph's despatch quoted to show this. — Several examples given of our enforcement of neutrality against England. — The French Minister of Foreign Affairs quoted to the same effect. — A striking example of the fearlessness of our people towards England given in the affair of the "Nautilus," where the General Assembly of Rhode Island detained one of His British Majesty's captains till he gave up six impressed American seamen detained on board his vessel.

IF there is any point well established in our favor on the pages of history, I had supposed it to be that we enjoyed a national reputation for professing and maintaining high principles of international neutrality. If the remark is limited to the time of Washington's presidency, there can be no doubt, I believe, that such a reputation is justly deserved. Probably next to our country's fame as being the place where Washington lived, there is no particular in which the republic is so favorably known in Europe and throughout the civilized world as that of being the honest and consistent advocate of neutral rights at the time of the French Revolution. And it was in her infancy, more than at any other time, that the United States enjoyed the opportunity of establishing this fame upon the basis of a manly and courageous self-respect, as well as in obedience to Christian precepts of love of peace, and promotion of good-will among men.

Does General Banks think that we chose our path of neutrality, in the trying days of the French Revolution, out of weakness and overpowering necessity? I maintain, that it was just because, when we *were* so weak and defenceless as at that era, we yet so manfully resisted the aggressions of France and England upon our independence, and so courageously fought the battle of neutral rights for other nations as weak as ourselves, that our vindication of neutrality deservedly became commendable and famous.

That a great and formidable power should force other equal or inferior powers to respect its rights of territorial sovereignty is a matter meriting no special comment. That such a power even should fulfil the duties of an impartial and yet hospitable neutrality, in affording that protection to the neutral rights of inferior or co-ordinate powers which the active practice of neutrality demands, is not altogether a new incident in international history. But for a new-born nation, five, or at most fifteen, years old, without a soldier or a sailor at its command, nay, without a dollar, as I might say, in its treasury, and having an unarmed frontier of thousands of miles by sea and by land lying open to aggression, to announce to nations four and five times its superior in numbers and a hundred-fold its overmatch in preparations for war, that its territory is sacred from belligerent enterprises and hostile undertakings; that it acknowledges no superior but the law of nations; that, in observance of that law, it shall *compel* the contending parties to comply with certain before-unheard-of but eminently just prescriptions of neutral conduct; and that, finally, *it holds itself accountable to injured powers for any damage sustained by them through its own non-enforcement of these prescriptions, and through its own non-fulfilment of the law of nations generally,* — was a new and unheard-of trait of national profession and practice in the world's history which might justly challenge attention and admiration. And it was just this, in my judgment, which made up the neutral deportment of the United States at the epoch in question.

Am I interrogated for my proofs of this position, I reply, that the fact has taken its place in the world's history, and has become an item of general reputation. I will not weary my readers' patience with going over the ground again in detail, which of late has been so much explored and turned up in recent discussions of our early precedents. Suffice it to say, that the more those precedents have been discussed and *disputed*, the brighter and fairer stands out the character of American neutrality, and the less occasion is there now for American statesmen to draw it in question.

Lest any of my American readers, however, shall have happened to fail of having their attention attracted to this bright page of their country's history, I venture to reproduce three or four practical illustrations of early American neutrality, not as yet become familiar points of historical information, by way of indicating the spirit in which that neutrality has been hitherto observed, and in which, it is the object of my discussion to prove, it should always continue hereafter to be enforced.

My first illustration is borrowed from the occurrence which brought the United States face to face with the French republic, for the first time after Washington's policy had been resolved upon, and his proclamation of neutrality issued.

Genet landed at Charleston, April 8, 1793, and sent the frigate which brought him to the United States — the "L'Embuscade" — round to Philadelphia, whither he himself directed his steps, by slow journeys, by land across the country. The "L'Embuscade" came into Philadelphia about the first of May, 1793, — the President's proclamation having, in the mean time, been published on the 22d of April, — bringing with her, as prize of war, the British ship "Grange," which she had captured in Delaware Bay, inside of the Capes, and within three miles of the land. Immediately on the complaint of the British minister that there had been a violation of the neutral jurisdiction of the United States, President Washington, through Mr.

Jefferson, Secretary of State, demanded of Genet's predecessor, M. Ternant, that the prize should be given up to the British Government. This was on the 15th day of May; and, on the next day, Genet himself arrived in Philadelphia, then the capital of the country, and, in concurrence with Ternant, shortly after decided to accede to the President's demand, and the "Grange" was put at the disposal of the British minister. This was the first practical enforcement of American neutrality.[1]

I pause for a moment to bring the surroundings belonging to this important historical incident to the reader's appreciation. Here was a newly organized and as yet hardly self-subsistent government, of barely four millions of subjects, and those widely scattered over a vast and thinly populated territory, without a fortified seaport or internal stronghold of any kind in its possession, without a ship or mounted gun in its navy, and with a sailor or a soldier that it could call its own, emphatically declaring to the first military power of Europe, — at that time certainly more than six times its superior in population, and holding all Europe at bay by its martial prowess, — that it must drop its prey, and make it over as a neutrality-offering to its hated enemy, because United-States neutral soil was inviolable, even to its best ally!

Would General Banks call that *accepting the situation, because we were too feeble to assert any will of our own?*

Let me briefly enforce this illustration with two or three others of a similar character, occurring within six weeks after the first executive resolve to enforce neutrality towards the European belligerents was decided upon.

A few days after the arrival of the "Grange" at Philadelphia, and while the question of her restoration was still pending, one of the prizes captured by a Charleston-fitted French privateer, which Genet had let loose while temporarily sojourning in that city, came into Philadelphia for sale; and the British minister complained that there had been another violation of the President's proclamation, for which he required redress. Genet at

---

[1] For particulars of this case, see 1 Am. State Pap. (Cong. ed.), pp. 147, 150; 1 Opinions of Attorney-Generals, p. 32; 3 Jeff. Works, p. 547; U. S. Gaz., May 1, 1793; *Ib.*, May 4, 29; 2 Marshall's Wash., 2d ed., p. 262.

this time had been fully accredited as minister, and now had to be encountered in defence of *his own* doings.

What was the President's course in regard to this new point in neutral procedure? Before, he had had to deal with a simple case of violation of territorial jurisdiction: now, he had to meet and cope with the French emissary upon the substantial business for which he had come to this country; viz., the turning of American ports into stations whence to fit out hostile expeditions against the governments with which the French republic was at war. Hamilton's advice (submitted to the President in a written opinion of May 15, 1793, — 4 Ham. Works, p. 394) was followed; and the two officers in charge of the prize, the British ship "William," were arrested, and held to answer to a criminal charge. The sale of the prize was stopped, and the prize itself taken into the custody of the Government, to be delivered up to the rightful owner when he should establish his lawful title.

I am tempted to give two short letters which passed between the French and American authorities relative to this affair, as illustrative of General Banks's thesis, that our conduct in preserving neutrality was only dictated by weakness, and not the result of principle. I quote from the American State Papers (Cong. ed. vol. i. p. 151):—

Genet to Jefferson (Secretary of State).

PHILADELPHIA, June 1, 1793,
Second year of the Republic.

SIR, — I have this moment been informed that two officers in the service of the republic of France, citizens Gideon Henfield and John Singletary, have been arrested on board the privateer of the French republic, "The Citizen Genet," and conducted to prison. The crime laid to their charge — the crime which my mind cannot conceive, and which my pen almost refuses to state — is the serving of France, and defending, with her children, the common and glorious cause of liberty.

Being ignorant of any positive law or treaty which deprives Americans of this privilege, and authorizes officers of police arbitrarily to take marines in the service of France from on board their vessels, I call upon your intervention, sir, and that of the President of the

United States, in order to obtain the immediate release of the above-mentioned officers, who have acquired, by the sentiments animating them, and by the act of their engagement anterior to every act to the contrary, the right of French citizens, if they have lost that of American citizens. I renew, at the same time, sir, the requisition which I made in favor of another French officer, detained for the same cause and for the same object.

GENET.

Jefferson to Genet.

PHILADELPHIA, June 1, 1793.

SIR,—I have to acknowledge the receipt of your note of the 27th of May, on the subject of Gideon Henfield, a citizen of the United States, engaged on board an armed vessel in the service of France. It has been laid before the President, and referred to the Attorney-General of the United States for his opinion on the matter of law; and I have now the honor of enclosing you a copy of that opinion. Mr. Henfield appears to be in the custody of the civil magistrate, over whose proceedings the Executive has no control. The act with which he is charged will be examined by a jury of his countrymen in the presence of judges of learning and integrity; and, if it is not contrary to the laws of the land, no doubt need be entertained that his case will issue accordingly. The forms of law involve certain necessary delays, of which, however, he will assuredly experience none but what are necessary.—I have the honor, &c.,

TH. JEFFERSON.

P.S.—After writing the above, I was honored with your note on the subject of Singletary, on which it is in my power to say nothing more than in that of Henfield.

I need not say, for the information of my readers, that Henfield was energetically and thoroughly prosecuted; nor that, when he was acquitted by the jury (probably through the belief that he had not intended any violation of the law), President Washington thought of immediately convening Congress to pass a statute which should make the offence plain and heinous to popular apprehension. As it was, however, citizen Genet undoubtedly found that American law took its course in trying citizen Henfield, an officer in the French service, arrested under the French flag, on board a privateer bearing the commission of the French republic, and for a crime which the French minister's "mind could not conceive, and which his pen almost refused to state." I will add, that, at the earliest opportunity without summoning a special session, the President called the subject to the attention of Congress in his next annual address; and that his recommendation, as we shall presently see, resulted in the passage of the act of 1794, June 5.[1]

---

[1] For the judicial particulars of the prize case, *the "William,"* see *Findlay* v. *ship "William,"* 1 Peters Adm. Rep. p. 12, decided June 26, 1793, where Judge Peters held, that, as a judge of an admiralty court, he had no jurisdiction to adjudicate upon a prize of war captured in violation of sovereignty, and restore it to its owner. The "William" was captured at the mouth of Chesapeake Bay, and, as alleged, within United States' jurisdiction; and was, at the same time, made prize of by a vessel fitted out, in violation of neutrality, at Charleston, S. C. Judge Peters, looking at the case in the light of a political and diplomatic question between the American and the French Governments, like that of the "Grange" just noticed, declined to take jurisdiction of the subject matter. This decision, in all probability, gave rise to the provision of the act of 1794, ch. 50, § 6, conferring the requisite authority upon the admiralty courts to restore prizes captured in American waters, or within three miles of the coast.

The reader will bear in mind the distinction between violating *the territorial sovereignty* and violating *the neutral laws* of the neutral nation. Thus the "L'Embuscade" was a French ship of war, *duly equipped elsewhere*, when she captured the "Grange." "The Citizen Genet," the French privateer which made prize of the "William," on the other hand, *had been unlawfully equipped in Charleston;* though Judge Peters did not take the latter element into account in making his decision (indeed, the point does not seem to have been raised at all), but repudiated jurisdiction on the former head. The Supreme Court, however, in the case of *Glass* v. *"The Betsey"* (one of the prizes of the same privateer, "The Citizen Genet"), in January or February following (3 Dall. Rep., p. 6), asserted the competency of the Federal courts to adjudicate upon captures made by vessels fitted out in violation of neutrality; and in August of the year following, 1795, actually decreed restitution of such a prize to its original owners, *though captured on the high seas*, it being subsequently brought into an American port, in the leading case of *Talbot* v. *Jansen* (3 Dall. Rep., p. 133). This jurisdiction continued to be asserted and practised by the United-States courts ever after, though the principle of its exercise troubled Chief-Justice Marshall, as it has other juridical writers who have questioned its regularity. See Chief-Justice Marshall's comments upon it, in the *Santissima Trinidad* case, when that cause was up before him for original adjudication in the Virginia Circuit Court (1 Brockenbrough Rep., p. 496–9), and again in the case of *The Gran Para*, 7 Wheat., 486, where the Chief Justice speaks of the American practice as one then become well settled. See also Mr. Harcourt's ingenious criticism on the point, in the letter of "Historicus" to the "London Times" of Nov. 4. (*Times*, Nov. 6.)

I am not aware that the point of restoring prizes under the head of violation of territorial sovereignty purely — i.e., "in cases of captures made within the

Washington's next example of enforcing neutrality had for its scene the commercial capital of the country, New-York City. On the 8th of June, 1793, one week later than the Henfield correspondence, just cited, Governor Clinton, the Governor of the State of New York, acting under instructions from the President, seized, *with a detachment of militia,* the French privateer, the "Republican," fitted out in violation of neutrality, and then just ready to sail on a cruise, and handed her over to the judicial authorities for prosecution. I will not stop to consider what was the ultimate issue of the proceeding, which I have elsewhere discussed with some detail. See "Precedents of American Neutrality," p. 49; only remarking, here, that the United-States executive held on to the offending vessel with a strong hand, notwithstanding the most vigorous and most violent protestations of the French envoy, and continued its forcible detention of the vessel till all possibility of an infraction of neutrality was at an end.

Here, again, I beg the appreciative reader who weighs the diplomatic moment, *of seizing by military force the commissioned privateer of the leading warlike power of Europe,* to answer for himself the question of whether it is likely that the policy which dictated such a step was either pusillanimous or subservient to foreign dictation.

---

waters of the United States, or within a marine league of the coasts or shores thereof," within the terms of § 6 of Stat. 1794, ch. 50, and § 7 of Stat. 1818, ch. 88 — was ever again made the subject of judicial consideration, after the case of the ship "William;" though the construction of the section just quoted has been incidentally alluded to here and there, as by counsel, *arguendo*, in *Talbot* v. *Jansen*, 3 Dall., p. 139; and by Livingston, J., in "*The Estrella*," 4 Wheat., p. 219.

For further particulars of this important case, see the "United-States Gazette," published contemporaneously at Philadelphia, for May 14, 15; June 8, 22, 26, 29; July 3, 6, and 10, 1793. See Cabinet Opinions, 4 Ham. Works, p. 394; *Ib.*, 463; 1 Am. State Papers, pp. 160, 161, 175; 1 Opin. Atty. Gen., p. 40.

For further particulars of Henfield's case, see Wharton's State Trials, p. 49; U.S. Gazette, June 5, and July 31, 1793; 4 Ham. Works, p. 461; 5 Ham. (J. C.) His. of Rep. p. 345. Though Henfield came into Philadelphia in charge of the "William," as prize-master, it would seem from the French Minister's note, as above, that he was arrested on board the privateer, "The Citizen Genet," which was lying in port at the same time.

And so I might go on with the three months' struggle which Washington kept up with French unneutral lawlessness as embodied in Genet's revolutionary career, and which struggle only culminated with the demand of the recall of the turbulent French envoy, on the 16th of August, 1793, in that despatch of the American Secretary of State, of that date, to Mr. Morris, our minister at Paris, which undoubtedly ranks among the ablest and boldest state-papers which this country has ever produced. (Am. State Papers, p. 167.) How far the fame of it belongs to Jefferson, whose signature it bears, or whether it was Hamilton's work, — as his son and biographer, Mr. John C. Hamilton, renders highly probable (Hamilton's History of the Republic, vol. v. p. 333, &c.), — I will not venture to affirm. But I will venture to assert, that its fame, by whichever of Washington's Secretaries it may have been composed, is the property of the nation, of which General Banks, I am sure, did not designedly intend to deprive his country, in the remotest degree, when he uttered his disparaging remarks about our early neutral history.

Of course, Washington's vindication of neutrality, and, I may add, nationality, did not end with Genet's ministership. I should be glad to cite other specimens of the first President's assertion of a just and independent policy of neutrality towards France during the remainder of his administration, particularly under the Secretaryship of Mr. Pickering, whose despatches in reply to Genet's successors will compare favorably, in my judgment, with those of any of Washington's secretaries; but I have adduced enough, I think, to enable the reader to judge whether, as towards France, General Banks's assertion holds good, that our policy was adopted, because "it answered the demands of other governments."

But I suppose General Banks will urge that the power to which he more particularly refers, as dictating our neutral course, was England. I believe that I cannot mistake his intention to indicate that Government, when he speaks, as he does in his Report (p. 2), of —

"the power that prompted the original enactment of the act of 1794;"

and, again (p. 3), of —

"prohibitions sufficiently stringent to satisfy and silence the claims of the nation most ambitious for supremacy upon the land and sea."

It was fear of *England*, then, that constrained Washington into a policy which "was not just, but necessary."

Does the Chairman of the Committee on Foreign Affairs forget that our relations towards England, at this period of 1793-4, were on so hostile a footing, that Chief-Justice Jay was sent out there on his famous mission, at that era, *not so much to make a treaty, as to save a war between the two countries?* Let me cite a half-dozen lines of historic proof to this point, not to convince General Banks of the historical fact, — for I do not doubt that he is already well aware of it, — but for the proper presentation of my point to the judgment of the reader.

A clause in Mr. Jay's instructions ran thus : —

"A full persuasion is entertained, that, throughout the whole negotiation, you will make the following its general objects: To keep alive in the mind of the British minister that opinion which the solemnity of a special mission must naturally inspire, of the strong agitations excited in the people of the United States, by the disturbed condition of things between them and Great Britain ; *to repel war*, for which we are not disposed, and into which the necessity of vindicating our honor and our property may, but can alone, drive us ; to prevent the British ministry, *should they be resolved on war*, from carrying with them the British nation ; and, at the same time, *to assert with dignity and firmness our rights and our title to reparation for past injuries.*" (1 Am. State Papers, p. 472.)

Following up his instructions, three weeks later, Mr. Randolph, Secretary of State, who had succeeded Mr. Jefferson in that office, writes to Mr. Jay at London, under date of May 27, 1794, among other things, as follows : —

"The late conduct of Mr. Hammond [the British Minister at Philadelphia] is that of a *minister foreseeing a rupture with the United States*, and collecting every scrap of exceptionable matter, however small, in order to swell the list of grievances in some future manifesto. . . . In the mean while, I enclose to you the proceedings at Newport, in Rhode Island, which involve too much delicacy to be delayed in the communication. But all these events, proceeding as they do from a state of inflammation which the British Government has it in their power to extinguish, manifest *the necessity of an immediate adjustment of our disputes.*" (1 Am. State Papers, pp. 474–5.)

These two letters were written within one month — the last within one week — of the passage of the act of 1794, June 5. And in view of the *exposé* of our relations towards England which they furnish, *for that very moment*, I think I may safely ask the question, whether England can be supposed to be one of " the favored nations whose supremacy we were intending to perpetuate " by that legislation.

But I go farther, and assert that fear had as little to do with influencing the neutral policy of Washington's Administration towards the British Government as favor or affection. Have General Banks and his committee forgotten with what an equal hand President Washington dealt out his measures of neutral severity towards repressing English violations of our territorial sovereignty, as well as towards those in the interests of France? I will not say that he had so frequent occasion to interfere with the former as with those in behalf of the latter power; but that he administered the law of neutral impartiality in the same spirit, and with equal fearlessness, towards one nation as towards the other, can, I think, be plainly demonstrated. I cite a few proofs in passing.

Here is an acknowledgment from Genet himself, on that head, under date of June 25, 1793. Genet is writing to Jefferson (1 Am. State Pap., 159) : —

PHILADELPHIA, June 25, 1793,
Second Year of the Republic of France.

I learn with infinite pleasure, by your letter of the 23d of this month, that the Government of [the State of] Georgia *have caused to be stopped a vessel, armed in that State, for the purpose of cruising against the French, and that the persons interested in this vessel will be prosecuted.* . . .

Accept, sir, &c. GENET.

July 9 (1793), M. Genet (1 Am. State Pap., p. 163), having requested the Governor of Pennsylvania to order the " Jane," an armed *English* privateer, out of the port of Philadelphia, Mr. Jefferson recites, in his letter of August 16 to Mr. Morris (1 Am. State Pap., p. 169), that the Government of the United States, finding that the privateer had bought new gun-carriages in Philadelphia to mount new guns which she had brought into port in her hold with her, and was opening new port-holes for those additional guns, *ordered the carriages to be relanded, and the port-holes to be stopped up;* which orders were complied with, and the privateer went out of port in the same outfit as that with which she had come in.

In the same sense, the French Minister for Foreign Affairs, writing to Genet from Paris, under date of July 10, 1793, after berating him soundly for his disregard of American neutral dignity and rights, says, "*We have never made an ineffectual demand on that Government* [the American], and we have always found there the most friendly disposition." ("Documens Historiques," Appendix to De Witt's Memoir of Jefferson, p. 526.)

But as illustrative of our treatment of the "most favored nation," if General Banks means to indicate England by that epithet, I beg my reader's leave to bring forward a little episode of our neutral history, which is not, indeed, strictly illustrative of American neutrality, but which is so strongly in point, to the question whether our Government acted under duress towards England at the period of 1793-4, that I think the reader would be sorry to have me omit it. It is a vindication of neutral rights on first principles, which never seems to have found its way into the text-books of international law, or the popular histories of the United States, but which is referred to as a grave State matter by Mr. Randolph, in the letter of May 27, 1794, just cited, and which undoubtedly occurred as a matter of fact in the way which I am about to narrate. I take my data from authentic original sources, in the Congressional collection of State Papers (1 Am. State Pap., p. 466, &c.).

In the month of May, 1794, His Britannic Majesty's sloop-of-war, the "Nautilus," Captain H. W. Baynton, came into Newport, R.I., in need of fresh provisions and supplies. Captain Baynton made application to the General Assembly of the State, which happened then to be in session at that place, for necessary leave to victual and furnish his ship. [Why such leave should have been necessary, except as illustrative of the disturbed relations of the country towards England, I do not understand.] The Assembly took the application into consideration, and, while deliberating upon it, were informed that the British vessel had a number of impressed American seamen among her crew, who were detained on board against their consent. The intelligence causing much excitement, the Assembly proceeded to investigate the matter.

They sent a message to Captain Baynton, soliciting his attendance, and, at the same time, requested the presence of all the judges of the State and Federal courts to advise with them how to deal with the emergency, in case the intelligence should prove true, and in case the British officer should refuse to release his American sailors. Captain Baynton, who happened to be on shore, made no objection to obeying the invitation, and attended the Assembly, in company with his lieutenant and the British vice-consul.

At the request of the Assembly, the judges conducted the inquiry. They informed the British officials of the statement which had been laid before them, and expressed the hope that they would furnish the fullest satisfaction upon the delicate subject of inquiry. The captain denied that he had any such seamen as were described on board his vessel, and so did his lieutenant. Captain Baynton demanded their names, and declared that he did not choose to take such seamen on board, and had never pressed any such among his ship's crew. The judges told him that they were not able to give the names; upon which he undertook to throw doubt upon the complaint altogether.

The judges, in reply, called a witness, who testified, under oath, that he had been told, by one of the ship's barge-men, that there were as many as thirteen American sailors on board the "Nautilus," and that three of them had been pressed. The captain still appeared to disbelieve the matter; and it was then proposed to him that a citizen or two should accompany him or his lieutenant aboard the ship, and make the necessary inquiry. The captain at first assented to this; but, on the consul's dropping something against the propriety of allowing a search of the ship, he recalled his consent, and refused to permit any such visit. Much argument was used to convince him of the propriety of so doing, but to no purpose. The captain maintained that his word ought to be sufficient, and he would go no further.

Finally, after the judges had exhausted their powers of persuasion, Captain Baynton broke up the conference with expressing his surprise at being thus cross-questioned, and demanded if he was to consider himself a prisoner. He was told that he was not a prisoner, and that no such step had been resolved upon. The judges then proposed to leave him and his lieutenant and the consul in a room by themselves, to see if they could not arrange something which should be satisfactory to all parties. This again was declined; and thereupon the two officers attempted to burst out of the hall into the lobby, but found themselves stopped by a crowd of people, who besieged the outer doors, and presently came back expressing apprehensions for their safety. The judges assured them of protection and perfect safety while with them, and again urged upon them some measure of satisfaction. This they peremptorily declined to give; and thereupon — the judges having first communicated the result of the conference to the Assembly — that body took up the subject in legislative deliberation, and passed the following resolve: —

LOWER HOUSE OF ASSEMBLY.

Whereas complaint hath been made to this Assembly, that sundry citizens of the United States are illegally detained on board of a certain sloop-of-war, called the " Nautilus," belonging unto His Britannic Majesty, commanded by H. W. Baynton, now riding at anchor in the road of Newport, within this State: It is hereby voted and resolved, that the said Captain H. W. Baynton and the lieutenant of said sloop-of-war, who are now on shore, *remain there* until investigation of the subject of said complaint be had before the judicial authority of this State and District.

To effect which purpose, it is further voted and resolved, that, on condition the said H. W. Baynton consent thereto, Messrs. Henry Sherburne, John L. Boss, Samuel Wardwell, Christopher Ellery, and William Davis be a committee from this Assembly to go on board the said sloop-of-war with Mr. Thomas W. Moore, vice-consul of his Britannic Majesty for the District of Rhode Island, and request of the commanding officer now on board said sloop-of-war an examination of the crew thereof, and report to the judicial authority of this State and District the names of any citizens of the said United States, there detained, as aforesaid; and that the said judicial authority take examination of the birth and residence of such citizens, and *enlarge those who, on such examination, are found to be citizens of any of the said United States. Voted, &c.*

SAMUEL EDDY, *Clerk.*

IN THE UPPER HOUSE.

Read the same day, and concurred. By order.

HENRY WARD, *Secretary.*

The report of the General Assembly, from which I have quoted and abbreviated as above, then proceeds to give the *denouement* of the affair as follows: —

" The officers were informed of this resolution; and, a conversation more cool and candid having taken place, the captain agreed that the gentlemen mentioned in the foregoing act of the General Assembly might go on board his ship. The consul agreed to go with them; and the captain sent a letter (which he first showed to the judges) to the commanding officer on board, directing him to give those gentlemen all the satisfaction in his power, as to there being any Americans on board. Those gentlemen proceeded on board, and were received with the utmost politeness. The books and lists of the men were shown, and the people called upon to declare whether there were then any Americans unwilling to remain on board. Six appeared (as, by the following copy, taken by the committee from the shipping-book itself, and by their own declaration) to be Americans. [The names and homes of the six American sailors are then set out in full.] — N.B. The entries appeared to be made by some officer of the ship, and no signature of the sailors."

The committee then certify to the entries being truly copied, and sign the report with their names in full.

The legislative report then proceeds: —

" The captain immediately declared that he was surprised; that four of them, he now believed, were Americans, but he was willing the six should be brought on shore, and as many as were Americans he would immediately discharge. His barge went again on board with his written orders, 'Send the six men on shore to be examined immediately.' The six sailors were soon brought on shore. The officers were convinced that they were all Americans, and the captain agreed that they might go where they pleased, and that in the morning he would send their clothing on shore, giving them written discharges, and certificates for their wages; and the consul freely offered to take the certificates, and give the sailors their money for them; whereupon entire good-humor appeared fully restored, and the officers with the consul retired. In the morning, the captain sent an officer on shore, who fully completed the business, agreeably to the captain's agreement."

The report of the legislature is signed by the United-States District Judge, and five State judges; and thereupon it was voted by the General Assembly, that the Governor be requested to send a copy of the report to the Secretary of State of the United States, as soon as may be. Accordingly, an official transcript of the proceedings, as above, finds its place in the United-States State Papers.

I will only add, that, Captain Baynton having made the *amende honorable,* the Assembly of Rhode Island voted thereupon that the Governor might furnish his ship with all the necessary supplies.

What sort of a reception Captain Baynton had from the British Admiralty when he reported his doings at home, or how this affair was ultimately arranged between the two governments in their diplomatic negotiations with each other, I am unable to answer. Our published State Papers throw no further light upon it, that I am aware of, beyond the mention contained in Mr. Randolph's letter, as above; and probably the British Government took no pains to bruit the transaction further. But no one, I think, who ponders on this little piece of homespun justice — where American judge-made and judge-administered law of nations fairly matched and equitably got the better of British press-gang usurpation — can fail to recognize, on the part of the American people, a spirit of self-help and a resolution to oppose foreign aggression at all hazards, quite incompatible with borrowing their policy from foreign dictation.

CHAPTER III.

Early American neutrality was as just as it was fearless; and this, from the necessity of the case, to satisfy French jealousy. — What occurred at the "Alexandra" trials in the way of quoting American precedents proves this. — American neutral law cited there with the greatest respect. — The Crown lawyers, however, hedged as to the "Alabama" question. — Hamilton entitled to chief praise for inaugurating American neutrality. — Hamilton and Jefferson's State papers a proud possession for the United States. — Authoritative vindication of our neutral fame. — Mr. John Ward. — Sir Robert Phillimore. — Mr. Dana's summary (note). — Citation of Mr. Canning's famous panegyric on American neutrality. — Mr. Rush quoted to the same point. — These authorities show how bad the starting-point of the new movement, in disparaging the country's fame, must be. — Why should not the neutrality of the republic surpass the expectations of monarchical Europe?

BUT, says the committee's Report, if our early neutrality laws were not forced upon us, they were not adopted because they were just in themselves. There, again, I join issue with the chairman, and the indorsement of his views by the House of Representatives.

I maintain that they were as just as they were the expression of a courageous independence.

One consideration alone, reasoning *a priori*, would seem almost sufficient to dispose of the question. Is it possible, that the United States, in view of their obligations to France, could have professed any other neutrality than that founded on the purest principles of international impartiality? While France was holding up the treaty of 1778 for our observance, under which the United States had received such great favors, and by whose terms they were so nearly bound to an alliance offensive and defensive with that country, could any other plea have stood a moment's examination than that having its basis in a neutrality pure and simple? In the nature of things, therefore, Washington and his Cabinet had immediate recourse to the writings of the best exponents of the law of nations, to define and to defend their course. Grotius, Bynkershoek, Vattel, and other authorities of that day, became as familiar at Philadelphia, as Wheaton and Kent and Lord Stowell have since become at Washington at the epoch of the "Trent" affair. Only there were much fewer persons to be found in 1793-4 who knew how to read and master the old international-law writers in Latin and French, than could be found in 1861 competent to examine and discuss the same class of topics, when treated by English and American publicists in their own mother tongue.

I cannot be mistaken, therefore, I believe, in supposing, *a priori*, that the neutral law of the United States, at the outset, was sought to be based on the justest and most scientific principles; and it is to this circumstance quite as much perhaps as to its fearless enforcement, that it owes its celebrity. If any proof were wanting to corroborate this idea, it would be furnished, it seems to me, by what occurred at the "Alexandra" trials (jury and law) in England, in 1863. On those occasions, for the first time for forty years, as they themselves confessed, the English judges and lawyers were compelled to study the elementary principles of neutral law, as embodied in the respective foreign-enlistment acts of England and the United States. But it was only in the jurisprudence of the latter country that they were able to find these principles expounded and applied. With belligerent law they had been sufficiently conversant, from the almost normal attitude of Great Britain as a warring Government; but neutral law was to them an essentially unknown province.

How, then, did American neutrality strike them? One and all paid homage to its early development under the hands of Hamilton and Jefferson. It would seem as if they could not get beyond it. On the one hand, Sir Hugh Cairns, for the claimants of the "Alexandra," insisted that Hamilton's "Instructions to Collectors" embodied all the law of nations on the subject; while, on the other hand, the Crown lawyers were in doubt whether those instructions did not go beyond it, and overstep the line of international obligation. By way of *hedging* on the "Alabama" question, as I believe I am justified in inferring, the Attorney and Solicitor Generals contended that the Instructions *did* thus surpass the limit of neutral duty. But all concerned agreed in recognizing the moral integrity and legislative and judicial skill, with which Washington's policy of neutrality, at that day, was inaugurated and practically enforced.

Beyond doubt, much the greatest share of praise, for the inauguration of this national policy, is due to Hamilton. He certainly first broke ground in the Cabinet in that direction, and ultimately carried President Washington with him. Besides being the originator, if not the draftsman, of the Neutrality Proclamation, and the author of the "Instructions to Collectors," and the writer of the various papers, "Pacificus," "Camillus," "No Jacobin," &c., in popular advocacy of Washington's foreign policy, he drew the act of 1794, as noticed by General Banks himself.

Jefferson, on the other hand, though in entire antagonism to Hamilton on the question of the French alliance and similar subjects connected with the observance of neutrality, was ultimately compelled to come into his views in the main; and, as the mouthpiece of the Executive, to set them forth in its communications with foreign powers. Whether, in those masterly despatches, he merely echoed the sentiments of the President and of Hamilton, simply clothing them with his own felicitous diction, or whether, to a large extent (as his biographers and friends assert), the matter, as well as the manner, of those famous compositions were his own, I will not undertake to decide. I will only venture to affirm, that neutral law, as embodied in the State papers of Washington and his Secretaries, and as enforced in the legislation and jurisprudence of his administration, furnishes as bright an example of exact and upright neutrality, based on scientific and impartial principles, as the history of the world can produce.

If I may be supposed to state this matter too strongly, through patriotic pride, I beg to quote two or three corroborating authorities from foreign sources, by way of meeting the disparaging statements of the Report from the House Committee on Foreign Affairs.

Says Mr. John Ward, the author of the "History of the Law of Nations," and of the treatise on "The Rights and Duties of

Belligerent and Neutral Powers," which Chancellor Kent says " has exhausted all the law and learning applicable to the question," in writing in 1801, four years after Washington's retirement: —

"Of the great trading nations, America is almost the only one that has shown consistency of principle. *The firmness and thorough understanding of the laws of nations, which during this war [the French Revolution] she has displayed, must for ever rank her high in the scale of enlightened communities.*" (Ward's "Rights and Duties," &c., p. 166.)

Says Sir Robert Phillimore, the present Queen's Advocate, and author of the most comprehensive and systematic "Commentary on International Law" that England has produced: —

"The conduct of the United States with respect to this matter [the principles professed by the armed neutrality of 1780] has been, *under the most trying circumstances,* marked, not only by perfect consistency, but by *preference for right and duty* over interest and the expediency of the moment." (Com. on Int. Law, vol. iii. p. 282.)

So, the same writer, after giving a summary of our practice and jurisprudence in seizing and condemning vessels captured in violation of neutrality, says, —

"In these doctrines, a severe *but a just* conception of the duties and rights of neutrality appears to be embodied." (*Ib.*, p. 427.)

So, again, in quoting Washington's language to the French Government in 1795, upon the point of our insisting upon neutral property being safe under the belligerent flag, — a point where the French were quite as outrageous towards us, as in insisting that we should allow them to use our ports as a basis of hostilities against England, — Mr. Phillimore characterizes the American despatch as "an *honest and courageous*" vindication of our rights.

But I have no intention of wearying the reader with a collection of authorities to corroborate a statement so generally accepted, and so much a part of every well-educated American's knowledge, as that our early neutral history is a just cause of national pride. I have cited the above two text-writers almost at random, because they happen to bring out the traits which I am considering; viz., whether our neutrality was not as honest and wise as it was independent and brave.[1]

There is one piece of national reputation, however, connected with our fulfilment of the dictates of public law, so *apropos* to this matter of enacting or repealing neutrality statutes, that I must ask the reader's indulgence to quote it. I mean what was said by Mr. Canning, when British Secretary of State for Foreign Affairs, in urging upon his countrymen the example of the United States, to induce them to retain on their statute-book the British Foreign-Enlistment Act, whose repeal was then under consideration, and which act, so far as I now remember, is the only British legislation ever borrowed from the United States.

The quotation is a familiar one to many of my readers; but it cannot well be overlooked, when we hear the Chairman of the Committee on Foreign Affairs of the House of Representatives of the United States gravely and deliberately declaring to that body, as General Banks did in the late debate of July 26, that "*he did not like to say much about the history of this [our neutral] legislation, because it was not an agreeable subject.*" (Washington Globe, July 30.) On the contrary, I believe no American can fail of having the subject made agreeable to him, by listening to the sentiments of approbation of our neutral policy, on the part of one of the greatest of British statesmen, whose political antecedents by no means inclined him to flatter us.

Mr. Canning, then, as one of the British ministry, having been largely instrumental in effecting the adoption of the Foreign-Enlistment Act in 1819, — four years later, in 1823, as Foreign Secretary, took up the word in Parliament, on behalf of the Government, to prevent its repeal. In the course of a memorable speech on that occasion, in the House of Commons (April 16, 1823), he used the following language: —

---

[1] Mr. Dana, in his valuable and extended annotation on neutrality, in his recent edition of "Wheaton's Elements of International Law," says, without specifying instances, "The course pursued by Washington and his Cabinet, in sustaining neutrality and impartiality, has received the commendations of the masters of public law in all nations." (Note to p. 540.)

"I do not now pretend to argue in favor of *a system of neutrality;* but, it being declared [by proclamation] that we intend to remain neutral, I call upon the House to abide by that declaration so long as it shall remain unaltered. . . . We have spent much time in teaching other powers the nature of a strict neutrality; and, generally speaking, we have found them most reluctant scholars. All I now call upon the House to do is *to adopt the same course which it has recommended to neutral powers upon former occasions. If I wished for a guide* IN A SYSTEM OF NEUTRALITY, *I should take that laid down by America, in the days of the presidency of Washington, and the secretaryship of Jefferson.* [After giving a brief historical summary of that system and practice, he then added:] *Here, sir, I contend, is the principle upon which we ought to act.*" — Hansard, Parl. Deb., vol. viii. new series, p. 1056.

Mr. Rush, our minister to London at that period, has set down in his diary some account of his meeting Mr. Canning, a few days after his paying this notable tribute to the United States, and of the interest which this speech excited among the foreign ministers then resident at the British Court. On his telling Mr. Canning, on this occasion (a diplomatic dinner given by the British Foreign Secretary, April 23, 1823, and attended by all the foreign ambassadors and ministers then present in London), "with what pleasure I had read it," Mr. Canning remarked, "that he had lately been examining the State papers of our Government at that era, and that they presented, in his opinion, especially the letters of Mr. Jefferson, while Secretary of State, principles well fitted to enter into a neutral code."

"The ambassador of the Netherlands," adds Mr. Rush, "who sat close by, appeared to listen with as much interest as I did to this tribute, from such a source, to the American defence of neutral rights; and another ambassador, from a larger power, who sat further off, and who had not been able to hear distinctly what Mr. Canning had said, sought me out on the day following, on purpose to ascertain what it was Mr. Canning had said to me about neutral rights. I told him; adding that what he had publicly said in the House of Commons, on the 16th, amounted in effect to the same thing." ("Residence at the Court of London from 1817 to 1825," p. 464.)

Had General Banks sat in Mr. Rush's place at Mr. Canning's

dinner-table in 1823, he certainly must have found American neutrality a more agreeable subject than he did in the House of Representatives in July, 1866; and I am quite sure that the General is the last man who would intentionally make any minister of the United States at the Court of St. James, at the present moment, uncomfortable or unhappy by designedly disparaging his country's fame.

I quote again from Mr. Rush, while I have his volumes in hand, a few more paragraphs illustrative of our neutral reputation. I do so the more readily, because, as is not unknown to many of my readers, Mr. Rush took an active part in inaugurating the Monroe Declaration, — being the channel through whom Mr. Canning, as British Foreign Secretary, first conveyed his request to the American Government that they would put forth that Declaration, and officiating as American envoy at the British Court, all through Mr. Monroe's two presidential terms. Standing in that relation to the country and the President, he, of course, next to Mr. Monroe himself, and his Secretary of State, Mr. John Quincy Adams, would understand the bearing of the new "Monroe" Declaration upon the former principles and practice of neutrality avowed and acted on by the United States. Says Mr. Rush in his "Occasional Productions," in a letter addressed to a friend, under date of 1851, and written six years after the publication of his diary of a "Residence," —

" From the commencement of the wars of the old French Revolution, and earlier, the State papers of the United States which aimed at upholding the fair rights of the neutral flag, and thus maintaining the domain of commerce and civilization, would probably form, were all collected and arranged, the best international code under this head to be found in any one volume extant of the same compass. . . . On page 465 [of the "Residence"] I have mentioned the manly homage which that eminent English statesman, Mr. Canning, when Foreign Secretary, and *who was not thought to have been over-friendly to us at earlier periods of his life*, ultimately paid in Parliament, when the war was past and gone, to some of our neutral doctrines. . . . They are doctrines that will probably receive more and more approbation from all nations, as time goes on, and continues to bring with it, as we may reasonably hope, further meliorations of the code of war. They are as replete with international wisdom as with American dignity and spirit. . . . Come what may in the future, we can never be deprived of this inheritance. It is a proud and splendid inheritance." (Rush's "Occasional Productions," pp. 164, 176, 177.)

I have dwelt thus much upon the point of our traditionary good name for an honest and independent neutrality, not because I have for a moment supposed that General Banks, or his committee, or the House of Representatives, were at all ignorant of that salient trait in our national history; still less because I am myself taken with the passing compliments of writers or speakers who naturally desire to say something agreeable to American readers; but because I desire to make it appear how bad that legislative scheme must be which requires for its starting-point such a depreciation or renunciation of our past neutral renown as this in question. If all monarchical Europe has hitherto admired the firmness and consistency with which the American republic have thus far upheld the cause of international law and good order, does it not argue a bad setting-forth, in a different direction, to hear a public man asserting that all *that* "properly belongs to another age, and is not of us nor for us"? (Report, p. 7) — nay, to hear the Chairman of the Committee on Foreign Affairs of the House of Representatives indulging in a sneer at England's "approving our conduct, as better than she had a right to expect"?

I beg leave to ask, whether it is not our crowning glory, that we have always demeaned ourselves better than England, or any other monarchy of the old world, supposed they had a right to expect of us.

But I must return again to the topic of subservience to foreign dictation which General Banks uses with so much vehemence against our later neutral legislation.

CHAPTER IV.

Notice of United-States neutral legislation since 1794.—A great mistake to suppose that the law of 1794 has been essentially changed by later statutes. — The amount of actual change considered. — The law of 1797 a mere patch to prevent American privateering from a foreign base. — Its efficacy afterwards mainly done away with. — The law of 1817 introduced two new provisions; viz. providing for unrecognized governments, and adding the "bonding" clauses. — As to the first, no question made. — As to the second, it is strongly denounced by the Report. — But Earl Russell has proved these clauses to be of no avail to stop an "Alabama," and they have really been almost shorn of their vigor. — The act of 1818 changed the law less than that of 1817, and only relaxed its severity. — Its features noticed, and the odium excited against it shown to be unjust. — Were the changes of 1797, 1817, and 1818 made at British dictation? — Supposing they were, what follows? — Instances noticed in which we altered our laws at the instance of England. — Note on law of 1838 in aid of the Canadian authorities, and English application for enforcement of neutrality in 1854. — These instances so many arguments for British liability for the "Alabama." — Mr. Canning cited to prove that England must do as she has been done by. — The "Artigas" precedent no authority to the contrary. — Note on that precedent, showing that the Portuguese would hold England liable under it for the doings of the Alabama, and that the precedent has not yet been developed. — True application of the argument, showing that England is bound to reciprocate our legislative favors; nor can she say that we volunteered or yielded too much. — Our own statesmen have acknowledged our obligation to adapt our laws to foreign protection, or else to respond for their insufficiency. — Contemporaneous declarations of Mr. Forsyth, Mr. Lowndes, Mr. Samuel Smith, and Mr. Middleton, at the date of 1818. — This view, so important to the "Alabama" reclamations, lost sight of in the new movement.

THUS far I have endeavored to confine myself to the earlier stage of our neutral history, — that of Washington's administration, and of Hamilton and Jefferson's enforcement, as two of Washington's principal Secretaries.

I pass now to hastily review the changes in our neutral laws which have occurred since that era down to the latest revision of 1818, constituting the present neutrality code of the United States. This review seems important, if not interesting, for its bearing upon our present grounds of complaint against England.

It seems obvious that General Banks, and the House of Representatives with him in their recent legislation, have labored under an egregious error, in supposing that a substantial change in principle, as well as an important modification of details, have been wrought in Hamilton's code of 1794, by the three successive acts of 1797, 1817, and 1818. To be sure, while the discussion of the committee's projected new law was going on, at the recent session of Congress, Mr. Jenckes, of Rhode Island, inquired of the chairman, —

"Whether the law now reported is not substantially the original neutrality law of the United States, the first one ever adopted by any nation."

To which General Banks replied, —

"The Bill reported, I will say, in answer to the inquiry of the gentleman from Rhode Island, is identical with that adopted during Washington's administration, and from which we have since departed." ("Globe," July 26.)

And again, just at the close of the debate: —

"The proposition submitted by the committee is, that we shall return to the statutes and policy of the age of Washington."

I shall have occasion hereafter, more particularly under the head of Fenianism, to examine how far the chairman's statement of the identity of his Bill with Hamilton's law is borne out by the Bill itself; but meanwhile I confine myself to the inquiry, what amount of departure from the statute of 1794 was really effected by the three later enactments referred to, and whether the prejudice sought to be raised against them in the recent congressional movement has been justly stirred up.

The first enactment of 1797 (chap. 1), adopted some three years later than that of 1794, and approved by President Adams *after* Washington's term of office had expired (not *before*, as General Banks seems to suppose at page 10 of his Report, where he says "the statutes of 1794 and 1797 enabled *Washington* to disregard public opinion and maintain neutrality between France and England"), was a mere legislative patch, adopted at the suggestion of the British minister, Mr. Liston, and had for its object to prevent American citizens from fitting out privateers *in foreign countries* against nations with whom the United States were at peace, or against the United States themselves. It did not inaugurate the first prohibition of privateering generally, as General Banks seems to suppose (Report, p. 2), but only privateering *from a foreign basis*, and against the home Government as well as foreign countries.

Probably this statute served a useful purpose, for the time being, in deterring from privateering against English commerce from French West-India ports, and to some degree against buccaneering upon our own commerce from the same basis of operations. I doubt, however, if a single conviction was ever had under the law, — for how could the United States deal with its subjects offending against neutrality in foreign parts, unless they afterwards voluntarily returned to American soil to subject themselves to its jurisdiction? — and when the statute came to be revised in 1818, it had all its neutral efficacy taken out of it, by the omission of the clause relative to depredations on foreign countries. This act may be dismissed, therefore, from further consideration, except to say, that General Banks, in his new project, — obviously intending to destroy its remaining vitality, and doubtless supposing that that vitality was of considerable importance, — strikes it out entirely from his Bill; with what effect, I shall have occasion to consider hereafter.

The act of 1817 (chap. 59) contained two new important features: first, in forbidding the fitting-out of vessels to cruise in the service of "any colony, district, or people," thereby supplementing the provisions of 1794, by providing for the case of unrecognized governments (a flaw disclosed by the case of *Gelston* v. *Hoyt*, 3 Wheat. Rep., 246), where the ship "American Eagle" had been fitted out for one of the Haytien combatants, Christophe or Petion, but which was held to be no offence, for the reason that neither of the chieftains had been recognized as "a foreign prince or state," under the statute of 1794); and, secondly, in requiring every armed ship, sailing out of an United-States port, to give bond that her owners shall not use her in a belligerent service, and in further authorizing the collectors of the several ports to detain any such vessel, whose "cargo principally consists of arms and munitions of war," until such bond shall have been given, or the President of the United States shall have been consulted.

With the first of these provisions (which is also copied into the British Foreign-Enlistment Act), General Banks finds no fault, that I am aware of. Its justice is so obvious, — if any nation undertakes to observe neutrality at all, — that I do not wonder at its being thus summarily dismissed.

With the second provision, however, embraced in two separate sections of the law of 1817, the General enters into a vehement contest; affirming that —

"It is impossible to suppose that provisions so repressive upon American commerce, so hostile to the cause of liberty in the [Spanish] colonies, and so strongly in favor of a government whose principles were so repugnant to the people as those of Spain, were voluntarily adopted. They [must have] had their origin in the interests of European governments, hostile to the cause of the colonies." (Report, p. 4.)

These same provisions, as re-enacted in the statute of 1818 (for nothing else contained in the act of 1818 differing from the prior laws of 1794, 1797, and 1817, could give rise to such declamation), are subsequently assailed in the chairman's Report (p. 7), —

"as disregarding the inalienable rights of the people of all nations; as *criminally* (!) restraining the rights of nations at peace, for the benefit of those at war; as intended to perpetuate the supremacy of favored nations on the sea; and as properly belonging to another age, and not of us, nor for us."

Now, if Mr. Adams, our present highly approved representative at the British Court, was unable to answer the objection urged by Earl Russell against these provisions (Earl Russell to Mr. Adams, Nov. 3, 1865: Blue Book, "The Shenandoah Correspondence," p. 128), — that had these same provisions been contained in the British act, and had they been enforced in good faith, they would have proved merely nugatory towards stopping either the "Alabama," the "Florida," the "Georgia," or the "Shenandoah," — is it worth while to spend so many hard words to indict this statute for its criminal severity? How can it have been so oppressively unneutral, when it was not stringent enough even to interfere with an "Alabama" outfit? And how can it have been "so repressive upon American commerce," when nothing short of an iron-plated ram, and perhaps not even that (as Earl Russell fairly shows), would have come within its terms?

To my own appreciation, both of these "bonding" clauses, as they are called, had most of their neutral virtue taken out of them, when Congress made them only applicable (1) to "vessels belonging wholly or in part to *citizens of the United States*,"— thereby leaving *foreigners* at liberty to clear unneutrally armed ships (see project of the act, Ann. Cong. 1816–17, p. 477, sec. 1); (2) when they limited the bond so as only to prevent "*such owners*" from cruising, or cruising hostilities, instead of making the bond guard against a belligerent employment of the vessel by "*any person to whom they* [such owners] *may sell or pretend to sell such vessel*" (Ann. Cong. 1816–17, p. 478, sec. 2); and (3) by requiring that any vessel, to be subject to detention, must have on board "a cargo principally consisting of arms and munitions of war,"— thus letting go at large a vessel armed to the teeth, and " manifestly built for warlike purposes," provided she adopts the precaution of taking *no such cargo* with her, and *is owned by foreigners*.

The statute of 1818 (our present code), though purporting to be a revision of the three previous acts, really introduced less change into former legislation than that of 1817. It is to be noticed, however, — contrary to what seems to be the opinion of General Banks (Report, p. 4, and Speech in the " Globe" of July 30), — that whatever change *was* made by it was in the direction of laxity, and in favor of tolerating belligerent enterprises, rather than the contrary.

Thus the starting-point of the act was, that Spain had an advantage over the South-American colonists, through the omission disclosed in the new act of 1817 (sec. 4) to provide a prohibition against a "prince or state's" augmenting the armament of their ships of war to cruise against the subjects of an unrecognized government; so that Spain could increase the armament of her war-ships in United-States ports, while Buenos Ayres could not do the same thing. (See the motion of Mr. Miller, of South Carolina, in the House of Representatives, Dec. 30, 1817, calling for an amendment of the act of 1817 in this particular, Ann. of Cong. 1817-18, p. 519.) This was duly provided for; and unrecognized governments — " colonies, districts, or peoples " — were put on a footing of equality with established " states and princes," by the insertion of the words " colonies," &c., in the last clause of sec. 5 of the act of 1818 as it now stands.

The other most noticeable changes brought in by the statute of 1818 were, the dropping from sec. 2 of the act of 1794 a clause of it offering pardon to offenders who shall turn State's evidences; the amendment of the act of 1797, already alluded to, in reference to privateering from a foreign basis; the omission from the act of 1817 of a clause of some importance, in the *bonding* sections, relative to "aiding or co-operating in any warlike measure;" and the lowering of the maximum of imprisonment for " fitting out and arming " a ship, &c., from ten years — of the act of 1817 — to three years, as originally fixed in the act of 1794. It will thus be seen, that what General Banks quotes Henry Clay as calling " an act for the benefit of Spain against the republics of America" was mainly the legislation of Washington's day, when we were asserting our self-respect and our self-existence against the overbearing and unscrupulous aggressions of France and England. And if, as the chairman, with a singular self-contrariety, takes pleasure in affirming, he is still willing "to adhere to the example and precept of our fathers " (Rep., p. 7), why, one may naturally ask, should he expend so much hostile invective against that legislation which departs so little from what he is willing to adhere to?

With this brief summary of our progressive neutral legislation, I return to the point of subservience to foreign dictation, which the chairman seems to have wielded with such success in attacking what were supposed to be the important modifications of neutral policy introduced by the three statutes just criticised.

I have shown, as I trust, that these enactments of 1797,

1817, and 1818 constituted in effect no departure in principle, or hardly in detail, from that early policy which the Chairman of the Committee on Foreign Affairs professes himself ready to stand by. Yet whatever changes, be their effect more or less, were wrought by these several laws, they are all obnoxious to the reproach, as General Banks urges, of being instigated or dictated by foreign influence. In 1797, it was England that called upon us to do her bidding, as she had done only three years earlier; and, in 1817 and 1818, it was England again, — this time in company with Spain and Portugal, — behind the President and Congress, enacting our laws for her purposes. "Shall we any longer submit to such a reproach?" is in effect the unanswerable interrogatory with which the Chairman of the Committee on Foreign Affairs overwhelmed the good sense of the House of Representatives.

I beg to differ from the conclusion drawn by the honorable and gallant chairman. Granting that we have accommodated our legislation once, twice, thrice, nay, four or five times, to the requests of European governments, and particularly to that of England, as I believe we really have done, what follows? That we shall profess ourselves ashamed of such international comity or complaisance, and resolve henceforth to refuse all good-natured acts, not towards England, but towards *all* foreign nations? On the contrary, standing on the vantage-ground which we now occupy, is it not a cause of national self-congratulation that we are able to say to England and the rest of the world, " Of course you will not repudiate the obligations which you have contracted by your requests of us for former legislative favors? Common gratitude demands a reciprocation in kind, whenever we shall have occasion to ask for it; and common justice, that, whenever you shall find yourselves unable to grant it, you should make good the omission by indemnifying us for any damages which we may have sustained by reason of your neglect. Is not this the fair construction of our relations?"

Thus take the case of England. In 1794, as Mr. Canning says in his speech on the Foreign-Enlistment Bill, June 10, 1819 (Hans. Parl. Deb., June 10, 1849), we obliged England by passing what I have ventured to designate as "Hamilton's Act" of that year. In 1797, as Governor Root, of New York, asserted in debate (Ann. Cong. 1816–17, p. 721), doubtless on good authority, we made an amendment to the last act, to meet the views of Mr. Liston, the British minister resident at that day in Washington; and in 1817, as Mr. Forsyth, Chairman of the House Committee on Foreign Affairs, made known in debate a few months later (Ann. Cong. 1818, p. 1409), we adopted still further amendments, to meet the representations of Great Britain jointly with Spain, Portugal, and France.[1]

---

[1] I do not adduce the instance of the act of 1838, intended to meet the emergency of the Canadian rebellion, as one of these pieces of legislative neutral comity, as Mr. Adams does in his diplomatic correspondence with Earl Russell (letter of Sept. 18, 1865, Blue-Book, 1866, "North America, No. 1, The Shenandoah, &c."), and as Mr. Cobden did in his speech in Parliament, July 23, 1861 (Hans. Parl. Deb., vol. clxxii. p. 1254); because, considering what Mr. Stevenson, our minister at London in 1838, had to say on that subject, in his communication to the British Government about the "Caroline" affair, I have had my doubts whether in strictness we can be said to have passed that law at the express solicitation of England.

Mr. Stevenson, in writing to Lord Palmerston, then Foreign Secretary, to demand reparation for the steamer "Caroline" affair, after speaking of the friendly movement of the American Government in behalf of neutrality, "and the steps taken to restrain its misguided citizens from interfering in the disturbances of Her Majesty's colonies," goes on to say, "These efforts, moreover, were spontaneous and uncalled-for. So far from being influenced or stimulated by any requisition on the part of Her Majesty's Government, they were prompted solely by its own views of duty and interest, and its love of peace." (Ex. Doc. 25th Cong. 3d. Sess. 1838–9, vol. iv. Doc. 183, p. 8.)

Perhaps the American minister was here referring only to the executive and military interference of the United-States authorities, and not to their measures of legislative co-operation with the British Government in helping them to preserve order in Canada. Perhaps, further, if Mr. Stevenson *did* mean to refer to special legislation at British instance, he was not correctly informed in London, where he had been residing for some time, of what had been done at Washington, in his absence, as to any request being there put forward by the British minister for the passage of the law in question. However, having happened to meet the statement in diplomatic correspondence, I have thought that it might be of some importance, and so in candor have felt bound to bring it forward.

I will add, that, even if Mr. Stevenson's remark can be considered as embracing legislative as well as executive friendly co-operation, yet that the question, whether we legislated to comply with a special demand, loses nearly all its importance in the view of Lord Palmerston's full admission in Parliament of our thoroughly friendly and satisfactory neutrality at that juncture. Says Lord

Now, if, at the time of the late civil struggle, the "Alabama," the "Florida," and all that class of rebel cruisers, could have been successfully detained, or even summarily declared forfeited, by alterations in British statutes corresponding to what we thus repeatedly enacted at the instance of England; and if, in consequence of British omission to make such alterations when thereto reasonably and seasonably requested by the United States, the United States suffered damage, — can there be any

---

Palmerston in the House of Commons, Feb. 2, 1838 (Hans. Parl. Deb., vol. xl. p. 717), — after stating that the British minister at Washington, Mr. Fox, had been in communication with Mr. Forsyth, the Secretary of State, about the occupation of Navy Island by the insurgents, and that Mr. Forsyth had assured him "that all the powers now vested in the executive should be used to preserve neutrality," — "In addition to this, the President [Mr. Van Buren], on the 5th, sent down a special message to Congress, stating that, though the laws as they stood were quite sufficient to *punish* an infraction of neutrality, they were not sufficient to *prevent* it; and asking the Congress to give the executive further powers for that purpose. Upon the receipt of this communication, a short discussion, in which many of the leading men, such as Mr. Clay, Mr. Calhoun, and others of high character, participated, took place in Congress; and, without exception, all who spoke expressed sentiments of the most friendly disposition towards that [this] country; stating a strong opinion that the laws should be enforced, and that if, as they stood, they were insufficient, stronger powers should be given to the executive. Nothing, in short, could be more satisfactory than the communications which had taken place between Her Majesty's Government and that of the United States."

Is there not here sufficient evidence to prove, that, if Mr. Fox did not ask, *in form*, for an amendment of the law, the United States, *in substance*, passed it for the furtherance of British interests? And, supposing the United States to have acted in advance of British solicitation, should their legislation be esteemed any the less an international favor to England?

I submit, then, that this may be fairly set down as a fourth instance of shaping our neutral laws to British requests.

The fifth instance of intervention for neutral protection by special request on the part of England, not indeed for legislative, but for executive, enforcement of neutrality, — I mean the application to the President by the British minister, Sir John Crampton, in 1854, to prevent the fitting-out of Russian privateers during the Crimean war, — is well authenticated by the official publication of the request itself. The British minister made the application concurrently with the French minister; but Sir John Crampton asks for the specific relief in question, *on behalf of* "*Her British Majesty's Government*" alone. (See Sir John Crampton to Mr. Marcy, Am. Sec. of State, of April 21, 1854, and Mr. Marcy to Mr. Crampton, of April 28, 46 British and Foreign State Papers, pp. 838, 840.)

Have Englishmen ever yet discovered any requital by England to the United States of these five several instances of neutral good-will and comity put forth at her special request, or for her special benefit?

claim better substantiated for indemnity before the tribunal of nations than that which we are now urging against the British Government on that score?

Our English friends hold Mr. Canning in high repute. Some of them even assert that he was the greatest Foreign Secretary that England ever had. Have they ever weighed how forcibly his declarations, in regard to the principle for which I am contending, bind England to reciprocate or indemnify, where she has demanded neutral favors from other nations?

It was in the debate upon " the Negotiations relative to Spain" in the British House of Commons, April 14, 1823, that Mr. Canning held this language as to international reciprocity: —

" There was a golden maxim which applied as well to politics as it did to morals, — ' Do unto others as you would that others should do unto you.' But to England I would say, ' Do unto others what you have made others do unto you.' For a quarter of a century this country has laid down the law of nations to the whole world; she has laid down most clearly the code by which neutrals must be guided." (8 Hans. N. S., p. 895.)

Mr. Canning said further, — I quote again from him in debate on the Foreign-Enlistment Act, in 1819 (Hans. Parl. Deb., vol. xl., p. 1105) : —

" It surely could not be forgotten, that, in 1794, this country complained of various breaches of neutrality (though much inferior in degree to those now under consideration), committed on the part of subjects of the United States of America. What was the conduct of that nation in consequence? Did it resent the complaint as an infringement of its independence? Did it refuse to take such steps as would insure the immediate observance of neutrality? Neither. In 1794, *immediately after the application from the British Government*, the Legislature of the United States passed an act prohibiting, under heavy penalties, the engagement of American citizens in the armies of any belligerent power. Was that the only instance of the kind? It was but last year [1818] that the United States passed an act, by which the act of 1794 was confirmed in every respect, again prohibiting the engagement of their citizens in the service of any foreign power, and pointing distinctly to the service of Spain or the South-American provinces."

Mr. Canning, on this last occasion, did not see fit to avow the renewed intercession of England in our neutral legislation at the very point of time (or possibly two years earlier than) when he was speaking; but as that intercession is distinctly asserted by Mr. Forsyth, Chairman of the House Committee on Foreign Affairs, who in that capacity would be the natural and necessary depositary of such a State secret, there can be no reasonable doubt, I think, that such intercession was in fact made at about the period of 1817-18.

Now, in face of these repeated interventions and of the binding consequences flowing from them, as avowed by one of their greatest masters of public law, — avowals directed, too, to the very precedent of the United States *versus* Great Britain, — how can British statesmen of the present day hope to escape from the responsibility of omitting to reciprocate, during the late civil struggle, the legislative favors which England has heretofore received at the hands of the United States? If Parliament and the British nation saw fit to indulge in the luxury of folding their arms and doing nothing over our difficulties with rebel cruisers and British ship-builders, is it any thing more than natural equity that England should now make good the damage occasioned by her delinquency? And is it any answer to our demands for indemnity, for Earl Russell, or any other Foreign Secretary, to point to our supposed short-comings in the fulfilment of neutral duties towards Spain or Portugal, at the period of the South-American contests? Supposing that *we have* omitted to pass all the statutes and make good all the reclamations called for by those governments at that time, — a matter which I should not for a moment concede, — is that any thing in point to the issue between the United States and England at the present juncture? As Mr. Canning would reply to Lord Russell and his successors in the Foreign-Secretaryship, "*England must do unto others what she has had others do unto her.*"[1]

---

[1] It is singular what stress English ministers and English publicists affect to lay on the "Artigas" precedent (as it is called), as concluding the United States from any claim against England for the outfit of the "Alabama," and similar Confederate cruisers. I beg to ask these English disputants, who seem so ready to

But would General Banks designedly and willingly cancel all this balance of credit against a government which he thinks so deeply in our debt as England, by enforcing his positions, that our neutrality was " not adopted because it was just, but because it was necessary ; " that what we enacted at England's

stake their whole case on the side-issue of whether we did justice to Portugal at the period of Mr. Monroe's administration, but who, it seems to me, had much better confine themselves to the direct issue now pending between England and the United States, — whether they have ever taken notice, that (if these Portuguese diplomats, whose word they so confidently rely on to prove our liability for tolerating " Artigas's " privateers, are good authority for the settlement of the present controversies) England is bound by her own doctrines and practice to make good every dollar of the " Alabama " reclamations.

Says the Chevalier Grehon (who succeeded Signor Correa, whom Earl Russell so highly compliments), — writing to Secretary John Quincy Adams, under date of April 1, 1822, about these " Artigas " reclamations, and in insisting upon their immediate satisfaction, — " But, if all efforts on the part of the Portuguese Government should be fruitless towards obtaining from that of the United States a [that] just and reasonable indemnity WHICH ENGLAND DOES NOT HESITATE TO MAKE IN ANALOGOUS CASES OF UNJUST CAPTURES, the Portuguese Government is fully determined to resort to the right of reprisals against the United States," &c.

Now, it may be that the Chevalier Grehon was quite misinformed about the practice of England ; but, if Lord Russell calls him as his witness against the Americans, is he not bound to adopt his whole testimony ? And I submit, whether that testimony, taken together, does not prove that England ought to pay for the doings of the " Alabama," even though the United States *wrongfully* declined to pay for the doings of the " Irresistible " and other such Baltimore-fitted plunderers of Portuguese merchantmen ?

I take this occasion to say that there remains a good deal more to be developed about the " Artigas " precedent, than what Mr. Adams, our present excellent representative at London, or — more recently than his discussion of the precedent — than what Mr. Dana, in his late annotation upon it in his new edition of Wheaton, have found time to explore and add to its previously known history. When the whole diplomatic and juridical history of that passage in neutral experience comes to be brought to light, and especially its British connections, I think it will cease to be quoted by Englishmen to the point of justifying a hasty recognition of rebel belligerency, or even as of much importance on the point of indemnifying for tolerations of unneutral preparations for hostile expeditions.

The writer of the present pamphlet had once nearly completed such an historical investigation of the matter, now some eighteen months since, at about the time of the precedent's being first brought to light, in the " Manchester Examiner " and " Times," and its being *exploited* by " Historicus " in the London " Times," and before Earl Russell had adopted it into the catalogue of *causes célèbres*. Nothing but the inability to procure in authentic shape, at that time, two or three State-papers, then thought to be of importance, prevented its publication. Probably, if the precedent continues to be pressed, it may be worth while to publish the new intelligence at the writer's command.

instance "was not demanded by international or natural law;" and that we yielded to the importunities of foreign powers, "because we were not in a condition to resist that which they pressed upon us"?

I submit that it is a better attitude for the American statesman to view his country's neutrality in the light of its European fame, as a manly and courageous assertion of our national self-respect and neutral independence; and that, when and so far as we have altered our legislation and neutral procedure at foreign solicitation, it has been in the view that European governments, and particularly that of England, have asked no more of us than what was just and honorable, and the same measure of international justice which they were prepared to mete out to us under similar circumstances in return.

So much for the English view of our neutral-law revisions, and the international obligations created by them. But will any Englishman venture to insinuate that his Government overstepped the line of international privilege, in making these requisitions upon the United States which we have been considering? Certainly, we have not, as yet, heard the disparagement — or should we call it praise? — from any quarter, that the United States *volunteered* too chivalrously and too liberally in behalf of neutral rights. On the contrary, the fact seems to stand in incontrovertible certainty, that all the way along, from Washington's day down, we have been acting with the avowed approbation, if not at the express urgency, of England herself, in advancing our neutral code. Is not Great Britain estopped, then, from asserting that we have meted out to her a superfluous or an extra-legal measure of international justice, and also from denying our right to insist upon a recompense accommodated to the very standard of neutral dealing which she herself has prescribed?

But did not the American idea of neutral obligations, at the very time of passing these neutrality enactments, correspond to the English sense of justice in soliciting them? And were not the American and English ideas in accord as to the just responsibility resulting from a nation's omitting to provide suitable preventive and protective neutral legislation?

Here, again, I venture to think, General Banks and the House of Representatives have misunderstood or misconstrued the motives of the legislation of Presidents Madison and Monroe's administrations.

Says General Banks's Report (in effect), "It was European domination that warped and overawed Congress and the executive at those periods."

As if Spain and Portugal were formidable to us in 1817 and 1818, after we had waged our second war with Great Britain with such equal-handed ability, when, as I have shown, we made ourselves independent of French and British domination at as early a day of the republic as 1794! Even Mr. Clay, the champion of the South-American patriots, went no farther in imputing foreign subservience to the motives which originated the acts of 1817–18, than our being "teased" into them by foreign governments. (Ann. Cong. 1818, p. 1406.)

But what was the true leading motive — that avowed by the very framers of these new laws themselves — for their proposed legislation?

Not "to perpetuate the supremacy of favored nations on the seas," as General Banks would have the House of Representatives and the country to believe, but *to guard the United States against the just claims of injured nations, if we failed to comply with our national duty of observing a fair neutrality towards them.*

Said Mr. Forsyth, the Chairman of the Committee on Foreign Affairs, in opening the debate on the revision of 1818 (March 18, Ann. Cong. 1818, p. 1409): —

"The origin of this act [that of 1817] has been imputed to the *teasing* of certain foreign agents near the United States. That the message of President Madison, recommending that act, was in consequence of the representations of foreign ministers, Mr. Forsyth said he was ready to admit, — not of reiterated importunities, but of a performance of their duty to their governments, by remonstrating against violations by citizens of the United States, of obligations which we owe, not to any one nation, but equally to all. A remonstrance had been made by the Portuguese minister, a garbled representation of which had been published; a similar statement of facts had been made by the minister of Great Britain; and another by the minister of France. All the foreign ministers here had, in short, represented that citizens of the United States engaged in cruises in patriot vessels (as they were called), which, fitted from our ports, committed depredations on the commerce of England, France, and Spain. What, asked Mr. Forsyth, was the duty of the President of the United States, if these facts were true? *Were not the United States bound to make reparation, if, without an effort to prevent it, we suffered depredations to be made by our citizens, and from our ports, on the commerce of nations in amity with us? The Government had heretofore recognized this principle, and had remunerated foreign citizens for property taken from them by citizens of the United States,"* &c.

So, Mr. Lowndes, of South Carolina, whom Mr. Clay complimented as "a powerful auxiliary in carrying through the bill" [of 1817], and "from whom when he found himself differing, he almost distrusted his own perceptions," in backing up Mr. Forsyth in defence of the law of 1817, said, —

" One consideration for such an act he would suggest, which it was too late *for us* to deny, is, *that we are responsible for injuries done by vessels of the United States, after they leave our ports, and before they arrive at a foreign port. For such depredations we are responsible, and have recognized the principle by paying claims founded on it. We have bound ourselves to respect the principle in a manner equally obligatory, by preferring claims founded on it against other nations,*" &c. (Ann. Cong. 1818, p. 1413.)

So, Mr. Samuel Smith, the able mercantile representative of the city of Baltimore, in speaking on the same side, said : —

" Our claim against Spain is for spoliations committed on our commerce by French privateers, whom she permitted to fit out from her ports, and bring in our vessels for sale. For this, *we justly demanded indemnity*. And what had Spain replied? *That we had a right to this indemnity, and that she will pay it when she shall be able.* Now, if a vessel, sailing out of our ports as a cruiser, obtains a commission we know not how, gives no bonds whatever, goes to sea, and commences the capture of Spanish property, *are we not responsible?* " &c. " *Of a war with the present power of Spain, nobody would think much;* but a rule applied to Spain might be applied by illegal cruisers from our ports to other powers, with whom a conflict would not be so very convenient. The House had been told that such conduct was not a cause for war: it might not perhaps create a war at this moment; but, whenever the power thus injured feels itself strong enough to make a war, you will find that it will be found a sufficient cause." (Am. Cong. 1818, p. 1423.)

These declarations of three of the most prominent advocates of the law of 1818 seem to me sufficient to show that a disposition to administer international justice, and to protect the country from reclamations for toleration of unneutral equipments, lay at the bottom of that legislation, rather than foreign dictation.

Cotemporaneous with this debate came another utterance from the Committee on Foreign Affairs on the part of the House of Representatives, on another topic, showing that the fear of liability to other nations for permitting unneutral equipments in American ports constituted the groundwork of congressional action at this period.

Says Mr. Middleton,of South Carolina, in reporting to the House of Representatives upon the subject of suppressing the piratical establishments at Amelia Island, under date of Jan. 10, 1818 (4 Am. State Pap., p. 133) : —

" The immediate tendency of suffering such armaments, in defiance of our laws [as those sent out from Amelia Island, a Spanish possession on the Florida coast, in immediate proximity to the American frontier], would have been to embroil the United States with all the nations whose commerce with our country was suffering under these depredations; and, *if not checked by all the means in the power of the Government, would have authorized claims from the subjects of foreign governments for indemnities at the expense of this nation, for captures by our people in vessels fitted out in our ports, and (as could not fail of being alleged) countenanced by the very neglect of the necessary means of suppressing them.*"

This language was caught at by the Portuguese minister, Signor De Figaniere, who afterwards urged what have been alluded to as the " Artigas " claims upon the United States, and was prominently put forward by him in support of those claims. (Ex. Doc. No. 53, 1st Sess. 32d Cong., 1851–52, p. 196.) Mr. Webster, to whom, as Secretary of State, the argument founded on our own admissions was addressed by Mr. Figaniere in 1850, did not pretend to dispute the justice of the general principle, so far as can be inferred from his keeping silence altogether in reference to the demand of the Portuguese Government. But the principle was no new one in American practice at the date of the Spanish South-American revolt. It had been acted on (as referred to by Mr. Forsyth and others in debate, as above) in Washington's administration, under Mr. Jefferson's secretaryship, in the well-known letter of Sept. 5, 1793 (afterwards made an annex to the British treaty), and had been more broadly and emphatically asserted by Mr. Pickering, who had succeeded Mr. Jefferson in the State Department (still under Washington's presidency, in 1795), in connection with the "Cassius" case, as I have had occasion to call attention to, in a discussion of that precedent, in the "Boston Daily Advertiser," of Aug. 21 and 22, 1865. The same principle was again brought under discussion in the claims under the Spanish treaty of 1819, dating back to the French occupation of the Peninsula, at the close of the eighteenth century, as alluded to by Mr. Smith, as above.

With this well-settled line of precedent and practice before them, in regard to national liability for toleration of unneutral privateering, how can the Committee on Foreign Relations have so far lost sight of the leading motive of our neutral legislation, — more decidedly avowed and insisted upon in 1817–18 than ever, — as to ascribe that legislation to a fear of foreign powers, rather than to a determination to protect the country from a just responsibility for the omission of her proper duties under the law of nations? And is the present, I would further ask, just the most fitting moment thus to ignore this most striking characteristic of our country's neutral history? I leave out of account the patriotism involved in such an omission. I only inquire whether such a mutilation of the country's record is judicious and timely.

CHAPTER V.

Refutation of the idea, that the neutrality laws are repealable, because only enacted temporarily. — General Banks's unfair quotation of the Adamses. — How we came to have Hamilton's act made temporary, and how it was only adopted at all, by John Adams's casting-vote. — John Adams's neutral record ; his endorsement of Washington's neutral policy; approves the act of 1797 and that of 1800, making the law of 1794 perpetual. — This Adams not the man to follow foreign dictation. — John Quincy Adams's neutral record; the master-spirit of our foreign neutral policy as Monroe's Secretary of State from 1817-25. — Both Monroe and J. Q. Adams, though identified with the Monroe doctrine, advocated a just neutrality. — Madison as well as Monroe voted against the law of 1794 in Congress ; but both afterwards changed their opinions. — Summary of Madison's and Monroe's neutral record. — The last even recommended to Congress the revision of the present law. — Does not this knock away the prop of the Monroe doctrine from the new scheme ? — J. Q. Adams's record as Secretary of State and President given further. — Charles Francis Adams cleared from any suspicion of favoring the new project. — Recurring to the temporariness of the neutrality acts, this very fact shown to be an argument in their favor. — Notice of Gallatin's change of opinion, and of the other leaders of the Jefferson school. — Allusion to the temporary acts of 1817 and 1838. — The great historic names of the republic all shown to be on the side of American neutrality. — How bad the policy which finds itself obliged to decry them. — Five general conclusions. — That our original neutrality was as brave as it was just. — That our neutral concessions constitute a fund of international credit to our account. — That, as to England, both expediency and consistency call upon us to stand where we are. — That the Monroe school of doctrine opposes rather than favors the new scheme. — That the argument of practical experience shows that neutrality makes part of American policy.

I CANNOT dismiss the subject of the disparagement of our past neutral history, without briefly replying to General Banks's unfavorable comment on the neutral enactments of the United States, founded upon their being, in several instances, of a temporary and unpermanent character. Several times in the course of his Report, or in debate, the General alludes to this feature in their provisions, as if their authors were at the time fully conscious that their laws were not good enough to go upon the statute-book as permanent legislation, and so made them fugitive and temporary. Perhaps his objections on this head are nowhere brought out more prejudicially, and, as it seems to me, more unfairly, than in a passage in his closing speech in debate, which I will quote in full for the sake of avoiding all possible misrepresentation.

Says General Banks, in that speech ("Globe," July 30), —

"The acts of 1797, 1817, and 1818 were departures from the policy of the Government, the principles of international law, and the legislation of every other Government. This Bill [the Committee's project] strikes from the statutes enacted since 1794 the unnecessary, unusual, and onerous restrictions and prohibitions upon the commerce of the country and the power of its people.

"I do not like to say much about the history of this legislation, because it is not an agreeable subject; but it appears distinctly in the history of the periods to which I have referred, that the changes in the neutrality law of 1794 were made to correspond, not with the wishes of the people or Government, or with a view to its interest or prosperity, but at the solicitation, and I might say at the demand almost, of foreign governments, and especially of Portugal and Spain, supported by Great Britain. We made our laws to correspond with their interests and wishes, rather than our own, because we were in a condition not to resist that which they pressed upon us. But it was distinctly stated by John Adams as President, by John Quincy Adams as Secretary of State, and more recently by Mr. Adams, representing our Government at the Court of St. James, that the legislation and policy of that day were adopted with a full comprehension that the time would come when the people of this country would be able to assert their own right, upon the judgment of the people alone, rather than at the dictation, or upon the representations, of representatives of foreign governments. The question for this House to determine is, whether that time has come. Sir, I think it has come."

Now, I take the fair import of this extract to be, that our neutrality laws have all been temporary make-shifts, which the three Adamses (at least) have concurred in saying should be relaxed or done away with as soon as our growing national strength would enable us to do so. In that sense, I conceive that no paragraph could hardly more unjustly represent the country and the historic family quoted than that. I contend that the Adams family always have been and still are identified with American neutral policy; and that they have been the consistent advocates of a permanent and well-established legislation, defining and enforcing that policy.

It is very true, that Hamilton's act, being at first limited to two years' duration, was adopted by the casting-vote of Vice-President John Adams, who then presided over the Senate, where opinions were equally divided in regard to it (Ann. Cong. March 12, 1794, p. 67). But the clause limiting its continuance to two years was an amendment to Hamilton's original proposition (Ann. Cong. 1793-5, pp. 66-7), and was doubtless adopted on account of the expected speedy termination of the French Revolution, or else to give an opportunity to the opponents of the act to watch its working in practice. I have no doubt, however, that Vice-President Adams would have voted for its perpetuity at once, if the opportunity had offered, since he sided throughout with the views of Hamilton; voting (among other things) for the clause prohibiting the sale of prizes, which the House afterwards struck out, and which was not finally made part of the act, as Hamilton earnestly desired.

The extension of the act of 1794 for two years beyond the period limited for its duration did not give rise to any debate or division in the Senate; so that I have no opportunity to quote Mr. Adams the elder again, on his legislative record in that connection. The extending act (which was again limited to two years' duration and "the end of the next session," at Mr. Gallatin's motion in the House of Representatives) was signed by President Washington on the second day of March, 1797. Two days later, viz., on the 4th of March, Mr. Adams, then having become President of the United States, expressed himself on the subject of maintaining neutrality, in his inaugural speech, as follows: —

"If *an inflexible determination to maintain* peace and inviolable faith with all nations, AND THAT SYSTEM OF NEUTRALITY AND IMPARTIALITY *among* [*towards*] *the belligerent powers of Europe which has been adopted by this Government, and so solemnly sanctioned by both Houses of Congress and applauded by the legislatures of the States and public opinion*, UNTIL IT SHALL BE OTHERWISE ORDAINED BY CONgress" [can bespeak the sentiments of my future administration, then Congress will find me acting up to that determination], &c. (Am. State Pap., p. 39.)

It was President John Adams who recommended (in his speech to Congress of May 16, 1797) the adoption of further legislation to prevent American citizens from fitting out privateers in foreign ports to cruise against our own commerce, and who afterwards approved the act of June 14, 1797, covering that subject, and extending protection to English commerce from similar depredations, as already noticed. This act, as General Banks himself observes, though conformable to English wishes, was *not* temporary, but "made permanent" at the outset. Finally, it was the same President John Adams who, on the twenty-fourth day of April, 1800, gave his official approval to the act by which Hamilton's neutrality statute became the permanent law of the land, and has remained such, in effect, to the present moment.

Surely this John Adams, with this legislative record, and the same John Adams into whose mouth Mr. Webster, in his eulogy, puts the speech in character, as he affixed his name to the Declaration of Independence, "Sink or swim, live or die, survive or perish, I give my hand and my heart for this vote," cannot have been the Adams who, according to General Banks, was yielding up his country's interests and the rights of all neutral nations to foreign dictation, and who meant to disavow all his acts of that description as soon as his country's circumstances would permit him to do so.

The neutral record of John Quincy Adams is even more pronounced in favor of the American system than that of his father. The part played by Vice-President John Adams, and afterwards by John Adams as President, in carrying out Washington's ideas of neutral policy, were, to a certain extent, only subordinate. But it fell to John Quincy Adams, as Secretary of State under President Monroe, to be the master-spirit of administering and enforcing American neutrality during nearly all the trying period of the South-American contests, when the relations of the United States towards the South-American republics on the one hand, and towards Spain and Portugal on the other, were widely different from what they had been towards the European contest of France and England in 1793, and down to the close of the eighteenth century.

It is quite aside from my purpose, and I fear it would be tedious to the reader, for me in this connection to enter upon any extended examination of Mr. Secretary Adams's opinions and official measures as to the neutrality observed by the United States from 1817 to 1825. Suffice it to say that Mr. Adams entered upon the policy initiated by President Madison and by Mr. Secretary Monroe, and carried out that policy with as courageous a vindication of the principles of Washington and Hamilton as any American statesman who has succeeded those illustrious founders of our system that can be named. I am well aware that Earl Russell supposes that he has found in Mr. Secretary Adams's State-papers *dicta* which make against our recent neutral demands upon England; but, for one, I am willing, as an American citizen, to abide by any thing which those dicta afford, and am quite satisfied with the explanation put upon them by his son and competent interpreter, who is at the same time his father's successor in the office of American representative at the British Court. Possibly had Mr. Charles Francis Adams's numerous and oppressive diplomatic duties permitted a more extended review of his father's Secretary-of-Stateship, or, rather, if possibly his personal relations to his father had not prevented his developing the whole of the elder Mr. Adams's merits in that important office at that important epoch, a yet more thorough vindication and illustration of Mr. John Quincy Adams's foreign neutral policy would have been produced.

As it is, it will be quite enough for me, in reply to General Banks, to show, that, though the second Adams inaugurated the Monroe doctrine, Mr. Monroe and himself were both staunch advocates for upholding and carrying *forward*, not *backward*, American neutrality; and that their policy in this particular was but a continuation of and improvement upon the measures of the previous administration.

Monroe and Madison, as appears by the congressional records, were both of them originally opposed to the adoption of the law of 1794, — Monroe in the Senate, and Madison in the House of Representatives (Ann. Cong. 1793-5, pp. 67 and 757). Indeed, Mr. Madison, in the House, was its chief opponent. Perhaps this would indicate Mr. Jefferson's hostility to the measure, as both Mr. Madison and Mr. Monroe were his well-known adherents and exponents. Certainly, however, all three shortly after changed their views; as all three, when they successively became Presidents, gave in their adherence to the neutral doctrines of Washington, and, it may be added, carried them out in good faith.

Passing at once to the period of the South-American revolt, it was President Madison, in September, 1815, who issued the proclamation of neutrality, forbidding citizens of the United States from setting on foot any military enterprises within neutral territory in aid of hostilities against Spain (4 Am. State Papers, p. 1). It was President Madison who, just before retiring from office, in his last annual message to Congress in December, 1816, recommended the adoption of "such further legislative provisions as may be requisite for detaining vessels actually equipped, or in a course of equipment, with a warlike force, within the jurisdiction of the United States," &c., — the obnoxious "bonding" measures of General Banks's aversion (4 Am. State Pap., p. 103). It was Secretary Monroe, on behalf of the State Department, who laid before the House of Representatives, in January, 1817, in furtherance of President Madison's recommendation, the particulars in which additional legislation was needed to enable the Executive to fulfil the neutral duties of the country (4 Am. State Pap., pp. 103-4). It was President Madison who, on the third day of March, 1817, put his signature to the law of 1817, chap. 59, containing those provisions "so criminally restraining the rights of nations at peace for the benefit of those at war," which are duly reprobated in General Banks's Report. It was President Monroe, the so-called author of the "Monroe" doctrine, who approved the act of 1818, chap. 88, on which the Chairman of the House Committee pours out his seven vials of wrath; and it was finally the same President Monroe, who, with John Quincy Adams for his Secretary of State, recommended to Congress in his annual message of December, 1819, a further revision of the neutrality laws, in the following terms (a paragraph of the message, doubtless furnished by the Secretary of State) : —

"It is of the highest importance to our national character, and indispensable to the morality of our citizens, that all violations of our neutrality should be prevented. No door should be left open for the evasion of our laws; no opportunity afforded, to any who may be disposed to take advantage of it, to compromit the interest or the honor of the nation. It is submitted, therefore, to the consideration of Congress, whether it may not be advisable to revise the laws with a view to this desirable result." (4 Am. State Pap., p. 628.)

In view of this recommendation coming from President Monroe and his Cabinet *more than a year after the law of April 20, 1818, had been tried in actual operation, and several months after the adoption of the British Foreign-Enlistment Act had become known at Washington,* I would respectfully ask of the Chairman of the Committee on Foreign Affairs, whether he believes that Mr. Monroe or John Quincy Adams would have preferred retrogressive to progressive neutral legislation, could they have returned to their official positions, and taken upon themselves to advise the American people in July last how to act in reference to discharging their neutral duties towards other nations. Does he believe that either or both of them would have been in favor of "scaling" down, instead of rising up in the scale of civilization? And does he believe that the authors of the "Monroe doctrine," one or both, were the men who were setting American legislation to the tune of European dictation?

I should be glad to trace Secretary J. Q. Adams's and President J. Q. Adams's neutral record down to a later point than this of 1819; particularly in the way of showing, how, though the neutrality statute of 1818 was not amended in conformity with President Monroe's recommendation, yet other important neutral legislation was inaugurated at that period, eminently serviceable to foreign powers, especially the amendment of the laws relating to piracy and the adoption of that remarkable statute (1820, chap. 110), by which the entrance of all armed vessels into the port of Baltimore was absolutely prohibited, except at the President's special permission: but I fear that such a discussion would lead me too far from my main purpose. I believe, however, that I have shown quite enough to meet General Banks's assumption, when he quotes John Quincy Adams as concurring with such opinions and measures as were sanctioned by the House of Representatives, under his own auspices, at its late session.

It is hardly worth my while, I think, to go on and answer General Banks's strange attempt to vouch in Mr. Charles Francis Adams's name in aid of retrogressive neutral legislation. If the burden of all the younger Mr. Adams's ministerial mission has been to hold the British Government up to Mr. Canning's doctrine, that England is bound to do unto the United States what the United States have heretofore done unto England, — as I think my reader's fresh recollection of its general tenor will bear me out in asserting it really *has been*, — is it probable that General Banks can pick out of Mr. C. F. Adams's whole official correspondence, during the past five years, a single sentence which will fairly bear the construction that Mr. Adams views our whole past neutral practice and policy as so much subservience to foreign dictation, which, if he could have his way, he would change at the first opportunity. Until the Chairman of the Committee on Foreign Affairs can produce at least one paragraph of Mr. Adams's writing which looks in that direction, I shall be slow to believe in any such suggestion of our worthy minister's self-stultification.

Perhaps I ought to add, in justice to General Banks, that I have not overlooked his citation from President Washington's Farewell Address (Report, p. 5), which Secretary John Quincy Adams quotes with approbation, in reference to the ultimate growth of the United States to that point where " they may choose peace or war with belligerent nations, as their interests, guided by justice, shall counsel." That declaration of Washington's, uttered in 1796, cannot by possibility be made to apply to neutral legislation enacted in 1817–18, and continued in force to the present day, and had as little to do with passing neutral laws at foreign dictation at all, in my judgment, as it has to do with pronouncing on the justice of the " Alabama " claims against England at the present moment. The Father of his Country was urging upon his countrymen a policy of peace and non-entanglement with foreign complications; but he had no more idea of condemning his own approval of Hamilton's Neutrality Act, and of recommending to succeeding administrations its repeal at the earliest possible moment, than he had of striking out of his own historic fame the glory that really belongs to his presidential initiation and enforcement of American neutrality, — perhaps the brightest laurel of his civic life.

But I return from this long, though I trust not unprofitable, digression, in vindication of the opinions held by the Adamses and the founders of the Monroe doctrine in regard to modifying, neutral law to the urgencies of foreign powers, to say, in conclusion of this topic of the unfavorable argument to be drawn from the temporary character of our various neutrality acts, that to my mind this point affords one of the strongest arguments in their favor.

I have already shown how Jefferson, Madison, and Monroe, who had all been opposed originally to Washington and Hamilton's neutral policy, ultimately gave in their hearty adhesion to it, and carried it forward by several degrees of advancement. The same is true of Mr. Gallatin, another historic name in our political history, except for whose exclusion from the Senate (on the ground of alienage) we should probably have never had the law of 1794 at all. Chief-Justice Marshall, in his Life of Washington (vol. ii. 2d ed. p. 327), takes notice of the fact, that, in the divided condition of the Senate on Hamilton's act [Marshall, I ought to say, does not call it such], it was only owing to Mr. Gallatin's having been unseated a few days before, on the score of his not having been a duly naturalized citizen for the length of time required by the Constitution, that the measure became a law. Now it so happened, that, when the act of 1794 came up for extension in 1797, Mr. Gallatin had found his way again into Congress as a member of the lower house, and so had an opportunity to renew his opposition to the law. Did Mr. Gallatin again attempt to get rid of that legislation? On the contrary, he declared himself in favor of making the act perpetual, except for some provisions in the first and second sections, which he thought of doubtful expediency (Ann. Cong. 1796–7, p. 2227) ; and, when the act came up again in 1800 for enactment in perpetuity, he withheld any further opposition, and, it would seem, voted in its favor, without further reservation (Ann. Cong. 1799–1800, pp. 656–65 ; Jour. House Rep., vol. iii. p. 662).

Now, if the law of 1794 thus made good its place in permanency on the statute-book, in face of the opposition of such men as Madison, Monroe, and Gallatin, all of whom eventually approved it, is it not a testimonial in its favor, rather than in its condemnation, that it began with being only experimental and temporary? So, again, the law of 1817 had in it a limitation of two years' duration. But its provisions (in the main), as we have seen, were made perpetual by the law of 1818, notwithstanding Henry Clay's vehement opposition ; much to the surprise, too, of the Portuguese minister, Signor Correa, who, according to the diplomatic correspondence of that day, waked up thirty days before the law of 1817, by its terms, would expire, — viz., in February, 1819, — and implored Secretary John Quincy Adams to procure an extension of that act, which he characterized " as so honorable to the character of the UnitedStates ; " a request which the Secretary of State was able to satisfactorily meet, by pointing Mr. Correa to the act of the 20th of April of the previous year, already in force, and of which he seemed to have been profoundly ignorant (Ex. Doc. 32d Cong. 1st Sess. No. 53, p. 170).

Since the revision of 1818, we have had another temporary neutrality act, applicable to the Canadian revolt of 1838, at the time of the " Caroline " affair, as referred to by General Banks, though with no disparaging allusion on the score of its temporariness. The reason for allowing this act to expire by its own limitation was doubtless that assigned by Mr. Buchanan, Chairman of the Senate Committee on Foreign Relations, at the time of its passage ; viz., that its terms were not sufficiently well considered, and its structure too untechnical (Benton's Abr. of Deb., vol. xiii. p. 641). It fulfilled the purposes of its enactment, however, highly satisfactorily during its two years' duration ; and the British Government, so far as I am aware, never urged its extension.

According to the best judgment, then, which I am able to give to the subject, the temporariness of our neutral legislation has been only experimental, and the result of deliberate forethought; and to argue from that circumstance, that the authors of this legislation felt themselves coerced to adopt it, and retained the mental reservation of intending to get rid of it at the earliest opportunity, seems to me an unworthy imputation upon the manliness and courageous statesmanship of some of the most independent and upright statesmen and lawgivers of the country. I repeat again, that I cannot and do not believe that the Chairman of the Committee on Foreign Affairs intended any such disparagement of the historic names of the Republic; but, in his effort to gain a foothold for subverting a long-cherished policy of the Government, he has been unavoidably driven to depreciate the motives of the measures and men identified with that policy. How bad, then, must be that proposed departure from old principles, which begins with questioning, even impliedly, the political firmness and independence of Washington and Hamilton, and which ends with confessing that the legislation approved by Jefferson, Madison, Monroe, and the two Presidents Adams, "is not an agreeable subject" for the American legislator to dwell on!

I dismiss this topic of General Banks's disparagement of our historical reputation, into which I have been led to an unexpected length by its attractive interest and undeveloped novelty, by expressing the hope that I have made good at least these five conclusions: —

First, That our policy of peaceful neutrality was initiated at the outset in the assertion of a brave and self-respectful national independence, as well as in furtherance of a just and true neutral impartiality.

Second, That, so far as we have yielded to the reasonable requests of foreign nations in originally adopting and afterwards advancing and consolidating that policy, we have not only gained for ourselves the respect and approbation of the civilized world, but have secured for the nation a balance of international credit which entitles us to a reciprocation of like legislative favors, or to a just indemnity for their refusal, on the part of those governments whom we have expressly benefited in times past.

Third, That, so far as our present relations with England are supposed to call for a new definition of our international attitude, both interest and a regard to consistency call upon us "to stand upon the old ways," and to hold up our past record to the courteous and considerate attention of that power as a motive for her making good to us those rights, or granting an indemnity for their omission, which we believe she has withheld from us during the late civil struggle.

Fourth, That if the Monroe doctrine, as it is called, is supposed to connect itself with the proposed new line of neutral (or belligerent) policy on the part of our Government, it is clearly made to appear that the authors and promoters of that doctrine would be the opponents of any such change, unless in the opposite direction to that inaugurated by the House of Representatives at its late session.

Fifth, That the experimental adoption of our neutral legislation at successive steps and by temporary enactments, confirmed as it now is by a consolidation of nearly half a century's duration, so far from proving that the time has arrived for abandoning that policy and experimenting upon a new theory, demonstratively shows that *that* legislation is suited to our Government in its international position and relations, and affords the best argument for extending, rather than contracting, the fundamental basis on which that legislative policy rests.

This leads me to the consideration of my next topic, — the proposed "scaling"-down of the American neutral laws to the alleged lower level of British legislation.

PART II.

THE TRUE ESTIMATE OF BRITISH NEUTRAL LAWS AND BRITISH NEUTRALITY.

CHAPTER VI.

General Banks quoted as to "scaling" American neutral laws down to the level of the British. — The assertion, that British neutral laws are laxer than our own, an unfortunate one. — On the contrary, British laws are decidedly the more stringent and complete of the two. — This natural, because they profess to be an improvement, and were adopted after a thorough discussion, in which Mackintosh, Canning, &c., took part. — The only wonder that the British improved so little upon Hamilton's model. — At least ten important heads of superiority on the part of the British code: — (1) Its provision against the incipient offences of "agreeing to enlist," &c., for the land service. — Illustrated by Fenianism, and case of Sir James Crampton's recruiting. — (2) In forbidding recruiting for foreign ships from among foreigners. — Illustrated by Laird's recruiting for the "Alabama" in his ship-yard. — It was useless for Sir Roundell Palmer to urge this point upon the Court of Exchequer, when the British Government had so scandalously neglected to prosecute Laird. — The American act, however, hits other violators of the law than "the natural-born subjects" of the United States. — Illustrated again from Fenianism. — (3) In embracing British subjects *everywhere*, while ours is limited to acts *within United-States territory*. — (4) In authorizing the detention of vessels about leaving with recruits "enlisted, or engaged to enlist," for foreign service. — It is under this provision that the crew of the "Alabama" ought to have been stopped at Consul Dudley's demand. — (5) In prohibiting the fitting-out of any transport or storeship for belligerent use. — Reference to American practice in Crimean War, and to the new provision authorizing free traffic in ships of war as merchantable articles. — (6) In forbidding the fitting-out *or* arming, &c., of a ship of war, when our act only prohibits "fitting out *and* arming," with an exception which General Banks takes pains to subvert. — Laird's iron-clads stopped on this use of the word "*or*" in the British act. — Importance of this word "or" in several of our leading cases ignored. — Did General Banks mean to strike hands with Chief-

Baron Pollock, of "Alexandra" fame? — Baron Bramwell's "quibble" and "evasion" noticed. — (7) In using the terms "in order that" in addition to "with intent" of our law. — Baron Pigott's friendly demonstration of this superiority alluded to. — (8) In employing the terms "persons assuming to exercise the powers of government," in addition to "colony, province," &c. — Illustration from description of Jefferson Davis in the "Alexandra" and "Pampero" cases. — Notice of Lord Curriehill's keen point, that neither the American nor the British act forbids the fitting-out of *privateers*. — The writer meets it with the American decisions. — Cases of Guinet and Quincy noticed. — The point may hold good of letters of marque.

THE Chairman of the Committee on Foreign Affairs thus states their motive for seeking to conform the new legislation of their proposing, to the tenor and terms of the British Foreign-Enlistment Act of 1819 (59th George III., chap. 69), which constitutes the only British neutral legislation now in force. I quote General Banks's oral explanation in debate, as more explicit than any thing contained in his written report: —

"The object of the committee has been to scale the [United States] neutrality act of 1818 to the standard of the Foreign-Enlistment Act enacted by Great Britain in 1819. The provisions of the Bill which has been read are essentially the same as the provisions enacted for the same purpose in the Foreign-Enlistment Act of Great Britain. With the exception of the section giving citizens of the United States authority to sell vessels, the material of which they are made, and munitions of war, to governments or citizens of governments with whom the United States may not be at war, there is nothing in this Bill which is not contained in that act, and there is no provision in that act which is not substantially embraced in this Bill." ("Globe," July 30.)

The Chairman had previously stated in his Report (p. 6), —

"Its restrictions [those of the British act] are nominal, compared with those of the American statute."

So that, by "scaling," I understand General Banks to mean that he proposes *to lower* the requisitions of the new American act to the level of the imperfections of the British statute; his line of reasoning being, that, whereas England has not been faithful to the fulfilment of her neutral duties towards this country in the late civil struggle, we now propose to put ourselves in a position to practise towards her, whenever it shall be deemed advisable, the same treatment which her imperfect legislation has enabled her to practise towards us.

When the Chairman of the Committee on Foreign Affairs of the House of Representatives asserts that "the restrictions of the British statute are nominal, compared with those of the American," he hazards a statement which I shall be sorry to have meet the eye of any English jurist or statesman. So far is it from being true that we shall have to *make a descent* in our legislation on this head, in order to come down upon a level with that of England, that I venture to affirm, that in many, if not in most, respects, the English statute is decidedly the more high-toned and comprehensive of the two.

Why should it not be so? It was passed the year after ours; it was professedly modelled upon ours, and with the *bonâ-fide* intent, as I believe, of improving upon it; and it had the benefit of one of the ablest and most thorough discussions that any measure involving the enforcement of international duties ever received in the British Parliament. When I mention that Sir James Mackintosh, Sir William Scott, Henry Brougham, Thomas Denman, James Scarlett, John Singleton Copley, all took active and prominent parts in the discussion; that Sir James Mackintosh made one or more of his most eloquent and celebrated speeches upon the Bill; and that George Canning, in closing for the ministry, replied to Mackintosh in one of his greatest efforts, in which he did us and himself equal honor for vindicating the good faith of the law of nations (as I have already briefly quoted in part), — I think I hardly need add any thing to show that the British Foreign-Enlistment Act is *primâ facie* as honest and thorough a piece of legislation as our own. The only wonder to me is, that the English publicists and statesmen were able to improve so little as they did upon Hamilton's model, in that part of the Bill borrowed from us; and I regard it as one of the greatest tributes to the genius of that extraordinary man, that all the legal talent of England combined, virtually confessed, twenty-five years after his act was penned, that it hardly knew how to better the groundwork of his scheme for enforcing international neutrality on the ocean.

Yet, with this actual or professed adherence to the American standard of maritime neutrality, there are numerous details in which the British statute is decidedly more comprehensive and wholesomely severe than our own, either as left by Hamilton, or as modified by the laws of 1797, 1817, and 1818. Some of these points of superiority relate to warlike preparations on land (on which subject English legislation had provided, to some extent, at a much earlier date than our own), and some to preparations by sea, and some again to preparations combining both land and marine operations. Under one or the other of these heads, I can name at least ten important points of superiority in the British statute over our own.

(1). *In the first place,* the British act is decidedly more comprehensive than the American, in denouncing unneutral enlistments, both in the land and naval service of a foreign government, by making it penal " *to agree* to enlist," or " to *engage or contract* to enlist," or to " *engage* " or " *attempt to engage* " *another person to enlist,* neither of which initiatory steps of raising foreign levies is forbidden by our statute. Our act (sec. 2) only punishes one who " enlists or enters himself, or hires or retains another person to enlist," &c.; thus making a positive and complete enrolment or hiring on neutral soil a prerequisite to the offence.

The importance of this distinction will be appreciated, when it is remembered that not a Fenian recruit nor a Fenian recruiter has been prosecuted for violating American laws *by recruiting on American soil* during the late Fenian demonstration in the United States, though the *engaging* to enlist, or *the attempting to engage* others to enlist, have probably been as open as the day in all the Northern cities. It was even made a question by Governor Andrew, at the time of Sir John Crampton's dismissal in 1855, — Mr. Andrew being then one of the counsel who defended a British recruiting agent, indicted for procuring British levies on American soil, — whether our statute goes any farther than to forbid enlisting in the *naval service,* merely, of a foreign government; its words being, " to enlist," &c., " *as a soldier,* or as a marine or seaman, *on board of any vessel of war,*" — nothing being said about *land service.* Judge Sprague, of the United-States District Court, overruled the point, doubtless quite correctly (*United States* v. *Kazinski*, 18 Law Rep., p. 255–7). Yet how much better in the British statute, not merely to distinguish between warlike operations "by land or by sea," "in land or sea service," &c., — as by sec. 2, — but also to denounce *the engaging*, and *attempting to engage*, in the business of recruiting?

I need hardly add, that, with its anti-Fenian bearing, the imperfect phraseology of the British statute on this head finds no imitation in General Banks's new project.

(2). *In the second place*, the British act is more complete than our own, in prohibiting any hiring or retaining of *any person whatsoever*, by way of recruiting, for foreign war-ships transiently sojourning in British neutral waters, without excepting the subjects or citizens *of the same nation as that to which such war-ships belong*, as the American statute does, in sec. 2. The effect of the American exception is, that if the United States happens to be a neutral power, and England and France, for instance, are belligerents towards each other, England can lawfully recruit from among British subjects for her ships of war, transiently stopping in American ports; and France, in like manner, from French subjects under like circumstances. Hamilton incorporated this provision into his act of 1794, — doubtless suggested by Henfield's case, where Genet, with a show of justice, tried to neutralize Henfield's offence by claiming him for an adopted citizen of France; and the provision has retained its place on the American statute-book, down to the present day.

The superiority of the British statute, in omitting this exception, shows itself in considering the provision of British law applicable to the recruiting for the "Alabama" in Laird's ship-yard, at the time of her original outfit. Had she then been a regularly commissioned Confederate ship-of-war, *built and equipped in the Confederate States, or elsewhere than in a British port*, it would have been entirely lawful for Laird, had the American exception obtained in the British act, to have filled up the ship's crew with *Confederate* seamen, on her coming into Liverpool for a temporary stop. As it is, our complaint against the outfitters of the "Alabama" (on the score of enlisting her seamen) is, not merely that she had not become a ship-of-war of a belligerent power, at the time of her quitting the Mersey, but that her crew were almost exclusively *British subjects*, and, to a large extent, *recruited from among Her Majesty's enrolled Naval Reserves.*

Sir Roundell Palmer, at the time of the "Alexandra" lawhearing (November, 1863), being then Attorney-General of England, and leading for the Crown, took occasion to call the attention of the Court of Exchequer to this superior completeness of the British statute, in the particular just noticed ("Alexandra" Law Hearing, p. 337); but I think the allusion an unfortunate one as an argument to help persuade Chief-Baron Pollock and Baron Bramwell to a strict enforcement of the British statute on other points, if it brought to their minds, as it naturally must have done, how little the penalties of the Foreign-Enlistment Act, with all its superior completeness, had thus far *been enforced* in the instance of John Laird and the other getters-up of the "Alabama" expedition. The Chief Baron might well have interrupted the legal representative of the British Government, with demanding of him why he should expect the Court of Exchequer to give judgment against the "Alexandra," when as yet no prosecution had been instituted by the Crown against the much greater offenders of the "Alabama," though more than a year had elapsed since "the scandal and reproach" of that transaction.

In that connection, as a matter of legislative detail, the Attorney-General might very properly have called attention — as he omitted to do, and as General Banks and his committee, for that matter, seem also to have failed to observe — to the superiority of the American statute in making the prohibition against *enlisting* simply (not against *recruiting*) on American neutral soil, applicable to *all persons whatsoever*, and not merely to "*natural-born subjects [of his Majesty]*," as the British act does, by its terms. When the Attorney-General says, as he does, page 338, in his argument, —

"Of course, the penalty against serving *ubicunque gentium* must be limited to natural-born subjects, because we cannot legislate for other parts of the world," —

he seems to have forgotten that the United-States statute, to which he had just been referring, forbids "*any person*" (be he native or foreign) from enlisting in *the land-service* of a foreign power on American soil. And why should it not? May it not trouble the peace of the United States, and tend to endanger its foreign relations, to have Irish Fenians or any other foreign would-be belligerents enlist or enrol themselves for war within its territory? And was it "*of course*" that England should have no statute, and take no pains to pass one, during our late civil struggle, to prevent Laird's ship-yards and other such establishments from becoming *Confederate* enlisting stations? *Englishmen* — i.e., "natural-born subjects" — were sufficiently prohibited from seeking such rendezvous, *to enrol themselves;* but not Confederate volunteers. I do not esteem the subject-matter one of great consequence, considering the paucity of Confederate sailors in foreign parts; but I cannot quite agree to the Attorney-General's "*of course.*"

(3). On the other hand, *in the third place*, the superiority of the British act over the American is decided, in forbidding British subjects from enlisting or engaging in warlike operations *anywhere whatsoever;* while the prohibition of the United-States law is limited to "any person *within the territory or jurisdiction of the United States*" (except in reference to fitting out ships abroad to prey upon American commerce, as already noticed in the criticism on the revision of the act of 1797, and which exception, as by § 4 of the act of 1818, is altogether abrogated in General Banks's new scheme). It would seem thus that citizens of the United States, under the laws of the United States as they now stand, may freely go abroad to enlist in a foreign service, — in fact, may at home, on American soil, agree to enlist in such service (provided they do not take money and "*enter themselves*"), — without committing any offence against United-States laws (see *United States* v. *Kazinski, ut sup.*); but that both these descriptions of belligerent undertakings are denounced by the British statute.

(4). *In the fourth place*, the British act is greatly superior to our own, as a preventive of infractions of neutrality, in authorizing (as by sec. 5) the detention of any vessel about leaving the British dominions with persons on board "who have enlisted or engaged to enlist," &c., in any foreign belligerent service; thus authorizing the stopping of any warlike embarkation for foreign parts, which our laws, as they now stand, do not, unless the number of persons thus collectively embarking brings it under another head, of "setting on foot a military expedition." Sec. 6 of the British act follows up this preventive provision, by making it penal for any shipmaster to take on board his ship any such recruits, "enlisted or engaged to enlist" in a foreign belligerent service, under a penalty of fifty pounds per head for each passenger. It further subjects the ship itself to seizure and detention, until the fine incurred as above is paid, or satisfactory security given for its payment.

These provisions are entirely new in the British act, and find no exemplar in our own statutes. It is under them that we lay much of our case (at least, as a volunteer disputant, *I* have ventured to do so) against England, for permitting the final start of the "Alabama" expedition from Beaumaris Bay, after Consul Dudley had notified the British Customs' authorities that Captain Bullock was going down the Mersey in the steam-tug from Liverpool, with his twenty-five or thirty Confederate recruits to join the "Alabama," then lying in that bay, some forty miles below Liverpool, — recruits, who, according to their own confession to the Customs' Surveyor, "were going to join the gunboat *as a part of her crew*," but for whose detention, or the detention of the tug herself, the Surveyor never raised his finger. ("Boston Daily Advertiser," Nov. 11, and Dec. 9, 1865.) Do General Banks and the House of Representatives mean to ignore this feature of the British neutral code, as unimportant to the final auditing of the "Alabama" claim? or must they admit again, in this instance, that "the scaling" is upwards, rather than downwards, in putting the United-States enactment on a level with the British?

I forget: these provisions *have* attracted the attention of General Banks and his committee; but with what indifferent success they have attempted to model from their terms, for the benefit of their new project, I shall have occasion to comment on hereafter.

(5). *In the fifth place* (to come to the head of fitting out ships, and maritime neutrality purely), the British Foreign-Enlistment Act, as a neutral measure, has the clear superiority over our own in forbidding the fitting-out, &c., of any "*transport or store-ship*" for belligerent use; a prohibition never contained in the American statute, and which would have materially narrowed that right of engaging in the carrying-trade of European wars (whether by chartering or selling vessels to the belligerents), which our Government so strenuously contended for at the period of the Crimean war, under the administration of President Pierce. Can General Banks point to any thing in the American revision of 1818, so "criminally restraining the rights of nations at peace for the benefit of those at war," as this provision of the British act? And would he consider that England meant "to favor the perpetuation of [her own] supremacy on the sea," by such a self-denying ordinance as this?

It does not blunt the point of my questions at all, that this clause of "*transport or storeship*" came into the British act at the hands of Sir James Mackintosh, its opponent, and with a hostile intent to the legislation [in order to put the South-American colonists on a par with Spain, as noticed by Sir R. P. Collier, the Solicitor-General, at the "Alexandra" law-trial, Rep., p. 425]; the fact still remains, that the words are there as a part of the existing statute, and in substantial conflict with General Banks's new proposition (sec. 10 of his Bill), declaring that "nothing in this act contained shall be so construed as to prevent citizens of the United States from selling vessels, ships, or steamers . . . to inhabitants of other countries, or to governments not at war with the United States." Does not the selling or chartering a transport or storeship to a belligerent service (for which the General would contend *totis viribus*) almost necessarily presuppose some degree of "fitting-out," or "attempting to fit out," or "being concerned in the fitting-out," of the commercial carrier, which is struck at and reached by the British statute as it now stands?

(6). *In the sixth place*, the British statute contains those much-belabored words, "equip, furnish, fit out, *or* arm;" while our own only denounces "the fitting-out *and* arming" a ship of war for belligerent uses, — a distinction between "*or*" and "*and*" which saved us from having Laird's iron-clads let loose against us in September, 1863; since, as all who have studied that dark crisis in our English relations will well remember, it was only the terms of the British act forbidding Laird from "equipping, furnishing, fitting out, *or* arming," or "attempting to equip, &c., . . . *or* arm," — short of arming, — which enabled the Palmerston ministry to take the decisive step of laying hands on the Confederate rams, the "El Tousson" and the "El Monassir," before they had got into that state of *arming* which Laird's legal advisers deemed within the bounds of impunity.

Now, I notice in General Banks's Bill, that, unmindful of the pitfalls disclosed by the "Alexandra" trial in England, and by the case of *United States* v. *Quincy* in our own Supreme Court, he proposes *to fall below* the level of British neutrality again, and only make the fitting-out culpable when consummated into full arming. Sec. 3 of his Bill reads, —

"If any person shall, within the limits of the United States, fit out *and* arm, or attempt to fit out *and* arm, or shall knowingly be concerned in the fitting-out *and* arming of any ship," &c., he shall be punished," &c.

And this provision, if hereafter enacted into a law, will, I am sorry to say, amount to an effective repeal of "*or*," and substitute "*and*" for "*or*" in the only place where "*or*" now obtains in this clause of our statute.

Whether this change of our own law of 1818 is the result of deliberate purpose, or only a piece of carelessness on the part of the chairman and his committee, jointly with the House of Representatives, I am unable to determine. I can only imagine with what amazement the proposed alteration will be read by English judges and lawyers who have been concerned in the "Alexandra" and "Pampero" trials, where these two conjunctions, "*and*" and "*or*," played such a conspicuous part in the discussions. To explain their significant effect, I may remark, in passing, for the benefit of those who have not examined the subject, that a country may as well have no neutrality laws at all on the subject of fitting out ships for the use of belligerents, as to compel its executive to wait till the outfitting vessel has taken on board its armament before authorizing the seizure. It was the salvation of our neutrality statute of 1794, and again of that of 1818, that, in the clause of "*knowingly being concerned in the furnishing, fitting-out,* OR *arming,*" there came in this blessed "*or*," in place of the previous "*and*," which had coupled together "*fitting out*" and "*arming*" in the earlier sentences. So that, in Guinet's trial in 1795 (2 Dall. Rep., p. 321), and again in Quincy's case (6 Peters Rep., p. 445), where the point was not raised till as late a day as 1832, and then on behalf of the defendant by Mr. Wirt, who had been Attorney-General of the United States, the Government were able to hold on upon the defendants, and establish for themselves two of their best precedents of neutrality, wholly by force of this little particle "*or*" in the statute.

Did General Banks and his committee mean to treat these learned discussions with contempt; or, when he drafted his new statute, was he purposely codifying Chief-Baron Pollock's famous *dictum*, that "equip, furnish, fit out, or arm, all mean precisely the same thing"?[1]

(7). *Seventhly,* The British Foreign-Enlistment Act is more comprehensive than our own, in using after the clauses "equip," &c., " or attempt to equip," &c., the phraseology " with intent,

---

[1] In speaking of Guinet's and Quincy's cases, as I have above, I am not unmindful that these two decisions have been severely criticised in the English and Scotch courts; and that Baron Bramwell in the English Court of Exchequer asserts with great positiveness, that Quincy's case "was wrongly decided." ("Alexandra" Law Hearing, p. 547.) Now, while agreeing to the position, that, on scientific grounds, *an attempt* ought not to be construed on stricter principles than the *complete offence* itself, I must yet contend, that the ruling against Quincy is fully borne out by the literal prescription of the statute. "*Ita scripta est lex*" seems to me a perfect answer to any argument drawn from the relation of principal and accessory, or based upon the theoretical idea of what the statute-makers *ought* to have prescribed. But will not the learned Baron agree, that it is quite as commendable and judicial to enforce the literal fulfilment of a positive statute, though unscientifically constructed, as to openly "evade" the object of the law — within his own admission — by insisting that its distinctive terms have no meaning? — [See Baron Bramwell's denunciation of what he calls "a quibble" during the law-hearing of the "Alexandra" case (p. 100), and his subsequent adoption of the same "quibble" in solemn judgment; all the while confessing that he was "evading" the statute, pp. 548, 549.]

or in order, that such ship be employed," &c. Our statute stops short with "*with intent;*" while the British, by adding "*in order that*," helps simplify a troublesome question of whose the intent must be, — whether the equipper's, or the belligerent state's, for whose use the vessel is equipping. This distinction was also largely discussed in the "Alexandra" and "Pampero" cases; and Baron Pigott, of the English Exchequer Court, from whom we got the best declaration of neutral law that the English courts have afforded during the late rebellion, has noticed the superiority of the British statute over our own in this particular. ("Alexandra" Law Hearing, p. 565, &c.) Did General Banks and the House of Representatives mean to turn their backs on this friendly light; or did they prefer darkness to light in this instance again, in leaving the old phraseology of the American act to stand as it is?

(8). *Eighthly*, The British statute has a wider scope than the American, and so seems more effectively neutral, in using after the words "colony, province," &c., the terms, "*or of any persons exercising, or assuming to exercise, any powers of government*," &c. The Government of Jefferson Davis and his associates, for example, both in the "Alexandra" and the "Pampero" proceedings, was set forth under these terms of the Foreign-Enlistment Act; the English and Scotch pleaders not considering it safe to rely upon any such designation of the Confederate authorities as would be afforded by the phraseology of the American statute, "colony, district, or people;" or rather the corresponding phraseology of the British act, "colony, province, or part of any province, or people." Possibly in these pleadings the Crown lawyers were over-cautious; but the American legislator, in reviewing them, might well have had the doubt suggested to his mind, whether Canning and his official associates were *scaling down* from the strictness of the American law, when they added to "colony, province, or part of any province or people," the cumulative expressions, "or of any person or persons exercising, or assuming to exercise, any powers of government in or over any foreign state, colony, province, or part of any province or people." At any rate, considering that the British lawyers and lawgivers have given us such a hint about the best mode of describing Jefferson Davis & Company in legal proceedings, would it not have been well for our legislators to have made a note of it for future judicial use?

Before passing from this common section of the two statutes, I believe that I ought to call attention to the keen point made in the Scotch Court of Exchequer, in the discussion of the "Pampero" case, by Lord Curriehill, an acute member of that court, that the American statute contains no prohibition at all against privateering; all its penalties, in his view, being directed against fitting out and equipping ships of war for the *public service* of foreign belligerent powers. The language which gives rise to this suggestion is, "If any person shall fit out, &c., . . . any ship or vessel with intent that such ship or vessel shall be employed in the service of any foreign prince," &c. Now, as the captain of a privateer, the learned judge argues, cruises for his own gain, and not in obedience to the orders of the power that commissions him, he cannot be said to cruise " in the service " of that power ("Pampero" Case, p. 193).

The British statute departs from the American in this particular: in providing — what at first seems an improvement upon the American act — that it shall be penal for any person "to equip . . . any ship or vessel with intent or in order that such vessel shall be employed in the service of any foreign prince, . . . or *with intent to cruise or commit hostilities against any prince* . . . with whom His Majesty shall not then be at war." Lord Curriehill attempted to satisfy himself out of this apparent divergence from the American statute, that the British legislators meant to provide against privateering under a commission, letter of marque, &c.; but, after reasoning out the matter with great intentness (pp. 194–7), he is driven to the conclusion, that, as the cruising with a hostile intent is a necessary ingredient, at all events, of the prohibited act of the statute, the first category of being employed in the service of the foreign prince overrides both distinctive provisions; and so, that the British act, like the American, leaves the coast clear for fitting out unneutral privateers for belligerents; in short, that, under both acts, it never has been, and is not now, an offence to fit out privateers to cruise against the commerce of a friendly power at war with another foreign friendly power.

A great gap this, one would say, in the British Foreign-Enlistment Act!—and one which it is wonderful that Sir Hugh Cairns, with all his acuteness, did not point out to his Confederate clients, when he was advising them how (in Baron Bramwell's phrase) "to evade" the laws of Great Britain, or one which it is alike wonderful that he did not hold up to the view of the learned Barons of the Court of Exchequer, when he was arguing before them the illegality of the seizure of the "Alexandra." That vessel, to be sure, was equipping for the public service of the Confederates, as both the Chief Baron and Baron Bramwell felt constrained to admit in their judgments ("Alexandra" Law Hearing, pp. 525, 549). But how refreshing it would have been to the Chief Baron — who was panting to prove that "a whole fleet of ships might sail through such an act" (as the Foreign-Enlistment Act) — to be reminded that the statute did not even interfere with privateering in the slightest degree!

Lord Curriehill's point, it should be added, made such an impression upon the Scotch Bench, that, under their approbation, the Lord Advocate on behalf of the Crown abandoned all that part of his information which sought to charge the "Pampero" as being fitted out for a privateer; and this, though all the judges (including Lord Curriehill himself) were intent upon construing the British act as much in accordance with American ideas of neutrality as the points under adjudication would permit of (p. 215).

Now, with all due respect for the acumen and discriminating ability of the Scotch Exchequer Lords, I cannot but think that the American courts and the American Bar have understood themselves in considering that the American act has sufficiently provided against privateering. Very certainly, both bench and bar, and the Executive and Legislature of the United States besides, have supposed, for upwards of seventy years, that the 3d section of the neutrality law, above quoted, covers the case of fitting out privateers as much as that of the public ships of war; and that "*being in the service of a state*" is shown *by making war* for it under its commission. In the very first prosecution by *indictment* (not civil proceeding) under the law of 1794, Guinet, who has been already referred to, was prosecuted, convicted, and sentenced for being concerned in fitting out the "Cassius" *for a privateer*. The indictment (given in Wharton's State Trials, p. 93, and found May 11, 1795) charges, that the equipping, &c., were "with intent that the same ship or vessel [the "Cassius"] should be employed *in the service of the French republic;*" and the facts in evidence proved that at that time *she was owned in shares* by eight Frenchmen.

Judge Patterson in his charge, among other things, says, "No man would proclaim on the house-top that he intended to fit out *a privateer*," &c.; furthermore, the counsel for the defendant went carefully into the distinction between ships of war, privateers, "letters of marque," and other armed vessels; and insisted that the Government must show (among other things) that the vessel *was to be employed in the service of the French republic* (*Ib.*, p. 98). As Guinet was sentenced to twelve months' imprisonment and a fine of four hundred dollars, I think it may be taken for granted that this leading case was thought to settle the criminality of fitting out privateers, for American law. (See the full particulars of the history of this vessel and of its arrest after it had become *a public ship of war*, in an article on the "Cassius" precedent, in the "Boston Daily Advertiser," Aug. 22, 1865.)

Quincy's case, in like manner, was an indictment for being concerned in fitting out a privateer, "with intent that such vessel be employed in the service" of Buenos Ayres. The vessel itself was a small pilot-boat of sixty or seventy tons, owned entirely on private account; and there was no particle of evidence offered of her ever having belonged to the Buenos-Ayrean Government. It seems to me almost incredible, if the point taken by Lord Curriehill could have exculpated Quincy, that Mr. Wirt, one of the ablest of United-States Attorneys-General, should not have raised it. But the truth is, that from Guinet's case down, including the adjudications on the prizes of the " Irresistible " (the " Gran Para," the " Nereyda," &c.), and on the case of the " Irresistible," herself, which was libelled for a forfeiture in 1819 (7 Wheat. R., 551), and a multitude of other decisions that could be named, it had become a settled principle of American procedure, that a privateer was to be considered as employed in the public service of the commissioning power; — just in the sense in which it was held that " L'Invincible," a French privateer, was protected from United-States process, by being a public ship of war to that intent and purpose (1 Wheat. R., 238).

Possibly the American practice on this head implies some disregard of statute phraseology; especially as the acts of 1794 (§ 2), 1797, and 1818 (§§ 2 and 4), all use the terms " privateer" or " private ships," and the act of 1797 seems to distinguish between " private ships " and " vessels of war." I am inclined to think, however, that his lordship's point will probably hold good of armed merchantmen sailing under letters of marque, or else without any commission at all, which do not make a business of *making war*, but only of fighting defensively when attacked, or which permit themselves to make an accidental capture, if opportunity offers, in the prosecution of a commercial voyage. So far, these vessels may not come under the designation of being " employed in the service of " the nation whose flag they carry. But to this extent, at least, the American legislator may well borrow a caution from the criticism of the keen-eyed Scotchman. I doubt, however, if the Committee on Foreign Affairs, or its chairman, would have availed themselves of its friendly light, — provided it had been brought to their notice, — considering their proposal to scale at least as low as any defect contained in the British code.

CHAPTER VII.

Continuation of points of superiority of British statute over the American. — (9) In forbidding the augmenting of any ship of war, whether in time of peace or war. — Chief Baron's comment on this point noticed. — American neutrality laws are not merely municipal and selfish legislation. — The further points of superiority noticed, of forbidding the changing of the guns of a warship at all, or the addition to it of *any* equipment of war. — Allusion, again, to Sir R. Palmer's hedging on the "Alabama" question. — (10) In prescribing severer penalties, at the unlimited discretion of the court, for violations of the law. — Allusion to ridiculously small penalties actually imposed upon Jones, Highat, and others, by British judges, in 1864-5. — Other points might be named, but these sufficient to show that the statement of "its restrictions being merely nominal" is not borne out. — Discussion of the objection that most of these provisions are dependent upon the will of the Crown. — Three answers: — (1) That this dependence only applies to a part of the provisions of the law. — (2) That General Banks himself imitates the same provision in sec. 10 of his own act. — This imitation shown to defeat the very object of the important section just quoted, and to be worse than the bonding clauses. — (3) That we have never had any reason to complain of the British Crown's suspending the British act. — Our real grievance towards England on this head is *not* that she had not a good neutrality code, but that she did not enforce it in good faith. — The trouble was in Earl Russell's pettifogging, Chief-Baron Pollock's shuffling, and the British Parliament's compromising with Laird. — To this might be added British hasty recognition of rebel belligerency, and neglect to amend the defects of the statutes. — Earl Russell has admitted the whole case, in conceding that the "Alabama" ought to have been stopped — Conclusion that General Banks has mistaken the character of the Foreign-Enlistment Act.

I HAVE to urge again, —

(9). *Ninthly*, that the British statute is more sweeping and more thoroughly neutral than our own, in enacting various prohibitions against augmenting the armament of foreign ships of war which come into port already armed, but which have occasion to refit or add to their warlike equipment. By the British act (§ 8), no foreign ship of war *at all*, whether belonging to a power *at peace* or at war, is allowed to add to or vary its warlike armament in a British port; while, by our own statute (§ 5), the modified prohibition against adding to the armament of such a ship of war is only levelled against a ship of a *belligerent* power. That is, the American statute does not pretend to interfere at all with increasing the number of guns, &c., of a foreign ship of war, at a time when the government to which the ship belongs *is at peace*, but only prohibits such augmentation when the ship is *the representative of a belligerent power*. The British act, on the other hand, directs its prohibition equally against such warlike equipment in time of peace as well as in time of war.

Chief-Baron Pollock, of "Alexandra" fame, is, so far as I know, the first person that has ever pointed out this distinction (Judgment in the "Alexandra" Law Hearing, p. 532). The point is doubtless well made; but when the Chief Baron comes to press it into the service of his argument, that the Foreign-Enlistment Act is wholly municipal, and for home use, having for its chief end to prevent British ports from becoming the scene of naval battles between foreign equippers of belligerent war-vessels, he needlessly and mistakenly, as it seems to me, depreciates and belittles the neutral honor of his country. At any rate, if he concedes that Great Britain took this provision of her neutral code from the American model (a matter which he did his best to prevent the Attorney-General from arguing, after giving full license to Sir Hugh Cairns, in his opening for the defence, to do the same thing), I am sure that he does not attribute to the American law the motive which actuated the framers and originators of that legislation. The American law *is not* and *never was* designed to merely promote municipal and selfish ends; and so, Chief-Justice Marshall declared in the "Santissima Trinidad" case (1 Brockenbrough Rep., p. 488), and so, in effect, the title to the act of 1817, ch. 58, decides, when it sets forth "An Act *more effectually to preserve* THE NEUTRAL RELATIONS of the United States."

However, it is doubtless going to the root of the matter of preventing all warlike equipment of foreign ships of war in a neutral port, to say that the thing shall not be done, as the British statute forbids, even in time of peace, without royal license; and, so far, that statute is more thorough-going than our own.

Under the same head of adding to the warlike force of ships of war, already such in fact, are to be noticed two other points of superiority of the British act over the American, also brought out by the "Alexandra" trial; viz., that the British act forbids the changing of the guns of such vessels *at all*, whether for those of a larger calibre, or for those of the same calibre but of a different construction; while the American law only forbids the changing "for guns of a *larger* calibre." The British act thus gets rid of all equivocations about the size of the substituted guns, and also of all dispute whether they may be rifled or of smooth bore, and the like, to which the American act may easily give rise.

Again, while the American statute only forbids (in the instance of these foreign war vessels) "the addition thereto of any equipment *solely applicable to war*," the British statute more summarily denounces "the addition [thereto] of *any equipment* of war."

It needs no argument, I conceive, to connect these manifest attempts to make the British statute more thorough-going than our own, with honest purposes and *bona-fide* neutral designs on the part of the British legislators who have proposed and adopted them. Only, I must protest again against any neutral code being estimated as such a selfish, municipal, and insular an affair, as Sir Roundell Palmer (who brought out these two latter points of superiority of the British statute in the "Alexandra" Law Hearing, p. 342) labors, in unison with the Chief Baron, to make it appear that the British system of neutral laws really is. Would the Attorney-General have consented to such a definition of his country's neutral attitude, and such a portraiture of British hunkerism and international illiberality, if it had not been for the shade of the American reclamations for the doings of the "Alabama," in the background?

(10). *In the tenth and last place*, the British statute is more severe in its penalties throughout than the American; though apparently the Chairman of the Committee on Foreign Affairs was of a different opinion when he brought in his Bill, accommodating its various prescribed penalties to those contained in the British act. The universal prescription of the latter act is, "fine and imprisonment, or either of them, *at the discretion of the court;*" with the exception of the punishment for masters of vessels who transport foreign levies out of the kingdom, which is fixed at a forfeiture of fifty pounds per head (sec. 6). General Banks, in imitation of this, reported his Bill originally, with every penalty left discretionary with the court, exactly in the terms just quoted; the provisions as to masters of vessels, as we have already seen, making no part of the existing American act. (House of Representatives' Document, No. 806.)

Upon the taking-up of the Bill in the House for consideration, the Chairman of the Committee — struck, perhaps, with this unscientific and un-American feature of his measure — moved to insert, in Sections One, Two, and Three, specific maximums of punishment, — so that, in Section One, the imprisonment should not exceed two years (one year less than at present by the act of 1818); in Section Two, the same maximum (also one year less than at present); and in Section Three, the same maximum of imprisonment as at present (three years), but with a reduction of the maximum of fine from $10,000 to $3,000: and in this shape the amendments were adopted by the House. Section Five, however (probably by some oversight), had the discretionary punishment of the first draft retained; so that, instead of the one year's imprisonment and the fine of $1,000 of the present law, the penalty is now left wholly " at the discretion of the court."

Now, going back to our starting-point, —viz., the comparative severity of the Foreign-Enlistment Act and of the American act in its present condition, unaffected by General Banks's project, — is it not a higher degree of severity for the British judge to have power to fine and imprison *ad libitum*, than for the American judge to be tied down to imposing a maximum of three years' imprisonment, and a limited amount of fine, for a violation of neutrality? And when the Chairman of the Committee on Foreign Affairs, not content with retaining this lesser stringency of the American law, proposes to reduce it still further, by lowering the maximums of imprisonment in three instances out of four, as has just been noticed (these four being the only remaining penal sections of the Bill, after striking out the clauses left for repeal in the project itself), is it hardly consistent with legislative candor to talk about scaling down to the level of the standard of the British Foreign-Enlistment Act?

Perhaps the Chairman of the Foreign-Affairs Committee, at the time of introducing his project to the House, was thinking of the paltry sentences actually imposed by the British judges, in the exercise of their discretion, upon Jones, Highat, and other such convicted violaters of the Foreign-Enlistment Act; but does that justify his general impeachment of the efficiency of the act itself, or permit him to leave the impression that we must lower the tone of our present laws in order to come down upon the same plane of neutral inefficiency with those of Great Britain?

I might go on to add to my catalogue of points of superiority of the British neutral code over our own, several others besides the ten thus above enumerated, though doubtless of less moment. But I trust enough have been adduced to make good my position, that in many, if not in most, respects, the British statute is decidedly the more comprehensive and searching of the two. Perhaps, instead of "its restrictions being merely nominal," the reader will be prepared to agree with me, that Canning borrowed from our code in good faith, and that if we would, in our turn, imitate again upon the model of the Foreign-Enlistment Act, we might "receive our own with usury."

On the other hand, I frankly concede, as General Banks urges, that the British statute is obnoxious to the objection of being more or less dependent on the royal fiat of the monarch for its vitality and operative effect. As any one will notice who glances at its terms, several of its denunciations against forbidden acts are predicated upon their being done "*without the leave or license of* **His** *Majesty being for that purpose first had and obtained;*" thus recognizing that His (or Her) Majesty's leave and license may quite legitimize the prohibited proceeding.

Now, in reference to this, I have to urge, in the first place, that this dispensing prerogative of the Crown does not apply to the statute universally and throughout, — as perhaps General Banks and his associates imagine; but only to certain features of the enlistment clauses, and those regulating the fitting-out of ships. On the contrary, the whole business of recruiting for foreign service on British soil (see latter clause of section 2) is left to the regular operations of permanent law; and so are the taking on board a vessel of domestic levies for foreign service, and the personal liability incurred by the captain for consenting to it, — as by the provisions of sections 5 and 6, already commented on.

In the next place, while fully agreeing to the vicious and inadmissible character of the dispensatory feature referred to, I am only surprised that General Banks should himself have adopted it — at the suggestion of Mr. Jenckes, of Rhode Island ("Globe," July 30) — in that part of his project upon which he lays most stress; I mean in the portion of his Bill putting beyond doubt the freedom of neutral commerce to traffic in ships and munitions of war. By section 10 of his Act, as amended by the House with his approbation, all the provision of that section (introduced into the statute for the first time, as a new feature), in regard to selling ships and material of war to foreign belligerents, which I have already quoted in connection with the clause of the British statute as to "the fitting-out of transports and storeships," is made dependent on the executive will of the President of the United States, in the following manner: —

"*Provided*, that the operation of this section of this act shall be suspended by the President of the United States with regard to any classes of purchases, whenever the United States shall be engaged in war, or whenever the maintenance of friendly relations with any foreign nation may, in his judgment, require it."

Now, as this clause can seldom or never come into operation "*whenever the United States shall be engaged in war,*" — the very fact of their being at war with any nation implying that they cannot so far be neutral, or in a relation of peace, to that nation, — the latter category, "*or whenever the maintenance of friendly relations with any foreign nation may, in his judgment, require it,*" becomes the normal prescription of the statute, and so places it upon the very footing which the chairman himself so much reprobates.

Plainly this principle of autocratic dictation ought never to find a place in American legislation. It is hard enough to comprehend how Englishmen, even at the date of 1819, should have left in the hands of the king's ministers the power of precipitating the kingdom into war, by allowing them to make the British dominions the recruiting-ground and the naval basis of foreign belligerents; but certainly, under the Constitution of the United States and the established practice of the American Government, no such power should be lodged with the President of the United States, as to be able to stop at pleasure all commerce "in selling vessels, ships, or steamers, built within the limits thereof, or material or munitions of war, the growth or product of the same, to inhabitants of other countries, or to governments not at war with the United States," which General Banks's new legislation proposes to confer henceforth.

With all respect, I would beg to inquire of the Chairman of the Committee on Foreign Relations, whether the too friendly aid which, seems to have been extended by the United States to Spain in her present contest with Chili, through an over-strict enforcement of our neutrality laws as against the latter power, and which, according to the chairman himself, "has been universally condemned" (Rep., p. 8), is not an exact illustration of that unneutral interference on the part of the Executive with our foreign commerce in times of war, which he now seeks to make normal and perpetual by express legislation. I would further ask whether such despotic stopping-short and letting-loose of *quasi* fighting-ships at pleasure is not an hundred-fold more objectionable in principle than the impartial and equally operative provision of simply taking a bond from the owners that *they* (not *their vendees* or *assigns*) will agree that their ships shall not violate the neutrality of the United States; — a restriction on commerce which, according to the chairman's denunciation, so "criminally restrains the rights of nations at peace for the benefit of those at war."

But, in the last place, I have to urge, more importantly than the two suggestions already made, — in reply to General Banks's assault upon the Foreign-Enlistment Act, founded upon its being dependent on the pleasure of the Crown for its vitality, — that thus far we have never had any occasion to complain of this feature of the British statute, *as applied against us;* and so that it can make no part of that list of grievances which impels the present movement to scale our neutral laws down to the level of the English standard. Admitting that *the whole* of the Foreign-Enlistment Act *has been* subject to the royal supersession during our late civil struggle, will the Chairman of the Committee on Foreign Affairs for a moment contend that we have suffered any injury in consequence of the exercise of the kingly prerogative referred to? On the contrary, notwithstanding the clamor of the secessionists, that the neutrality of Great Britain has worked to their prejudice in its recognizing and respecting the Federal blockade, and in its refusing (to both parties) the right to carry in and sell prizes, and in various other particulars, who has ever heard that it was even *proposed* by the British Government to suspend the operation of a single section of the Foreign-Enlistment Act for a single day? There were proposals enough on their part, to be sure, to better it, which, I am sorry to say, never came to any thing, practically; but when and where was it ever suggested by any responsible public man in England, that the Crown should interfere with the law, as it then stood, to set it aside in a single particular, or for a single moment?

No: the burden of our grievance against England, *toned down to its lowest basis,* is *not* that she had not on her statute-book a neutrality code as good as our own, and one sufficiently complete to guarantee to us our neutral rights, but *that, having a law quite sufficient to afford us neutral protection, and one decidedly superior to our own, she did not adequately and in good faith enforce its provisions.* Executively, it was Earl Russell's pettifogging mode of administering it, in for ever insisting upon proof sufficient *to convict*, instead of *primâ-facie* evidence adequate *to detain;* Judicially, it was Chief-Baron Pollock's shuffling partisanship, in depriving us of a precedent declaring the "Alexandra" forfeited, at as early a day of the rebellion as June, 1863; and, Legislatively, it was the British Parliament's openly sanctioning and approving of a compromise with the violators of the law, in which "the law itself bought out the guilty prize," in the shape of paying

John Laird & Sons a bonus for their Confederate rams, — thereby confessing that Great Britain had to pension the builders of the "Alabama" not to involve her in war, — of which we have a right to complain.

Earlier than all this, no doubt, we may bear in remembrance the unfriendly haste with which she took the rebels by the hand, and, besides acknowledging them as belligerents, virtually asked them to come into the congress of nations, and help declare the oracles of international law; and later, that, when we pointed out how our commerce was perishing through the divided voice of her judiciary and the supineness of her Executive, she refused to strengthen the Crown with any further legislation, and indulged in the luxury of doing nothing, and pitying (?) our misfortunes. But it needs not either of these latter suggestions to make good those claims against England which General Banks and the House of Representatives hold in such sensitive recollection.

The "Alabama," for instance, — to touch no other example, — might and should have been seized under British laws *as they were*. That these were effective enough for that object, has been solemnly admitted by the British Government's parade of its superserviceable attempts to stop her before she took wings; and the Foreign Secretary has irrevocably clenched the admission, by confessing, more than once, that her escape was "a scandal and a reproach" to British laws, and that he could only explain it by official "treachery." Furthermore, the same Foreign Secretary found those laws potent enough to enable him to seize the half-finished rams, when, as he has since twice declared in the face of the British nation, it would, in his opinion, have been a just cause of war for the United States against England, if he had refrained to exercise that power.

Now, in the face of these admissions by the highest exponent of British responsibility, is it good logic or good comity for the United States, while holding England up to the fulfilment of her international duties, as defined by her own self-imposed and so-called "*municipal*" laws, to announce to her, and, in the same breath, to the rest of the world, that we do not mean to practise, ourselves, under any such stringent code as hers hereafter?

I beg General Banks's pardon. He says, —

"There is nothing in this [his] Bill which is not contained in that [the British] act, and there is no provision in that act which is not substantially embraced in this Bill."

Either the General or myself, then, must be mistaken about the provisions of the British statute above cited. I make my quotations from an authoritative reprint of the British Foreign-Enlistment Act, published by the Queen's printers in 1863, and contained in the Appendix to the "Alexandra" Jury Trial, where the British and American neutrality statutes are brought together in juxtaposition for the use of the English Bench and Bar. Supposing it to be genuine, I give its text, together with that of the American act, in the Appendix hereto, for the benefit of my readers. I should be glad to have the Chairman of the Committee on Foreign Affairs establish the spuriousness of the copy of the British law from which I borrow, and so do away with the points of comparison which I have attempted to set up, as above. Until that is made to appear, however, I must adhere to the conviction that our legislators were not sufficiently informed for their task, when they undertook to disparage British neutral legislation as altogether inferior to our own.[1]

---

[1] Perhaps I ought to notice, that General Banks himself assumes the liability of Great Britain to the United States, for permitting the outfit of the "Alabama," and similar infractions of neutrality, on some of the same grounds as those which I have ventured to put forth as above (Report, pp. 9 and 10). Yet, as the assumption seems in entire contrariety to the general drift of his Report and legislative scheme, I can only regard it as one of those evidences of arguing at cross-purposes, or of a diversity of intents in the preparation of different parts of his Report, which I have already had occasion to notice.

PART III.

UNWORTHY PROMOTION OF FENIAN BELLIGERENCY.

CHAPTER VIII.

The new project an outspoken declaration in favor of Fenian belligerency. — Fenianism the tocsin of the new *coup d'état*.—Extract from the Report to show this. — Can the suppression of the Fenian raid upon Canada be a just starting-point for the repeal of the neutrality laws ? — President Johnson both deserves and receives the support of the country for that step. — The people approve it, as they have the former exercise of the executive prerogative in similar cases. — Many Irish-Americans opposed to Fenianism. — Starting from the Fenian raid, what better proof could be afforded of the necessity and value of the neutrality laws than that affair ? — Would not General Banks have imitated the conduct of General Meade in suppressing it ? — Probably he would have been glad to return good for evil to the Canadians. — Irishmen, whether naturalized or not, have no right to trouble the peace of the United States with old grievances. — Quotations from Pitt, Wilberforce, and Grote, no more to the point than the Scandinavian myths. — Would not General Banks, as President, have done the same thing as President Johnson ? — Would the General throw open domestic questions of our own to British discussion, like this of Fenianism with the English ? — Sections 6 and 8 of the neutrality statute, which it is proposed to repeal, quoted ; also General Banks's remarks in explanation of his project, and correction of probable misreport of their tenor. — Are the Fenians "a people," within these remarks ? — Is not England also a people ? and was not Sir John Crampton dismissed for recruiting on behalf of the British "people" ? — The Fenians really not prosecuted as soon as they ought to have been. — No such provisions as sections 6 and 8 in the British laws ; but they are less necessary from British insular position. — The British act, however, has something nearly as good, which General Banks has ineffectually tried to imitate. — These sections of our law have made part of it since 1794, and most efficiently. — Were they not enforced against Genet and the French "people" ? — The idea of indicting a solitary Irish recruit, and letting the mass-agitators, like Roberts and Sweeney, go free, an absurd one. — Allusion to Roberts being introduced to the floor of Congress. — Application of some of General Banks's sentiments about extending the rights of neutrals, and restricting those of belligerents, to the case of the Canadians. — The Canadian put forth as the speaker. — Would General Banks approve his own logic more than his own law, if he were one of those Canadians? — This criterion alone enough to dispose of the whole question. — Perhaps, however, Fenianism has not been so well provided for in the terms of the new law as the Canadians and English have been led to believe.

HOWEVER objectionable the Report and Bill of the Committee on Foreign Affairs, as sanctioned and adopted by the House of Representatives of the United States, may appear to be on the score of their unjust depreciation of the national fame and their unfounded disparagement of the British neutral code, they present a still further aspect, yet more obnoxious to censure than the two characteristics already considered. I refer to their pronounced and unmistakable declaration in favor of Fenian belligerency.

Indeed, General Banks, on behalf of the committee, hardly hesitates to avow that the Fenian movement is the more immediately inciting cause of his sudden onslaught upon the neutrality system of the country. Other exciting inducements are, to be sure, alluded to or borne in mind by him: such as British unfriendliness during the Confederate rebellion, already noticed; French encroachment upon Mexican liberties, more than hinted at by the significant importance attached to the Monroe declaration; and, more recently, the censurable co-operation (as he esteems it) of the United States' Executive with monarchical Spain as against republican Chili. All these combine to impress upon him the importance of seriously considering whether the country ought not to change its attitude of passive neutrality into one of active intervention in the affairs of foreign nations. But it is more especially the Fenian call to the Celtic clans to rally and raise the standard of Irish independence — recovering *Ireland for the Irish* — which seems to have finally struck the tocsin for the new *coup d'état*.

Says General Banks in the concluding paragraphs of his Report, which, like the final residuum of a chemist's process, may doubtless be taken as the ultimate desideratum of his speculations: —

The recent memorable invasion of Canada offers a signal exhibition of the spirit and character of our Government. Great Britain has given us no cause to respect her sense of justice, or her regard for right. . . . She gave her sympathy to rebels, of whose Confederacy slavery was to be the headstone of the corner. . . . And when, in adherence to our own policy, by reluctant, questionable, and even violent execution of our laws, we preserve to her possessions, the loss of which would be the precursor of other calamities, and reduce her to the rank of a subordinate power, against a race to which our country is deeply indebted, and which has suffered for six centuries inexcusable and ineffable wrong, she mildly approves our conduct, as better than she had a right to expect. . . .

"They [the committee] cannot withhold from Ireland an expression of their hopes for the restoration of its independence. They believe, with Pitt, that Ireland is entitled to the same privileges as England, and Irishmen to the same rights as Englishmen. They believe, with Wilberforce, that England owes reparation to Ireland. . . .

"American opinion . . . reveres English history at large, but regards the Irish part of it with resentment, wonder, and scorn. We believe with [Grote] 'that England cannot study the history of Ireland without losing her self-respect, nor the character of its people without advantage.'

"The sympathy we extend to all nations struggling for independence is strengthened in this case by a sense of obligation due to these people [the Irish] for their assistance in the development of our country. But independent of any consideration of this character, if to our sense of *their* wrong we add the recollection of *our own*, the popular interest in their favor is sufficiently explained. The intervention of our Government under such circumstances is proof of our fidelity to our obligations to other nations, and ought to satisfy the world that we have no desire to disturb its peace. It is rather to maintain our relations with other nations that we ask the favorable consideration of the measures herewith reported." (Report, pp. 11 and 12.)

Thus it is the addition of our own wrongs to those of Ireland, both inflicted by the same overbearing and tyrannical England, which constitute, in General Banks's view, the motive and occasion of the new demonstration. Fenianism and antagonism to Great Britain, then, are the two great watchwords by which we are to interpret this revolutionary attempt to undermine and set aside the long-cherished policy of the American Government.

Now, so far as the suppression of the late Fenian raid upon Canada by executive interposition is concerned, I must needs express my surprise, that the Chairman of the Committee on Foreign Affairs can seriously contend — I might almost say, *pretend* — that what happened in that connection last June, on the Canada border, in the way of a quiet and honorable discharge of our neutral obligations towards our provincial neighbors, the Canadians, and towards the more distant parent Government, our international allies, the English, can be tortured into either a fitting motive or a justifiable occasion for this ferocious attack upon the long-standing neutrality code of the United States.

Do General Banks and the House of Representatives really believe, that the people of the Union condemn President Johnson for simply obeying his oath of office in seeing to the enforcement of the laws of the country, or that his moderate and mild-tempered arrest of the misguided Fenian movement can have created a call for taking away from him altogether the power of suppressing such warlike outbreaks in future? If so, I must confess that the legislators of the Capitol hold a very different estimate of the good sense and love-for-law of the American people, from the opinion which, for one, I have grown up to entertain for them in these particulars.

I maintain, on the contrary, that not only have the great mass of the voters in the United States applauded this action of the President's, as the people of the United States have heretofore sustained Presidents Washington, Adams, and most of their official successors, — including President Van Buren, at the trying period of the "Caroline" and "McLeod" affairs in 1838, — in upholding the neutral policy of the country; but that no better test could be afforded of the salutary and peace-preserving efficacy of that system of laws which is now sought to be subverted, than is afforded by this very instance of the Fenian crusade.

My readers will not expect — probably do not desire — that I should argue the question of the relative popularity gained or lost by President Johnson in putting down the Canadian invasion, and so attempt to make good the first of my propositions. I leave it, therefore, to their decision, unargued. I will only add, that, in settling that issue according to their own judgments, I desire them to take into account the true American sense of the country, and not merely the opinions held by its Irish voters; though I believe it may be confidently predicated, even of this latter class, that a large portion of them view the movements both of Roberts and Stephens, and their respective adherents, with undisguised dislike.

It is, then, to the test and criterion of our neutrality laws afforded by Fenianism, that I wish now more particularly to direct my discussion.

If the Chairman of the Committee on Foreign Affairs would carry his hostility to our neutral system so far as to favor the repeal of all the neutrality laws, — and *that* certainly *seems* to be his drift, as I shall presently have occasion to quote, — I beg to ask him, where the country would have found itself last spring, if it had encountered the uprising of the Fenians, at that time, without a statute to make known and prescribe to its Executive and the people their respective duties? What could a President of the United States have done in President Johnson's place, at that juncture, without any statutory power to control and repress that conglomeration of Irish filibusters which thronged up to the Canada frontier, and filled our northern cities and villages with its excitable and excited swarms? If Washington felt himself powerless to deal with a few American recruits, like Gideon Henfield, in 1793, who were disposed to jeopardize the national neutrality by enlisting on board French privateers; and after ineffectually causing him to be indicted and tried *at common law*, and *under the law of nations*, for an infraction of neutrality, had to demand of Congress the law of 1794, to specially invest him with powers adequate to preserve the peace of the country, — what opposition could President Johnson have offered to the late Fenian crusade in sufficient season to have saved a warlike conflagration, but for the much-reprobated neutrality code of 1818, perpetuating this very section of the law made to fit Henfield's case?

Possibly General Banks thinks it unfortunate that the Fenians were not allowed to have free swing in attacking and sacking Canadian cities, or, at least, to the extent of retaliating in kind for the St. Albans raid of 1864. I cannot believe it; and do not doubt, that, had General Banks filled General Meade's place, he would have carried out the President's orders as cheerfully — perhaps as successfully — as the gallant commander just named. Perhaps, with his known magnanimity, General Banks would all the more cheerfully have set the Canadians an example of returning good for evil, in view of their having so little claim for the protection afforded them. It must be, then, on the general principle of allowing free scope to patriotic impulses, under our free institutions, — *short of levying war on United-States soil*, — that the Chairman of the Committee on Foreign Affairs indulges in those invectives about Irish rights and British wrongs which I have above quoted.

For would General Banks contend, on his responsibility as an American lawyer and legislator, that it is lawful for any set of native-born — or, if he prefers, *naturalized* — Irish-American citizens, to make the United States a basis of hostile operations, whence to carry on war against a friendly power, because the parents or ancestors of those citizens — or, if he prefers, because *those citizens themselves* — have suffered political grievances when residing at a former period in Ireland? If they have quitted that country and cast their lot here, what right have they to stir up strife in their new domicile, and embroil the hospitable republic which has so kindly received and sheltered them? If they are *not* naturalized or domiciled American citizens, but are merely emigrant British subjects, transiently resident with us, *a fortiori*, what right have they to be carrying on war from our territory?

If such an invasion of Canada, then, as consummated, would have been a great international wrong, and a just cause even for offensive war on the part of Great Britain, why do General Banks and the House of Representatives undertake to palliate, nay, to patronize it, by reviving the story of Ireland's misgovernment and England's oppression?

What have the opinions of Pitt and Wilberforce and Grote to do with the present duties of Irish-American citizens, more than the myths of the Scandinavian gods? Why go back to the "six centuries of inexcusable and ineffable wrong," and talk about "a reluctant, questionable, and even violent execution of our laws" "against a race to which our country is deeply indebted," when the Chairman of the Committee on Foreign Affairs knows that every Fenian crossing the Canada line with a musket in his hand was a flagrant offender against the laws of the United States and the peace of the Union, whom it would have been his duty, had he himself filled President Johnson's place, to have ordered to have stopped, at all hazards and with any extremity of force? Furthermore, does General Banks mean to concede to the British House of Commons the same right to discuss questions of the domestic policy of the Union — for instance, the admission or exclusion of the rebel States from representation in Congress — that he and his committee claim to exercise in reference to Irish participation in English privileges?

Is it in behalf of oppressed Ireland, then, — either as a matter of political effect or of serious statemanship, — that the Committee on Foreign Affairs have proposed, and the House of Representatives of the United States have unanimously voted for, the repeal of the two following clauses of the present American Neutrality Act : —

" SEC. 6. — If any person shall, within the territory or jurisdiction of the United States, begin or set on foot, or provide or prepare the means for, any military expedition or enterprise, to be carried on from thence against the territory or dominions of any foreign prince or State, or of any colony, district, or people with whom the United States are at peace, every person so offending shall be deemed guilty of a high misdemeanor, and shall be fined not exceeding three thousand dollars, and imprisoned not more than three years."

" SEC. 8. — . . . It shall be lawful for the President of the United States . . . to employ . . . the land or naval forces of the United States, or the militia thereof, . . . for the purpose of preventing the carrying-on of any such expedition or enterprise from the territories or jurisdiction of the United States against the territories or dominions of any foreign prince or State, or of any colony, district, or people with whom the United States are at peace."

I beg the reader's attention to the explanation given of this proposed repeal by General Banks in his place in the House, he having omitted any reference to it in his Report. I emphasize a few passages with italics, to help the reader to the General's points : —

"The effect of that [the sixth] section [of the existing law] is to enable the Government to hold *a single man, a society or association of men*, responsible for acts committed *by a people*. It is not contained in the English law. Instead of this, the [new] Bill proposes that *every man* engaged in any enterprise prohibited by the provisions of this act or the laws of the country shall be held responsible for what *he himself* does, and shall be punished for any violation of the law. . . . The Government is remanded to *the persons* by whom the offences are committed. . . . [The Bill] prohibits and punishes the organization of any expedition within the United States against other governments by making *every man engaged therein responsible for his crime*. It gives to the President, the same as the law of 1818, power to use the land and naval forces to execute the law, and also to compel foreign vessels, if necessary, to depart from the country."

I suspect that there is some misreporting of the chairman's words, by the stenographer, in this last sentence; and that, instead of saying, "It gives to the President, the same as the law of 1818, power to use the land and naval forces to execute the law, and also to compel," &c., it should read, "It gives to the President, the same as the law of 1818, power to use the land and naval forces to execute the law *in regard to detaining vessels with their prizes, and to restoring such prizes where the capture had been made in violation of neutrality;* it also gives the President power to compel foreign vessels, if necessary [as by sec. 9], to depart from the country." I make the suggestion, because, with the proposed repeal of the last clause of sec. 8, above quoted, it cannot be true (within General Banks's reported declaration), that the new law leaves with the President the same power to use the land and naval forces to execute the law, which he now possessed under the present law. On the contrary, the proposed law expressly repeals the provision under which, as I understand, General Meade was ordered to use the United-States troops to suppress the Fenian outbreak, and under which, I venture to say, he rendered an honorable and patriotic service to the country by so speedily and yet so quietly bringing it to the ground.

Now, giving the application of the motive for this repeal of part of sec. 8, and of the whole of sec. 6, of the old law, which I have imputed to it, viz., a design to favor "the restoration of the independence of Ireland," I ask the reader to consider for a moment the chairman's reasons for recommending it. The complaint against the old provisions is, that they may render " a single man, a society, or an association of men, responsible for acts committed *by a people.*" And the remedy proposed by the new law is, that every man shall only be held accountable for his own doings. That is, — you shall no longer indict single or collective Fenians for setting on foot or providing means for any military expedition to be carried on against Canada or Ireland from United-States territory, nor shall the President of the United States have authority to employ the land and naval forces of the Union for the suppression of any such Fenian invasion *so long as, or because, Fenianism is the cause of a people.* You may indict an Irishman for making war against England *on his own hook*, as a solitary Irish belligerent, — and would he not be an Irishman indeed to be such a belligerent? — but, when he is the exponent of the cause of a people, he is not to be a subject of prosecution under American neutral laws.

Since when — I would ask — have General Banks and the House of Representatives found the Fenians to be "a people"? And, pray, is not England "a people" as well? And did we not give Sir John Crampton, the British minister at Washington, his passports, in 1855, for undertaking to make the United States a recruiting-ground against Russia in the Crimean War? It seems, that, after allowing the Fenians to hold public meetings and openly "prepare the means for a military expedition" against Canada, Ireland, England, or where not, and after allowing such sort of proceedings to go on *with perfect impunity for months*, General Banks now takes it hardly that *there was a law* by which they might have been prosecuted, and *were not;* and now proposes to repeal, not only that wholesome provision of the statute, — sec. 6, above quoted, — but also the one under which General Meade actually interfered with their movements in a stage of flagrant hostilities, — sec. 8, also above cited.

It is very true, as General Banks urges, that these provisions are not to be found in the British code; and so far he can find a chance to "scale" downwards from our neutral level. But had the Committee on Foreign Relations duly weighed how much less applicable to that kingdom the insular position of England has rendered these provisions than to the continental position of the United States? and how far the deficiency is supplied by the provisions of the Foreign-Enlistment Act, already referred to, forbidding any vessel (for of course the exit from England must be by vessel), or master of a vessel, to carry away any recruits or enlisted soldiers from British territory? — provisions which the Committee have made a show of incorporating to some extent into their project, but which are so inartificially ingrafted upon the House Bill that I venture to pronounce them perfectly nugatory. Besides, too, as I have already hinted, if ever so skilfully incorporated they are incapable of being so adapted to our continental location as to secure our neutrality on the Canadian and Mexican borders with equal efficiency as that of the British act in regard to the islands of the United Kingdom.

But, again, if these repealed provisions, against setting on foot military expeditions, &c., are not a part of the British neutral code, they are certainly not a part of that legislation of our own, of the era of 1817–18, which the Committee so inveigh against, as shaped after foreign dictation. These sections, which General Banks proposes to repeal, were part of Alexander Hamilton's original draft of the law of 1794, our first and famous code, and have been repeatedly tested in American practice since, down to the present day. Pretty plainly, they were meant to hit the warlike schemes of Genet and the French Government at that day; and did successfully answer that purpose, if the fame gained by us for their enforcement, on which I have already dwelt at such length, is any proof of their value and efficiency. Pray, are the Committee on Foreign Relations ready to maintain that the French republic of 1794 — that fiery democracy, which had on foot, at one moment, fourteen armies, fighting all Europe — was not as much of "a people" as the Fenians of 1866? or that "our country was not as deeply indebted" to the French of Louis XVI.'s day as to the Irish of the present?

Again, if General Banks concedes that the individual Irish belligerent who enlists or procures others to enlist ought to be prosecuted, does he consider it good logic that the men or the association of men who "set on foot a military expedition" ought to be let alone, and have *carte blanche* to get up a war? — that Patrick or Michael, who is deluded into putting his name to a paper containing he knows not what, shall be sent to prison, if complained of; but that Roberts or Sweeney, who disturb the whole body politic with Fenian musters and Fenian marchings to and fro, shall be put above the reach of the law, because acting in the name of "a people?"— nay, if report speaks true, that the said Roberts shall have the freedom of the floor of Congress, in order to advise legislators how to draw the teeth out of the statutes, and make Fenianism both safe and respectable?

One word more on this topic of Fenianism, and I will pass from it. Supposing that I quite mistake the object of the repeal of the sections above considered, and supposing that I misjudge the chairman's and the committee's motives generally in alluding to the Fenian movement at all, I cannot forbear to make that movement a criterion of another portion of General Banks's proposed policy, which, he will doubtless fully concede, embodies and sets forth one of his fundamental ideas. That I may do the General no injustice, I will quote his exact language in explanation of the idea referred to (Report of the Committee, &c., p. 7) : —

"The highest interests of civilization demand that the liberties and rights of neutrals should be extended, and the privileges and powers of states at war diminished. Upon the recognition of this principle depends the progress of nations, the independence of states, the liberties of the people. To restrict the rights of neutrals and enlarge the power of belligerents is to reject the teachings of Christianity and the improvements of civilization, and to return to the doctrines of uncivilized nations and the practices of barbaric peoples."

Now, I desire to ask the honorable chairman, whether, in his opinion, it is not "enlarging the power of belligerents" most flagrantly and most injuriously, to give *carte blanche* to the Fenians to set on foot and prepare the means for military expeditions from United-States soil against British possessions, and to strike from the President's hands, at the same moment, the power of employing the land and naval forces of the Union to suppress the prosecution of such enterprizes. I desire to ask him, further, whether, in his candid judgment, it is not " restricting the rights of neutrals" most scandalously and most unchristianly, to permit the Fenian faction to drag the great body of the American people, who desire to keep themselves neutral as to any quarrel between England and Ireland, and who, I doubt not, regard Fenianism as a huge swindle or a fanatical delusion, into a groundless war with England about Irish grievances of six centuries' standing.

Then, as to our Canadian neighbors, whose inoffensive territory is to be overrun and subjugated in order to make a standpoint for belligerency against remoter England, — how does General Banks think, that some of these phrases, which I have just quoted from his Report, have struck the Canadian ear, in the light of those alarms and preparations to meet an unknown invader, which have harassed the dwellers of that province for the last six months?

" *The highest interests of civilization demand that the liberties and rights of neutrals should be extended.*"

Pray, will not the Canadians have said, "That means *our* liberties and rights, does it not? We are neutrals, — are we not? — whose liberties and rights ought to be extended. And can it be an extension of them for the American Congress to adopt a law which will compel us to sleep with our arms under our pillows, perpetuating and legalizing the miserable embroilments from which we thought ourselves so happily delivered by the late enforcement of United-States neutrality?"

" *To enlarge the power of belligerents is to reject the teachings of Christianity and the improvements of civilization, and to return to the doctrines of uncivilized nations and the practices of barbarous peoples.*"

"Can General Banks" (these same Canadians would, doubtless, further urge) "have seriously put forward such a sentiment as this, for an inducing motive to repeal those provisions of American law against filibusterism, which have, during the late Fenian raid, proved our best protection against the designs of turbulent and fanatical Irishmen, and whose biting and efficacious terms have constituted such a study of their leaders, lest the demonstration of the executive will at Washington should at any moment stamp out their reckless incendiarism?"

"'*Unchristian and uncivilized to enlarge the power of belligerents*,' says General Banks. And yet, in the same moment, he strikes hands with Roberts and Sweeney to get up an invasion of our borders and carry on as unjustifiable a war against our peaceful, neutral province as was ever waged 'by an uncivilized nation or a barbarous people.'"

Has the Chairman of the Committee on Foreign Affairs ever held up these sentiments of his Report to his own consideration from the Canadian point of view? And would he venture to say, if he himself were one of these Canadian dwellers, that he could approve his own logic any more than his own law?

I leave this topic of Fenianism here; sure that the manifest injustice and injury to be wrought through its protection and encouragement by the new congressional movement, as tested in the case of provincial Canada alone, supposing no other friendly neutral country is to be affected by it, are such as to leave no doubt of the inexpediency of the United States' embarking in the new scheme inaugurated under General Banks's auspices.

But possibly there has not been as much legislative harm as yet consummated by the new project, supposing it in its present shape to ultimately pass the Senate and become a law, as our Canadian and British friends have been led to imagine and deprecate. This leads me to consider the amount of repeal or modification of existing statutory law actually involved in the adoption of General Banks's project, as amended by the House of Representatives, and how far the aim and *animus* of the new movement are thereby expressed and put into legislative shape.

PART IV.

DEFECTIVE EXECUTION OF THE ATTEMPT TO DETERIORATE ("SCALE") THE NEUTRALITY LAWS OF THE UNITED STATES.

CHAPTER IX.

The new project does not propose the immediate repeal, but only a temporary revision or "scaling"-down, of the neutrality code. — So much of the old law retained as hardly to excite notice of any change; not enough of repeal to quite come up to the programme of the Report, yet so much that it deserves grave attention. — The inquiry how much has actually been repealed, sheds important light upon the whole subject. — The scheme is to take the old statute into a new draft, leaving out the obnoxious clauses, and then amending. — Seven sections retained almost identical with those of law of 1794; five sections left out, and a formula of repeal adopted that all provisions and penalties, "inconsistent with the provisions of this act, are hereby repealed." — What provisions and penalties are inconsistent? — Not the provisions against setting on foot a military expedition, nor that giving the President power to use the army and navy to suppress it. — Nor the "bonding" clauses. — In general, most of the provisions supposed to interfere with Fenianism hold their place. — No thanks, however, to the good-will of the House, which was earnestly bent on their repeal. — This illustrated by the repeal of the clause giving half penalties to informers. — Particulars of the congressional debate on that head. — Mr. Jenckes's motion to give the whole penalty to the United States. — Mr. Thaddeus Stevens's suggestion that that would prove fatal to any further prosecution. — General Banks's silence. — His statement refuted, that there is no such provision in the British act as that of the American. — The British act gives informer half *penalties*, if not half *forfeitures*. — Note canvassing the distinction. — It seems that the British act *meant*, at least, to correspond to the American. — Are bounties to informers necessary? — If so, did General Banks mean to strip the law of all its efficiency? — Doubtless, the new scheme substitutes *"and"* for *"or"* in the clause relating to fitting out ships of war. — Nugatory amendments. — The provision against masters of vessels carrying away enlisted recruits contains no *scienter*. — Hence a Cunard steamer might be innocently subjected to forfeiture. — The same clause has no grammatical consistency, unless one "person" is made "to take on board" another "person" *puss-back*. — The same defect exists as to augmenting the force of a ship of war, unless by a *chaise-a-porteur* process. — Clause as to punishing offences without United-States jurisdiction noticed; a punishment without a crime. — The new important provision as to the right of trading in ships of war also fails altogether of its appropriate expression. — This provision dwelt on to secure its better enactment. — Ludicrous mistake of Mr. Jenckes, of Rhode Island, as to Hamilton's use of the term "complaints," in § 7 of present law. — Illustrated by the legislative anecdote of mistaking "heath-hen" for "heathen." — General Banks's Bill "to *preserve* the neutral relations of the United States" quite on a par with this.

ACCORDING to the new project (as has already been in part suggested, in noticing General Banks's Report), the Committee on Foreign Affairs do not purpose the entire, immediate repeal of the existing neutral code of the United States; but, after recommending "a thorough revision of the statutes affecting our neutral relations" hereafter, content themselves for the present with reporting in their new Bill a law which omits certain of the most obnoxious provisions of the existing statute, and which then takes the remainder of the statute, with three or four additional and amendatory sections, into a new draft. In this sense, the committee's Bill retains so much of the existing law, in the new draft, that the casual reader of it would hardly suppose that any thing had been disturbed, and that the statutory project did not at all answer to the revolutionary designs broached in the chairman's Report.

Personally, I must confess to sharing myself in this feeling of disappointment, at contrasting the project of the law actually recommended with the revolutionary changes and fundamental reconstruction implied in General Banks's Report; yet, on more careful examination, it will be found, I think, that more repeal has been attempted than meets the eye, and, has already been suggested, than is indicated and explained in the preliminary Report itself. As a whole, however, the new legislative scheme cannot, it seems to me, be thought to quite come up to the programme of that great movement forward in the path of national destiny, which, according to the chairman's idea, has already reached the hour of its inauguration; but, on the contrary, it resolves itself into little better than a temporary political manifesto, intended to express congressional resentment for British unfriendliness, and congressional sympathy for the cause of Irish independence.

But, if the reader cares to follow the unanimous action of the American House of Representatives upon this important subject, I will endeavor to very briefly point out how far the new legislation succeeds in expressing the views of its promoters. I believe the inquiry will help shed important light upon the subjects hitherto discussed, particularly upon the disparagement of the Foreign-Enlistment Act, and the promotion of Fenianism.

As has just been suggested, a large portion of the existing law finds its place in the new draft.[1]

Seven sections of that law (there being thirteen in all) are retained in the committee's project nearly *verbatim*, with a slight modification only of penalties, as already noticed. These are Sections One, Two, Three (with a slight addition, hereafter commented on), Five (with a similar addition), Seven, a part of Eight, and Nine. These seven sections are almost identical with the original legislation of 1794, of Hamilton's proposing; and, so far, the first part of General Banks's reply to Mr. Jenckes is borne out, in which he says:—

"The Bill reported, I will say, in answer to the inquiry of the gentleman from Rhode Island, is identical with that adopted during Washington's administration, and from which we have since departed."

Whether the identity is retained in the remaining sections, and who it is that departs from it, I leave to the reader to infer from what has already been said about the history and analysis of the existing statute, and from what follows as to attempted repeals.

Then, for the purposes of repeal, five sections or parts of sections of the existing law are left out in the new draft. These are Section Four (the clause forbidding the fitting-out of privateers in foreign ports to cruise against American commerce,

---

[1] For the reader's convenience, I subjoin, in the Appendix, the new act, as it has passed the House, and now awaits the action of the Senate.

already considered), Sections Six and part of Eight (directed against setting on foot military expeditions, and giving the President power to stop them, already noticed under the head of Fenianism), and Sections Ten and Eleven, the *bonding clauses*, as I have termed them. These five sections and parts of sections constitute all that is specially doomed to annihilation. The new draft, then, embraces some new *additions*, which may be noticeable hereafter; but with these five sections ends all matter of *subtraction*.

To effect the repeal of these obnoxious sections, the House — not without examination of the matter, but following the lead of Messrs. Bingham and Conkling, who expressed themselves opposed to a specific and sweeping repeal, lest it should abrogate provisions not intended to be sacrificed — adopted the following formula of repeal : —

"Sec. 12 [of new act]. — *Provided*, That all acts and parts of acts inconsistent with the provisions of this act, or inflicting any other penalty or forfeiture than are hereinbefore provided for the acts forbidden herein, are hereby repealed."

The question now arises, how far this formula, as thus crudely and rudely phrased, effectuates the objects of the committee, and how great an inroad will thus be made upon existing neutral legislation, provided the Bill, in its present shape, receives the sanction of the Senate, and ultimately becomes a law.

In reply to this, it is plain, that, unless the provisions thus sought to be repealed are "inconsistent" with those left standing in the new project, or unless the penalties or forfeitures prescribed by the old provisions are "*other*" than those "hereinbefore provided" (i.e., by the new act), there is no abrogation of those omitted sections.

Now, submitted to these tests, I venture to say that it will be found that no repeal in fact will have been wrought of either of the sections in question by the proposed formula, supposing it to be matured hereafter into a law. Thus, take the most important one, — the clause forbidding the setting on foot of any military expedition, &c. (sec. 6 of the existing law). Is it inconsistent with any thing denounced against accepting a commission, or enlisting or recruiting, for a foreign service, or fitting out and arming a ship, &c., — within the list of offences left standing in sections 1, 2, 3, &c., of the new draft, — that one should be punished for setting on foot a military expedition within United-States territory? The body of the offence was plainly thought to be something different from the other offences of the old statute; and will it not remain, in like manner, something different from the same offences, when merely reproduced in the new draft?

Nor, again, are the *penalties* denounced by this same sec. 6 any thing different from, or "*other than*," those of the accompanying sections of the existing act. Doubtless, the true construction of this latter category of the repealing clause of the new project is, "*other penalty or forfeiture than are hereinbefore provided*" *for the same description of offence.* Setting on foot a military expedition, for instance, is a different crime from arming a ship; and it is perfectly consistent with punishing this latter, that there should be another and a different penalty attached to the denunciation of the former. The meaning of the category is obviously satisfied by the reduction of the penalty of the old act, *as applied to the same subject-matter*, to the limit of punishment specified in the new project. Thus, so much of sec. 2 of the old act — against enlisting and recruiting — would be repealed, as that the maximum of imprisonment shall be *two* years, instead of *three;* because, in this instance, "the penalty hereinbefore provided" of the new act, "two years," is "*other*" than the penalty of the old act, or "three years."

So, again, "the bonding" clauses of the existing statute — General Banks's special reprobation — are perfectly consistent with any other co-ordinate sections of that statute, or the same provisions transferred into the new. Possibly, the new provision in regard to selling ships may have been supposed by the Chairman of the Foreign-Affairs Committee, at the time of reporting the new law, to be wholly antagonistic and irreconcilable to those sections. But, for myself, I cannot see why it is not perfectly consistent with allowing the sale of ships, &c., to require that their *American* owners shall give bonds that *they* will not employ them in hostilities against a friendly foreign power. Plainly, the clause (of sec. 8 of the present law) authorizing the President of the United States to employ its land and naval forces to suppress any military expedition is not inconsistent with this new section, as there is no penalty or forfeiture mentioned in that clause, or in any part of sec. 8, at all.

So the provisions and penalties of sec. 4 (of the present law), against fitting out privateers abroad for hostile aggressions against our own commerce, are neither "inconsistent" with, nor "other than," the prohibitions and penalties of the new draft. The subject-matter is evidently foreign to any prohibition of that scheme, and the appropriate penalties not at all conflicting with those now made applicable to a wholly different grade of crimes.

I conclude, then, on the whole, that, if a design to encourage and promote Fenianism had any thing to do with the attempted abrogation of the five sections in question, our British and Canadian friends need not give themselves any uneasiness at present about the injurious consequences likely to flow from the future ratification by the Senate and President of General Banks's *coup d'état*, unless that project receives some more effective legislative touch than any thing contained in it at present. No thanks, however, to the good intentions of the promoters of the new scheme! — for doubtless their aim and object were as absolute and equivocal as if they had expunged bodily from the statute the obnoxious portions of the law sought to be repealed. No thanks, either, to the House of Representatives! — for they have shown themselves ready to go any length in the direction pointed out, and, as it is, may have wrought incalculable mischief by the moral support which they have lent by their legislative action to the cause of filibustering generally.

This leads me to notice another important item of repeal, which, I am sorry to say, has in this instance been more successfully consummated. I refer to the attempted abrogation of the clause of the existing act (sec. 3) by which one-half of the forfeiture is given to the informer; a provision, in the opinion of Mr. Thaddeus Stevens, of Pennsylvania, quite indispensable to the enforcement of any future prosecution for a violation of neutrality.

As the circumstances connected with the adoption of this proposition by the House indicate, better than any thing else which can be quoted, the hostile disposition of a portion at least of that body towards any neutrality laws, I am tempted to reproduce, from the official report of the "Globe," the entire episode relating to this topic. It will not be found to be of any considerable length, and is well worthy of attention.

General Banks (or his committee), in taking sec. 3 of the existing act into the new draft, — the very important section of the present law, by which all equipment of ships for a belligerent use is forbidden, — had left out a part of the concluding sentence of that section, which now reads, "And every such ship or vessel, . . . together with all materials, &c., . . . shall be forfeited, . . . one half to the use of the informer, and the other half to the use of the United States;" so that, in the new draft, the section stopped short with "*shall be forfeited.*" To this (in debate), Mr. Jenckes, of Rhode Island, moved to add the words, "to the use of the United States of America;" so "that" (in his explanation) "the forfeiture shall go entirely to the Government." General Banks accepted the amendment, and it was adopted by the House; thus leaving, in its amended shape, the whole clause to read as follows: "And every such ship, &c., . . . together with all materials, &c., . . . shall be forfeited to the use of the United States."

After the process of amending all parts of the project had been gone through with to the satisfaction of the House, and the Chairman of the Committee on Foreign Affairs had entered upon the explanation of the various details of his measure, when he came to notice this feature of the abolition of bounties to informers, he commented upon it in the following terms (I italicize the fourth line) : —

" The Bill [before the House] also repeals the provision giving informers one-half the fines and forfeitures that may result from the execution of the law. *No such provision is contained in the English act.* The amendments proposed by the gentleman from Rhode Island [Mr. Jenckes], and adopted by the House, provide that all the proceeds of the prosecution shall be paid into the treasury of the United States."

General Banks, having then proceeded to the consideration of certain other topics, was shortly after interrupted by Mr. Stevens, of Pennsylvania, with the following interpolation (the italics, again, are mine) : —

" Mr. STEVENS. — I ask the gentleman to yield to me for a moment.

" Mr. BANKS. — Certainly.

" Mr. STEVENS. — I understood the gentleman to say, that, as amended, the Bill gave the whole forfeiture to the United States. Is that one of the amendments which has been adopted by the House?

" Mr. BANKS. — The amendment has been adopted by the House.

" Mr. STEVENS. — *Then I do not think there will ever be a prosecution. I suppose that is the object of it.*"

General Banks made no reply to Mr. Stevens's keen comment. Did he mean thereby to signify that he was consenting to the death of the present law?

But, when the Chairman of the Foreign-Affairs Committee says that "no such provision is contained in the English act," had he overlooked sec. 10 of the Foreign-Enlistment Act, which I venture to reproduce, for his consideration, from the same official reprint already so much drawn upon? —

" 10. *And be it further enacted*, That any penalty or forfeiture inflicted by this act may be prosecuted, sued for, and recovered by action of debt, bill, plaint, or information, in any of His Majesty's Courts of Record at Westminster or Dublin, or in the Court of Exchequer, or in the Court of Sessions in Scotland, in the name of His Majesty's Attorney-General for England or Ireland, or His Majesty's Advocate for Scotland, respectively, or in the name of any person or persons whatsoever ; wherein no essoign, protection, privilege, wager of law, nor more than one imparlance, shall be allowed ; and, in every action or suit, the person against whom judgment shall be given for any penalty or forfeiture under this act shall pay double costs of suit ; and every such action or suit shall and may be brought at any time within twelve months after the offence committed, and not afterwards ; and *one moiety of every penalty* to be recovered by virtue of this act *shall go and be applied to His Majesty*, his heirs or successors, and *the other moiety to the use of such person or persons as shall first sue for the same*, after deducting the charges of prosecution from the whole."

Now, I will not assert, of this section, that it technically confers upon informers one-half of all *forfeitures* created by the Foreign-Enlistment Act; but it is beyond question, that it holds out to them the bounty of one-half of all "*penalties*" thus created. That it *intended*, further, to vest forfeitures in informers in the same manner as it does penalties, I think will be admitted, when it is considered, (1) that, by its terms, "any penalty *or forfeiture*, inflicted by this act, may be prosecuted, sued for, *and recovered* . . . in the name of His Majesty's Attorney-General, &c., . . . or *in the name of any person or persons whatsoever;*" (2) that, by sec. 6 of the act, *forfeiture* and *penalty* are used synonymously; and (3) that in sec. 7 (the section relating to fitting out ships), there is no specific appropriation of the subject-matter forfeited *to the use of the Crown*, as in the corresponding clause of General Banks's project: on the contrary, the prosecution and condemnation of such subject-matter is put upon the general footing of custom-house seizures, leaving the distribution of the proceeds of the prosecution to fall under the regulations of sec. 10, or else to be governed by the general principles of law applicable to forfeitures.

For these reasons, I am strongly inclined to the belief that not only did the British act intend, throughout, to confer upon informers one-half of its specific forfeitures, as much as one-half of its prescribed penalties; but that, on technical grounds, the informer, in such cases as the "Alexandra" for instance, could as much claim his one-half of the proceeds of the forfeited vessel (provided he had first brought his *qui-tam* suit, and provided the Crown had not taken the initiative by *indictment*) as he could his one-half of the pecuniary penalties authorized by other provisions of that act.[1] But — it may well be asked, in

---

[1] This point has never been discussed, that I am aware of, in any of the recent English or Scotch cases; and I know of no authority bearing upon it, unless the

view of the provisions cited from sec. 10 — is General Banks justified in asserting, that there is "no such provision contained in the English act" as that giving to informers "one-half of the fines and forfeitures resulting from the execution of this act," and thereby inducing Mr. Stevens to vote for what he considers the death of the measure, in the process of "scaling" the American law down to the level of British neutrality?

Whether the policy of giving to informers one-half of all penalties and forfeitures is a wise principle of legislation, or one so important to the enforcement of any system of neutrality as Mr. Stevens believes it to be, is hardly within the limits of my present purpose to consider. Doubtless, the most competent judges of human nature have esteemed some such system of rewards indispensable to the due execution of various portions of the penal code, particularly of the laws connected with smuggling and the collection of the revenue. The British Foreign-Enlistment Act, it will have been seen, proposes to accommodate the enforcement of neutrality forfeitures, so far as concerns ships and their appurtenances, to the practice regulating revenue prosecutions. I do not know that the parallelism between the two kinds of offences is not sufficient to put both upon the same footing, as to stimulating the zeal of prosecutors, by pecuniary bounties. Yet I would venture to suggest, that there may be good reasons why there should be a controlling power in the fiscal head of the Government to apportion the reward to the informer, in case of the condemnation of a valuable ship at something less than half its value, which do not apply to ordinary revenue penalties. Such a power, I believe, is supposed already to exist in the Secretary of the Treasury, in

---

case of *Dobree* v. *Napier* (2 Bingham's New Cases, p. 781), decided in the English Court of Common Pleas, in the year 1836, upon a side issue in pleading, and without much discussion, can be considered an authoritative expression of judicial opinion upon it. That case, I must admit, in some degree lends a partial sanction to General Banks's unfavorable comment on the British statute; but, on common-sense principles, I would cheerfully appeal to any legislator or lawyer, whether the construction which would cut off the informer from his half-bounty in a forfeited ship, as much as in a pecuniary penalty, is not a technical and forced one, which, in all probability, was outside of the purpose of the enactors of the British law?

reference to forfeitures for unneutral offences. If so, there is all the less occasion for Mr. Jenckes's repeal, approved of by General Banks, and so warmly endorsed by Mr. Stevens.

So, too, the proper enforcement of international law seems sometimes to require that the Government, and not the individual informer, should be the party to set in motion a prosecution for violating neutrality.

That some bounty, however, either on revenue-collection principles or on some other footing, should go to the informer, in case of a prosecution for infraction of neutrality, seems plainly desirable. Now, as General Banks and the House of Representatives left it, — at the point of Mr. Stevens's interruption, — the new project is to be stripped wholly bare of any such stimulus to legal enforcement. Was this duly considered, in justice to the portion of the law intended to be preserved? Or was it, again, consistent with General Banks's borrowing from the British act, and introducing into his own measure the very section relating to custom-house proceedings, and then discarding the concomitant provision of that act, conferring half fines and penalties upon the prosecutor?

There is another point of attempted repeal, of almost equal importance with the clause authorizing bounties to informers, as to which, the new project, I am sorry to say, has succeeded in doing its work equally effectually. I refer to the substitution of "*and*" for "*or*," in the clause relating to "being concerned in fitting out *or* arming," &c., already dwelt upon (see Part II.). I fear there can be no doubt, that, within the purview of the new Bill, a redraft of sec. 3 — reading, as it does, "If any person shall fit out and arm, . . . and knowingly be concerned in . . . fitting out *and* arming of any ship," &c., and accompanied with a general form of repeal, to the effect that "all acts and parts of acts, inconsistent with the provisions of this act, are hereby repealed" (as above considered) — amounts to a thorough merging of "*or*" into "*and*," as being wholly "*inconsistent*" with it, — as inconsistent, for instance, as substituting *darkness* for *light ;* to which substitution, in fact, the proposed change bears a striking resemblance.

Before leaving this portion of my subject, I deem it worth

my while to briefly notice two or three other matters of legislative detail embraced in the new scheme, which have not for their object, indeed, further repeal of existing provisions, but which seek to bring in new and supposed improvements, borrowed mostly from the British act; and which, in their present shape, are any thing but improvements. I deem them important to comment upon, not merely because they show the sudden haste and immaturity of arrangement with which the new measure must have been precipitated upon Congress, but because, as they make part of a scheme, which, as General Banks has more recently asserted,[1] is sure to pass that body and become a law, it behooves the Senate to consider, whether, with such imperfections on its head, that scheme is one quite fit for their adoption.

One of the most noticeable of these amendments is that seeking to engraft the provisions of the sixth section of the British act — making it penal for the master of any vessel to carry out of the kingdom recruits enlisted for a foreign belligerent service — upon the terms of our own. By section three of the new project, —

"If any person shall, within the limits of the United States, . . . have on board any person or persons who shall have been enlisted, &c., . . . with intent to enlist or serve, in contravention of the provisions of this act, every person so offending shall be deemed guilty," &c.

Now, the corresponding provision of the British act contains the important element of a *scienter*, or "*knowingly*," which the new project leaves out. By the former, —

"If any master, or other person, having or taking charge or command of any ship or vessel, . . . shall *knowingly and willingly* take on board, . . . or shall *knowingly* engage to take on board, any person or persons who shall have been enlisted, &c., . . . such master or owner, &c., shall forfeit and pay the sum of fifty pounds, . . . and such ship or vessel, so having on board such person or persons, shall and may be seized," &c.

---

[1] In his address to his constituents at Charlestown, Oct. 8 (see "Boston Journal," of Oct. 9).

DEFECTIVE LAW-MAKING. 115

So that while by the British act the sea-captain must, with his eyes open, "knowingly and willingly" take on board his vessel the recruits enlisted in violation of neutrality, before he can subject himself and his vessel to penal procedure, by General Banks's Bill (if literally followed) the bare fact of the captain's having on board such a recruit, though ever so innocently and unwittingly, is enough to render his vessel forfeitable to the law. To exemplify the proposition, as it bears upon Fenianism, and in quite a different way from what I presume was ever intended by its authors: If a Cunard steamer should receive a Fenian passenger to transport to Ireland for hire, or if such passenger should even smuggle himself on board the steamer without any person's knowledge, and there be found (said Fenian having been unlawfully enlisted on American soil), the steamer and all its appurtenances would become forfeitable to the United States, though the captain and all owners and agents of the line should be utterly ignorant of the passenger's being a Fenian, or even of his being on board the steamer at all.

When Messrs. Roberts, Sweeney, & Company come to look at this improvement (!) upon the present law, in the point of view suggested, possibly they will be tempted to exclaim, in Falstaff's phrase, "Call you this backing your friends?"

But then, on the other hand, Messrs. Roberts, Sweeney, *et al.* need not disturb themselves about this unwelcome feature of the Bill, considering that, by reason of its defective etymological construction, the whole clause must fail of any legal validity. The new section does not read, "If any sea-captain or other person shall have on board *his vessel* the unlawfully enlisted passenger," &c., but, "If *any person*" (without mention of a vessel) "*shall have on board*" "*any person.*" The British act, it will have been noticed, commences, "*If any master*, &c., ... of *any ship or vessel* ... shall knowingly and willingly *take on board* [i.e., such ship or vessel], &c., ... *such master* shall forfeit and pay the sum of fifty pounds." This is leaving the matter quite enough at loose ends, so far as the inference of "*on board*" is sought to be made applicable to the previously mentioned "*ship or vessel;*" but where no such term as "*master*" has been previously employed, nor any thing to connect the first-mentioned "person" with "a vessel," it is hard to see how "*any person*" could "have on board *any* [*other*] *person*," unless it is an offence for one man to carry another *puss-back*.

More seriously, at any rate, I commend this legislative patch to the attention of the Committee on Foreign Relations of the Senate, to whom the House Bill has been referred, as a piece of nugatory amendment which they will have to re-form, before it can convey any legal designation of a prohibited offence.

The same copying, from a British model, of the patch on the elbow, or, rather, of leaving the elbow naked where the British act had patched it over, as that just noticed in the instance of the third section of the new project, is also observable in the fifth section of that project. In this last section, our legislators have forbidden "any person . . . [to] have on board any person" (as before), — with a view to augmenting the force of a ship of war already armed. It is rather difficult to comprehend how the process of one person's *having on board another* can conduce to the end here sought to be effected, unless the war-ship is going to be recruited by a sort of *chaise-a-porteur* process.

The Committee on Foreign Affairs borrow, also, from the British act (sec. 9), the following provision, constituting sec. 9 of the new project: —

"SEC. 9. — *And be it further enacted*, That offences made punishable by the provisions of this act, committed by citizens of the United States beyond the jurisdiction of the United States, may be prosecuted and tried before any Court having jurisdiction of the offences prohibited by this act."

Now, as every "offence prohibited by this act" is expressly limited, in every one of its sections, to something done "within the territory and jurisdiction [or "within the limits"] of the United States," it is hard to see what object can be served by providing *a place of trial* for impossible offences. Possibly the Committee had forgotten that they had struck out of their scheme section 4 of the existing statute, which enacts against **an** offence committed abroad; but as that section sufficiently provided, by itself, for a venue of trial of the offence therein specified, it would seem a piece of unnecessary imitation of the (obnoxious) British act to borrow its *fetters* after the *criminal offence* itself had been discharged.

Then, the important provision of sec. 10 of the new act — which, in its spirit, quite meets some of the views which I have had the honor of advocating in reference to free traffic in ships of war, as articles of commerce, in connection with the notice of the "Meteor" case, already referred to — quite inadequately effects the intent of its authors, as I am inclined to believe. The first part of the section (for it is with that alone that I have occasion to deal at present, having already sufficiently commented on the latter part) reads thus: —

"SEC. 10. — *And be it further enacted*, That nothing in this act shall be so construed as to prohibit citizens of the United States from selling vessels, ships, or steamers, built within the limits thereof, or material or munitions of war, the growth or product of the same, to inhabitants of other countries, or to governments not at war with the United States."

Now, I suppose the main intent of this new provision is to preserve to our neutral industry and trade, within the scope of our own judicature, the right of dealing in vessels *adaptable to war, at a time when a foreign war exists,* and *with the belligerent powers, or their subjects, as purchasers.* And yet neither of these three ideas finds expression as above.

Of course, all vessels, whether built within or without the limits of the United States, are an undoubted subject of free commerce with belligerents, on our part (we being neutrals), unless prepared for war, — subject (it should be said) to the liability of capture as contraband, when declared to be contraband by the laws of the capturing power; and, when our laws are uttering their legislative behest, they cannot, of course, undertake to annul or contravene any such foreign definition of contraband, but only to point out what acts are punishable, within their own scope, or on the part of our own citizens. So that, until something is said about the vessel being adaptable to war, the first point — of its being no offence under United States' laws, and in cases brought within their jurisdiction, "to sell vessels, ships, or steamers, built within the limits thereof" — is not once brought out, and declared with any significance.

The second and third particulars, of such a sale *during the existence of a foreign war,* and *to belligerents as purchasers,* is so obviously left unexpressed and unlegislated, that I will not add a further word of comment.

Then, again, what can be the motive in this new provision — intended to express the unhampering of neutral commerce from its present "criminal restrictions," as I understand it — for confining the sale of "vessels, ships, or steamers" to those *owned by citizens of the United States, or built within the limits thereof?* Will it promote American ship-building to provide that a foreign merchant who is doing business here, perhaps permanently, cannot sell the American ship, which he is thinking of buying or which he may already own, to a foreign belligerent, because he (the merchant) is not an American citizen? Or will it encourage American commerce to forbid the American merchant from selling his vessel — for which he has received an advantageous offer from the same belligerent — *to* that belligerent, in case such vessel shall happen to be of foreign build? In fact, I submit that both of these new provisions would amount to "criminal restrictions" of themselves (in General Banks's phrase) on the existing privileges of American commerce, under the neutral laws of the United States as they now stand, bad as General Banks believes those laws to be.

Then, again, can the Chairman of the Committee on Foreign Affairs find any authority in any *dictum* upon the subject of neutrals' selling materials or munitions of war to belligerents, which limits such materials and munitions to being "*the growth or product of the same*" (neutral country)? No such limitation, certainly, is contained in Mr. Jefferson's famous declaration to Mr. Ternant, the French minister, in 1793, to the effect that "our citizens have always been free to make, vend, and export arms;" and no such limitation was contained in President Pierce's presidential declaration upon the same subject, at the time of the Crimean War in 1854. Why should it be brought in now to fetter our citizens, when the question is, not of narrowing, but of enlarging, neutral commercial privileges?

I ask this on the supposition that a foreign war prevails, in which we are neutrals, and that the question is one of selling such materials or munitions to belligerents, neither of which categories is brought out by the provision in question.

On the whole, without any intention of making an *exposé* of the defects of this (new) section, but, on the contrary, hoping that, in an amended form, it may make good its place on the statute-book, as a counter-declaration of what American law now is, in opposition to the condemnation of the steamer " Meteor " in the United-States District Court for New York, I most sincerely regret that the views of those promoting the passage of this section are so inadequately and ineffectually expressed by the statute-form in which the Committee and the House of Representatives have embodied them. It is bad enough to have subjected the control of the whole subject-matter to executive dictation, as already noticed;[1] but it is worse still to have missed the mark at which the legislation was aimed, so totally and so thoroughly. I pray the Senate Committee on Foreign Relations not to allow this section to go upon the statute-book with its present imperfections on its head, and without taking more time to point its meaning than the House of Representatives and its committee have allowed themselves to devote to it.

One other stricture upon the legislative execution of the new neutral statute, and I have done.

Mr. Jenckes, of Rhode Island, has incorporated into the new act an amendment upon the old which borders upon the ludicrous. At any rate, it serves to show what need there is that even a very skilful lawyer should be well acquainted with the cotemporaneous history of a statute before he undertakes to add to or improve upon its terms.

---

[1] I say this, of course, without any invidious reflection upon the present head of the nation, who, I have taken occasion already to remark, in my judgment, deserves the approbation and support of the country for the just and independent stand which he has taken against Fenianism.

Sec. 7 of the existing law (taken *verbatim* from sec. 6 of stat. 1794, ch. 50) reads as follows: —

"SEC. 7. — That the district courts shall take cognizance of complaints, by whomsoever instituted, in case of captures made within the waters of the United States, or within a marine league of the coasts or shores thereof."

According to the "Globe" (July 30), Mr. Jenckes moved to amend this, when the Neutrality Bill was under discussion, "by inserting after the word 'complaints' the words 'informations, indictments, or other prosecutions;'" and, General Banks having signified his acquiescence, the House adopted the amendment; so that the whole section reads thus: —

"SEC. 6. — *And be it further enacted*, That the district courts shall take cognizance of all complaints, informations, indictments, or other prosecutions, by whomsoever instituted, in cases of capture made within the waters of the United States, or within a marine league of the coasts or shores thereof."

Here, it will be seen, Mr. Jenckes uses "complaints" as a technical form of procedure, — *ejusdem generis*, — as "informations or indictments;" in the sense of a complaint for assault and battery, trespass, and the like, before a justice of the peace. Now, on reference to the cotemporaneous history of the statute (as referred to in a previous note to page 15, discussing the prize case, the "William"), it will clearly be found, as I think, that Hamilton, in framing the section, was not thinking of the form in which the proceeding should be embodied, but was indicating that the district court, on *representation made* by any person, whether President, Attorney-General, foreign minister, consul, private owner of the prize, or who not, should take jurisdiction of the matter, and frame, if need be, the proper process to bring the case into judicature.

The substantial thing was the conferring of jurisdiction upon some judicial tribunal, and thus relieving the executive from embarrassment about the mode and means of proceeding. Thus, take the case of the prize made by the French frigate, the "L'Embuscade," in Delaware Bay, already referred to. If Ternant and Genet had refused to restore the capture to its

British owners, what course could President Washington have taken to enforce its surrender, without a statute conferring authority upon him or some other Federal functionary to act in the premises. Should he have issued a warrant, or ordered a seizure of the prize without a warrant, himself? Or should he have communicated his requests to the judicial authorities, and solicited their concurrent action in vindication of the rights of neutral sovereignty?

Hamilton, as it seems to me, providing for just such another future possible violation of our territorial sovereignty as this, frames the provision, that, upon any one's — whether the President, United-States District Attorney, foreign minister, consul, party aggrieved, or who not — complaining of the grievance to the district court, informally, or in any manner to be thereafter regulated by rule of court, and asking for its redress, the court may assume jurisdiction of the subject-matter, and grant proper process to enforce satisfaction.

In this sense, the provision was undoubtedly general, and left too much to judicial intendment. Still, as a relief against a sudden executive emergency hereafter, and with a view to furnish something to amend by in future legislation, it constituted an expedient and valuable enactment.

Now, is it promotive of the scope of this act, and supplying the desired additions to its deficiencies, to treat "*complaint*" as *a form of process*, and, assuming that the authors of the law intended that *a ship of war or its prize should be seized on process borrowed from Burn's Justice, or some other justice's form-book* (!), go on to remedy the defect by suggesting that informations and indictments may become co-ordinate processes as well? It reminds one of the story of Puritan legislation, which, I dare say, may have already at some time reached the ears of the learned member from Rhode Island, but which I will venture to reproduce for the sake of its illustration of his legislative amendment.

The question before the Yankee General Court was, upon passing "An Act for the preservation of the *heath-hen* and other game." An unlettered member from the back settlements, more used to hunting Indians than to spelling out statutes, coming in upon the House of a sudden, without any initiation into the business then before it, struck with the title of the Bill just as it was passing the Speaker's hammer, and believing that he must do something to arrest a legislative abomination, arose and delivered himself of the following speech: "Mr. Speaker, I don't care about preserving the *heathen* generally, and haven't much objection to them; but I must except *Indians*. I move you to amend the Bill so that it shall read, 'An Act for the preservation of the heathen and other game, but *except Indians*.'"

I venture to think that the honorable member from Rhode Island hits as wide of Hamilton's ideas in adding "informations, indictments," &c., to his Bill, as the backwoodsman did in excepting Indians from the statute devoted to the preservation of the heath-hen and other game.

Perhaps, however, I may fairly add, that Mr. Jenckes is guilty of no greater legislative *faux pas* in his interpretation of Hamilton's proviso (supposing my own construction of it is the just one) than the Chairman of the Committee on Foreign Affairs has made in entitling his new project, as he does, "A Bill more effectually to *preserve* the neutral relations of the United States!"

This leads me fairly to my last topic; viz., to inquire how the neutral relations of the United States may, in fact, be best preserved and promoted; or, in other words, what is our expedient policy in future on the score of neutrality.

PART V.

THE EXPEDIENT FUTURE OF AMERICAN NEUTRALITY.

CHAPTER X.

Though our past neutral practice has resulted to our advantage as well as our fame, should it not change for the future, with our changed condition? — The writer does not purpose a new neutral theory, like a new Monroe declaration, but rather to state negatively what our future neutrality ought *not* to be, and then to add some suggestions towards an improved neutral system, affirmatively. — The repeal of the present neutral code of the United States will not (1) advance the Monroe doctrine on this side of the Atlantic; nor (2) increase our influence on the European side; nor (3) prove a step forward in national progress; nor (4) is it expedient out of ill-will to England, who might be of the greatest aid to us as a fellow-champion of neutrality; nor (5) is it expedient as to the other nations besides England, against whom we have no ground of complaint; nor (6) is it expedient on any ground of the temporariness of neutral legislation, which, in truth, ought to be as permanent as extradition laws; nor (7) is it the lesson taught us by our late civil-war experience. (8) The advancement and consolidation of that code is the "coming" movement in American foreign policy. — Has our neutral stand-point shifted with our growth? — Now that we have grown to be a great people, can we dispense with the rules of international morality? — A nation is responsible, like an individual, for the discharge of its duties. — The element of our growth, then, does not vary our international duty. — The new movement based largely on the idea that England has imposed upon our good nature. — Supposing it to be so, England does not stand to us for all the world. — Must we not keep up our neutral relations to France, Spain, &c.? — Ought we to abolish our neutral laws as to England and France (for France has also imposed upon us), and leave them standing for other powers? — Now, as to England, do we not owe to the existence of these neutral laws, and the jurisprudence founded on them, that England did not make common cause with the rebels? — Surmise as to the possible result of such a step, which, in Lord Russell's phrase, would have been "an engagement for the suppression of liberty." — Some good, then, has come out of this neutrality policy, so far as it concerns England. — General Banks quoted as to our having stood bail for the peace of the world long enough, and also as to the moment having come for a new *coup d'état*. — That *coup d'état* can have nothing to do with the Monroe doctrine, though it may connect itself with promoting filibusterism. — Notice of the Monroe doctrine. — Exemplification of it by Fenianism. — Is the new act in reality "an act in aid of filibustering"? — And would the reputation gained by its adoption help us to greater weight in European affairs?

I TRUST that it has sufficiently been made to appear, in an earlier portion of this discussion, that our past neutral policy has redounded to our national fame, if it has not to our national advantage. I propose now to devote a little space to the discussion of what ought to be our line of future neutral conduct. Undoubtedly, as the late Congressional Report declares, the circumstances of our national condition are largely changed from what they were seventy, or even fifty, years ago; and it is worth considering, whether the conduct of our foreign relations, and the structure and aim of our domestic neutral legislation, should not change with them.

Lest the space to which I propose to limit myself should prohibit the adequate development of some of the leading ideas which I have in mind upon these topics, I hasten to say, at the outset, that I do not propose to initiate the discussion of any new Monroe doctrine, or other scheme of foreign policy, — marking a new point of departure in our political history, — but shall rather content myself with exposing, from a negative point of view, in what our future neutral policy ought *not* to consist, and then, in a more affirmative direction, explaining how, without tearing down the present structure of our neutral system, we ought rather to widen and deepen its foundations, and enlarge and strengthen its superstructure, than to undermine and ultimately overthrow it.

As a negative statement, then, of what our future neutral policy ought *not* to be, I should say that the frittering-away or the total repeal of the neutrality laws would *not* be, —

(1) A carrying-out of the Monroe doctrine, or a necessary prerequisite to making the country's influence more potently felt in the disposition of the affairs of state of the American continent.

(2) Nor would it be a desirable step towards giving the United States a greater weight in European politics.

(3) Nor would it be a step forward in the path of manifest destiny or of national aggrandizement; but, on the contrary, a retracing of our former progress in the ways of civilization, and a more detrimental course to us than to any other maritime power of the globe, whether inimical or friendly.

(4) Nor would it be a step forward, so far as our relations with England are concerned, to consummate this ultimate or immediate overthrow of the neutrality laws out of special discourtesy or ill-will towards her. On the contrary, if we have reason to complain of British unneutral conduct during the late civil war (as leading British statesmen concede), we are bound to acknowledge that we have derived important benefits from her observance of neutrality, poor as it may have been; and, at any rate, that, if England would first set herself right as to past grievances, — which it would require but little sacrifice of consistency for her to do, considering these acknowledgments of her governmental authorities referred to, and considering, further, how potently her own interests prompt to that construction of neutrality contended for by the United States, — it would redound to the highest interests of the two nations separately, as well as to the advancement of the common cause of civilization, to have the United States accede to that urgent appeal already made to them by England for co-operation and fellowship in the development and extension of the sphere of neutral rights.

(5) But, if such repeal or doing-away with the neutrality code can be thought to be justifiable or expedient as towards England, *and for the motive above assigned*, then it is unjust and unjustifiable as towards those other friendly foreign powers from whom we have received no such objectionable or unneutral treatment, and with whom our relations have been preserved on a just and desirable footing of friendly neutrality by means of this same system of neutral laws.

(6) That such frittering-away and repeal of the neutrality code is inexpedient, because such a code is not a temporary and shifting scheme of external policy; but, on the contrary, ex-

presses the permanent and universal law of international dealings, which, like the extradition treaties for crime, has for its object the suppression of domestic crime and the forwarding of international justice; and which ought, therefore, to have as little connection as possible with the passing politics of the day.

(7) Nor, finally, is such frittering-away and repeal of all neutrality restraints the moral inculcated by our late civil struggle. On the contrary, that event, like the occurrence of a great conflagration, warns us that we ought immediately to seek to guard ourselves for the future against the recurrence of some of those injurious practices — such, for instance, as the affording foreign aid to domestic rebellion, and the tolerating the hostile equipment of naval armaments in foreign friendly ports — from which we have suffered so injuriously, and of which we now so justly complain.

(8) *Affirmatively*, the revision and reconstruction of the American neutral code — with a view to its improvement and perfection, instead of to its subversion and abrogation — constitutes the true "coming" movement in American foreign policy.

In development of these points, I do not propose to treat them *seriatim*, in the order above set forth, but rather to prove their justice, as I best may, by some general discussion of the province of neutral laws, and how far our own stand-point towards them has been shifted by the events of the recent civil war. I begin with the latter branch of the subject first.

General Banks's Report and the late action of the House of Representatives seem to have at bottom two great motives for some fundamental change in our neutral policy: —

(1) That we have become a great and powerful nation.

(2) That, under our past self-inflicted neutral restraints, *we have been imposed upon by the warlike powers of Europe*.

As to the first, so far as it asserts a fact, I shall not be unpatriotic enough to deny it; so far, however, as it implies a motive for altered national conduct hereafter, I should demur to the proposition in full, unless it shall first be shown that our past action has proceeded upon mistaken principles and unworthy motives. Because a man has become rich, shall he thereupon declare that he can now " afford to become," not " *honest,*" but *dishonest?* If, when we were poor and " a little people," we could dare to be honestly neutral and justly impartial, shall we say, now that we have become " a great nation," that we can afford to act as lawlessly as we please, and follow out our own " wicked will "? that, as we have become strong enough to afford to be pugnacious, we mean to put ourselves in fighting attitude, and repeal all our old-fashioned rules and ordinances, so that nothing shall stand between us and a free practice under the law of might making right?

If this *is* the first fruit of our matured national strength, I beg to dissent from the proposition with my whole energy. On the contrary, would not the dictates of common decency — not to say the manifest behests of Divine Providence — impose upon us the obligation, *a fortiori*, of respecting the laws of international equity, now that it has become a so much easier matter to obey their injunctions? And as " much is required " of the individual " to whom much is given," is not the obligation, in like manner, all the more imperative upon us as a great power, to make good use of our national example in the conduct of the world's affairs?

There is nothing, then, I apprehend, in the circumstance of our national growth, to vary the position of the question, whether it is expedient to adhere to our past policy of neutrality, provided (as I have endeavored to show) that *that* policy has been founded upon just and theoretically true principles of international law.

But the more difficult question to answer is, whether we have not been trifled with, or, if the questioner pleases, *been imposed upon*, for our peace-loving neutrality, by the powers of Western Europe, and particularly during the late civil struggle?

The Chairman of the Committee on Foreign Affairs, and the House of Representatives with him, in its brief discussion of the the Committee's Report and Bill, seemed to think that we had experienced from England such a poor return of neutral favors conferred, and had witnessed on her part such a disregard of the neutral restraints of the law of nations, that it was hardly worth while to pretend to keep up towards *her*, at least, a further compliance with those restraints ourselves. Is that a justifying motive for a fundamental change of our foreign policy?

In the first place, England does not stand to us for all the world. Are not France, Spain, Russia, Holland, Italy, and other governments of Europe, — to say nothing of the growing empire of Brazil and the Mexican and South-American republics, — something to us, in the matter of shaping our neutral relations for the future? Supposing that it is expedient for us to keep no terms with Great Britain on points of neutral law, have we not other related nations, friends or foes, with whom we must keep up an intercourse, either of friendship or hostility, or of impartial neutrality? And do we not need laws to express and regulate the terms upon which that intercourse shall be maintained?

I assume, then, that General Banks and his coadjutors would agree that the legislation must be special which should strike out all provisions of the neutral code so as to exclude England from any possible benefit under it, and leave it standing for the rest of the world. Perhaps, in fairness, any such exclusion should also except the case of France, at least so long as its present Emperor presides over and shapes its policy; for have we not, in many respects, as good grounds for complaint against French disregard of international restraints during the late struggle, as we have against English?

But then, in answer to this *bête noire* of English ingratitude and English trifling with any system of neutral law, I beg to ask our American legislators, whether, after all, we do not owe to the existence of our own neutral code, and to the precedents of our own neutral record, the fact of the British Government's declining to side with our rebel enemies, and allowing themselves to be drawn into their quarrel so far as to declare open war against us? For my own part, I think there can be but very little doubt of it; and but for the existence of the Foreign-Enlistment Act on the British statute-book, and but for our own record of neutral legislation, jurisprudence, and executive action, such as we had made it up to our own credit, in our past relations with Great Britain, I think it is as morally certain the rebel emissaries would have precipitated Great Britain into hostilities with us over the letting-loose of Laird's iron-clads, as that Jefferson Davis and his associates confidently relied upon that firebrand of provocation to light up a war between the two nations.

What effect such a declaration of war on the part of Great Britain against us at the darkest period of our civil struggle would have had upon our national future, it is fortunately quite unnecessary to surmise. Possibly, it might have had the same effect upon us, if England and France had jointly combined with the rebels to attempt to smother our liberties, as it had upon revolutionary France to have united Europe combine to invade her. But short of wading through such a sea of blood as would have flowed from that "engagement for the suppression of liberty" (as Lord John Russell, in his younger days, said of the British prosecution of the American war of 1775), I believe, under Providence, we owe the peaceful continuance of our relations with the British nation during the late Confederate sedition, largely, if not chiefly, to the existence of a common neutrality code in the two governments, and to a well-settled interpretation of it on this side of the Atlantic, forbidding and frowning on such operations as those drawn in question.

So far at least, I venture to say, we have derived good from the existence of the code under which General Banks and the House of Representatives believe our good nature has been imposed upon; and so far, at least, it is a mistaken basis of fact for the assertion, that Great Britain has paid no respect either to her own laws or to the neutral precedents set her by the United States. Whether Great Britain has in other respects honestly acted up to her own code, and made due account of the debt of neutral honor which she has contracted with the United States at former periods, I have had occasion elsewhere to notice, and shall probably return to the subject in another connection hereafter.

Meanwhile, on this topic of suffering international imposition, General Banks seems to have struck the key-note to his own opinions, and to those probably of many of his fellow-legislators, when he said in his Report (p. 10), —

"We can no longer stand bail for the peace of the world. We have stood guard for other nations long enough."

And again, in debate (partly cited already) : —

"The question for this House to determine is whether that time has come [foretold by the Adamses] when the people of this country would be able to assert their own right upon the judgment of the people alone, rather than at the dictation or upon the representations of representatives of foreign governments. Sir, I think it has come.

"If we want any thing to prove our power, let us look at the history of this country for the last five years," &c.

Now, if this is intended for a declaration, that it is time to propose a new affirmance of the Monroe doctrine, or a carrying-out of that doctrine in some new and as yet undefined direction, I have to reply that the authors and originators of that doctrine never made the taking-down of the barriers of neutral restraints any condition precedent towards applying and carrying it out. On the contrary, as has already been shown, there were no stauncher upholders of the American neutral system as they found it, and warmer advocates of advancing it still further, than Messrs. Monroe and John Quincy Adams. In their view, at any rate, the fulfilment of our duties of impartial neutrality municipally was entirely consistent with a more vigorous assertion of American independence from European intervention, externally and diplomatically. How then can the proposed repeal or emasculation of the neutrality laws do any thing to favor the promotion of the Monroe doctrine, unless upon principles entirely at variance with those professed by its original promoters and godfathers?

Perhaps the new movement proposes to give a greater vitality to the Monroe doctrine, by increasing the facilities of our citizens and others to acquire territory by filibustering; and the consideration given to the subject of Fenianism seems to show, that, in that phase at least of the subject, General Banks and his coadjutors seem ready to take away any legal barriers that would impede our making our intervention in our neighbor's affairs felt practically. But will it be pretended, that filibusterism is identical with the Monroe doctrine or its enforcement?

On the contrary, President Monroe's original declaration, and the practical construction since given to it by President Adams and Congress, has for its object, rather to prevent the filibustering of European nations, than any encouragement of it on the part of our own people. That the American continent shall be free from European interference or colonization, and that the American governments, whether monarchical or republican, shall be left to themselves to work out their own salvation, is its substance; and our own Government disclaims for itself, in the same breath, that it will any more interfere on its own part, or so permit its citizens to do what it promises to refrain from, itself.[1]

Thus construed, the Monroe doctrine, though providing for American intervention externally, — that is, in the way of antagonistic action to the intervention of the European powers, — is, in its essence and spirit, repressive of filibusterism, instead of promotive of it. If the Fenians were British subjects coming over to the American continent with a view of revolutionizing Canada on British account, as, for instance, into an independent British monarchy, the spirit of the Monroe declaration would incite our Government to frown upon it, either as a disturbance of existing American governmental institutions, or as a scheme of European colonization. In that sense, would not the United States be equally bound to restrain its own citizens from doing what it forbids to the British interlopers? And would it vary the problem, that the filibustering Irishmen pass through American territory on their way to invade Canada, instead of making a descent at once upon Canada from British soil?

I conceive, then, that the authors and founders of the Monroe doctrine never purposed, by its means, to foster and promote filibusterism, or, any more, that modern phase of it which finds so much favor at present at the capital of the country, — Irish Fenianism.

---

[1] For a lucid and luminous discussion of the Monroe doctrine, see Mr. Dana's note to Wheaton, 8th ed. p. 97, note 36.

I grant, that, if there are a party in this country who favor the annexation of Cuba or Mexico by filibustering means, it will help on their project, to throw down all neutral restraints and leave our citizens and others at liberty to set on foot military and naval expeditions to invade our neighbors' territory. But would General Banks and his supporters once admit that the upshot and aim of their new movement is to render filibusterism easy? Would they consent, in that view, to submit their new bill to the people, under the title of " An Act to make easy the invasion and forcible possession of the countries adjoining the United States"?

If the proposed change in our neutral policy, then, has no affinity to the re-affirmance or enforcement of the Monroe doctrine, considered with reference to other countries of the Western continent, has it any more connection with helping us to intervene more efficiently in European affairs?

To that it is enough to answer, that such intervention never has constituted, and, it is to be hoped, never will constitute, a feature of American foreign policy. Even the promoters of the new scheme declare themselves quite contented, on this head, with abiding by the principles of the Farewell Address of Washington, and the non-intervention policy of President Monroe's administration, as set forth in the answer to the application for aid to the Greek patriots in 1823. But I would make the further suggestion, whether the efficiency of any intervention on our part, in European politics, would be likely to be very much bettered by our prefacing it with a declaration that we have cut loose from the long-established restraints of neutral observances, and are now prepared to set forth on a course of free and easy territorial aggrandizement.

CHAPTER XI.

Further answer to the question, whether our neutrality has not exposed us to imposition. — Very probably it has; e.g., in the matter of impressment. — But did the war of 1812 set that right, or help British fame either? — The necessity of keeping up her own press-gang, not so much the motive to oppress us, lay at the bottom of that piece of British conduct. — Granting freely that we have been imposed upon, is a resort to arms the best safeguard against its repetition? — Are we prepared for standing armies, and to hold ourselves always ready for war? — Napoleon the First's remark quoted as to American military improvidence. — That improvidence will doubtless continue (perhaps justly), and therefore we ought to rely upon a just cause, and not martial force. — In what does a just code of neutrality consist? — Are not neutrality laws a stay against barbarism? — Proof of this from American neutral fame. — Summary of the American record to justify this fame. — The attitude of the United States from 1793 till 1817, covering the French Revolution, the French empire, &c. — This attitude continued through the South-American contests, and a lapse of fifty years, covering the Canadian Rebellion, the Crimean War, &c. — What would have resulted from a course the opposite of this, but retrogression towards barbarism? — The United States can less dispense with such a policy than any other country. — They are, and must be, a peace-loving and law-abiding people. — Their naval weakness in comparison with their commercial development alluded to. — But has not the United States been taught a lesson by the late civil war? — Can they get over the argument drawn from their own practice? — And would not the existence of a statute covering the "Alabama" outfit have been of infinite service to them, then? — Could the English have got away from it, much as they insist upon the municipal scope of their neutrality laws? — But, now that the precedent of the "Alabama" has exposed the flaw, must not the United States legislate accordingly, to preserve their rights hereafter? — Note as to Lord Curriehill's point. — Mr. Dana sides with him unconsciously; but quære, whether they both (in common with General Banks) have not mistaken the object of the statute of 1797? — Another illustration afforded by General Banks's proposal to substitute "*and*" for "*or*" in the fitting-out section. — What would be said to us, and done to us also, if we made such a substitution? — Another illustration afforded by our doctrine, that a nation is liable to another injured nation, in damages, for not observing proper neutrality; exemplified by our demand of indemnity for the "Alabama," and then retaliating on England, in kind, at the first opportunity. — England takes us at disadvantage unawares afterwards, and what shall be done? — If the answer is, "Fight," then it is conceded that war becomes normal, and barbarism reigns as of old. — The result is, either we must practise a just neutrality or adopt standing armies and the reign of brute force.

BUT it may be said, that a full answer has not yet been given to the suggestion that we ought not "to stand bail any longer for the peace of the world," and that our peace-loving neutrality has subjected us to imposition.

I dare say it *has* subjected us to imposition; and I believe British impressment of American seamen, for instance, was no better than trifling with our national good-nature and forbearance. That subject, to be sure, does not immediately connect itself with neutrality; though, as impressment was always practised in connection with the exercise of the belligerent right of search, it may be said to be an over-peaceful acquiescence on our part in an unjust and insulting pretension. "Well," I would reply, "supposing it was an imposition, did we help it by going to war for it, as we did, in 1812? Both parties left off, on that point, where they began, — did they not?" "And did it better the standing of Great Britain any, among the nations of the earth, to take up arms upon such an issue?" I might further ask.

But I might better reply, "Supposing that we did suffer some imposition in that matter, for which we got no redress by war, was not the real root of the trouble, that we were asking Great Britain to abandon, not the international wrong of re-taking her own seamen from American vessels, but the municipal institution of her own press-gang, to which she clings down to the present moment?"* For how could she consistently renounce the right of reclaiming her native-born seamen, wherever she could find them on the open sea, when she was asserting the right of pressing into the naval service, on British soil and within the very precincts of the King's Bench, the same class of her own subjects? This, of course, amounts to no justification of our grievance, but is only a vindication of her own consistency.

---

* Mr. Stephens is my authority for this, — Stephens's Commentaries, 5th edit., London, 1863, vol. ii. pp. 616-17.

Well, granting, if we must, that we have suffered imposition from Great Britain, in the matter of her impressing American seamen, and, more recently, in her outfit and encouragement of Rebel cruisers; and granting, further, that we have been treated with like want of consideration by France in the matter of the Berlin and Milan decrees at a former day, and more recently with unneutral disrespect in her reception of the "Florida" into an imperial dockyard, and in the whole Mexican intervention and other friendly impertinencies; and granting, further, that all the leading European powers have been over-free of their advice and patronage, not to say importunity, to the American republic about neutral observances, — does it follow that a recourse to arms and warlike armaments will prove a sufficient safeguard against the repetition of such uncourteous or unhandsome treatment hereafter?

If the authors of the new movement are ready to propose standing armies and great naval equipments, in indorsement of their more aggressive policy towards other nations, then doubtless, for the time being, their political theory will work. But are the United States prepared for "this standing menace to their own liberties," and this permanent incubus upon their economical republicanism? Are they even ready to free themselves from the reproach of the first Napoleon, that, with all their resources, they will constantly put themselves in the power of an inferior invader, by their short-sighted parsimony in providing against foreign attack?

I assume that our people will not consent to imitate Europe in this matter of standing preparations for war, — and in my judgment, to a large extent, wisely, — and therefore I feel confident that a neutrality relying upon principle, and which appeals to the moral sense and respect for justice of mankind at large, is a better preservative of our rights than a threatening and quarrelsome attitude, which falls back upon the law of might and the coercion of war as the ultimate vindicator of its pretensions. But this leads me to expose, as briefly as possible, in what a just code of morality consists; and whether the progress of civilization demands its reduction to the smallest and fewest particulars, or its expansion and development into a comprehensive and permanent scheme of legislation and jurisprudence.

It has already been suggested, that the abolition of all our neutrality laws would be a step backwards towards barbarism. Has not this point, I would ask my reader, been heretofore pretty forcibly demonstrated by the historical review of our neutral record? What else does our neutral reputation signify, but the praise of mankind, bestowed upon a just and impartial respect for the rights of other nations? What other lesson can be learned from our national adherence to the code of Washington's day through so many succeeding trials and crises, but that that code contains an element of permanence which ought never to be dispensed with?

Let us for a moment run over the line of its birth and continuance again, to possess ourselves of the certainty of its containing this element. In 1793 we behold no statute in force to guide our people in the strait and narrow path of neutral impartiality. Washington's Proclamation, Chief-Justice Jay's Charge to the Grand Jury,* Henfield's indictment, and Hamilton's Instructions to Collectors, supplied the deficiency imperfectly for upwards of a year. But for the guidance and instruction of our people, accustomed to obey law and anxious to learn its bidding, a statute is necessary to declare the international sense of municipal duties and the proper regard for foreign rights incumbent upon them. The statute is passed (after a great discussion) by the casting-vote of the President of the Senate, to hold for the experimental term of two years and until the end of the next congressional session. The law is tested in operation, and it works admirably, both internally and externally. Again the question of its re-enactment recurs, and, for the sake of further experiment, it is submitted to another probationary period like the former. Again its adoption is secured for that period, without dissent; and, after answering the public exigencies for that repeated term, it takes its place in permanency upon the statute-book.

This code, designed (as its authors and first expounders de-

---

* At Richmond, May 22, 1793 (Wharton's State Trials, p. 49).

clared) to come in aid of the law of nations, then retained its operation for seventeen years longer, — carrying us through Napoleon the First's wars, the Berlin and Milan decrees, the Orders in Council, the revival of the Rule of 1756, our own Embargo and Non-intercourse Laws, and our second war with Great Britain (in which last we changed our attitude before the world from that of neutrals to belligerents), till it brought us to the South-American contests of Spain with her colonies. Then, undoubtedly, the law was strained to its utmost capacity, to meet the exigencies of the situation; but, with this heavy strain and with repeated and powerful assaults upon its vitality, it survived the crisis, and, with some amendments in detail, came out of the struggle with stronger testimonials than ever to its merits and essential necessity.

So firmly had its principles and practical operation now commended themselves to the approbation of the civilized world, that even belligerent Great Britain — so shortly before, the foe and warlike antagonist of the neutral republic, — now paid it the unheard-of compliment of imitating its example, and following in essentially the same footsteps of its international-law declarations. Since that period, a lapse of fifty years — embracing the Greek Revolution, the Canadian outbreak of 1838, our own statute of that year in stricter assertion than ever of American neutrality, the Crimean War of 1854, and various other political revolutions, German, French, South-American, and Mexican — has furnished other repeated and convincing tests of its value and efficacy, either in substance or in various of its details. Would not these antecedents lay a groundwork of presumption that the subversion of such a code would be a step backwards for American civilization?

But my position assumes, further, that the United States could less afford to dispense with some such code than any other maritime power. This is my reason; that, while we are and must be essentially a peace-seeking and peace-loving people (without the existence of a standing army and navy, and without any need for them, unless we mean to embark in the embroilments of European politics), our main reliance upon obtaining neutral justice from other nations is the profession and practice of that justice ourselves, upon the truest and most thorough principles of public law. Just as the well-ordered citizen studies and practically obeys the requisitions of municipal law, surrendering to it the gratification of redressing his own wrongs, and learning from it the lesson of using his own rights so as not to injure those of his neighbors, so the United States, as a law-abiding and a law-respecting nation, must owe its neutral redress to the development of the permanent public law of nations, and the general prevalence of a disposition to obey its injunctions, rather than to the opposite theory of might making right.

I hardly need allude to the disproportion that always has existed, and probably always will exist, between the magnitude of the *commercial* and the smallness of the *naval* American marine, — greater in our instance, perhaps, than in that of any considerable power of Europe, — in further corroboration of this idea. The suggestion is so obviously decisive of the importance to us of a substantial neutrality by sea, if not on land, that I forbear expanding or dwelling upon it.

This leads me, however, to consider the point already made, whether our gain does not lie in the direction of expanding still further our neutral code (whether with or without concert on the part of other governments) rather than in contracting or altogether abrogating it.

Have not the fearful precedents of the ravages of the "Alabama," the "Florida," and the "Shenandoah," taught us a valuable lesson in the way of guarding against the recurrence of such destruction of our unarmed and unprotected merchant marine hereafter? If, as is doubtless the case, we shall have to go largely outside of the neutrality law of either country, and invoke the aid of the law of nations, to help us make good our claim against England for co-operating in these neutral (or *un*-neutral) enormities, is it not a startling caution to us, that hereafter the argument shall not be thrown in our teeth, "Well, your own laws would not have prevented American citizens from doing the same thing"?

Without conceding that this retort is founded on fact, and can justly be made in the instances named, is it not, nevertheless, an almost incontrovertible argument in the mouth of a relucting friendly power? Thus, take the very cases of the "Alabama," the "Florida," and the "Shenandoah:" suppose that American law had codified into its municipal prescriptions that a combination to equip a hostile cruiser in neutral waters, and then to give her her warlike armament outside of the territorial line, — a matter put with such force by Secretary Seward, in his despatch to the British Government of Oct. 6, 1863 (Dip. Cor., 1863–4, p. 447), as the international obligation now resting on Great Britain in reference to the "Alabama," — suppose, I repeat, that the American neutral statute had expressly forbidden such a combination, and had provided the means for its prevention as well as for its prosecution, would not the path of redress to us for such grievances as we have sustained in the instance of those vessels have been more patent and incontestable than at present?

I know that Lord Palmerston, Lord Russell, Sir Roundell Palmer, Chief-Baron Pollock, and other exponents of British opinion, have declared, over and over again, that the British and American statutes are mere municipal ordinances, not intended to set forth the limits of international law, but only domestic legislation, intended to bear exclusively upon the subjects of either nation. Let that proposition go for the present unchallenged. I purpose, presently, to give it due attention. Yet I ask again, Who can doubt that the existence of such a provision on the American statute-book as the one I have named would have struck British legislators with appalling force? They might have reasoned that British law recognized no such principle, and declaimed loudly upon the loose generalities of the law of nations; yet who would question, for a moment, that the bare existence of such a provision on the printed pages of the statute code of the United States would have constituted an incontrovertible appeal for American indemnity?

Now, again, suppose that Lord Curriehill's point should command general assent, — that there is no provision in either statute against fitting out privateers, — how would the absence of such a provision have a tendency to affect any future reclamation of ours, against any other nation, for unneutral wrongs on that score? Would it not be said, "Not only did the Americans *not* put a prohibition of that sort on their own statute-book, to forbid United States citizens from participating in such practices; but, *after they were duly notified that there existed such a flaw in their own statutes, they designedly omitted to supply the deficiency*"?[1]

Or suppose that Congress, sanctioning General Banks's present Bill, should designedly substitute "*and*" for "*or*" in the clause of "fitting out or arming," already considered under Part II.; and then, in a future war with England, we should be calling France or Holland to account for a repetition of the

---

[1] Since writing the above, I notice that Mr. Dana, in his extended note to Wheaton on the neutrality laws and jurisprudence of the United States, already alluded to (8th ed., p. 542, &c.), without apparently having had an opportunity to study the decision in the "Pampero" case, and, in fact, without apparently being aware that the point had been raised in that case, unwittingly lends countenance to Lord Curriehill's position. In discussing the legal *status* of a privateer, Mr. Dana remarks (note to p. 564), "Her commission, being a mere commission to make captures, which she may exercise or not at her option, *does not put her into the class of vessels in the service of a sovereign state.*"

I emphasize the important words of the extract, which tally so well with Lord Curriehill's idea, that a privateer cannot be said "*to be employed in the service of any foreign prince, to cruise,*" &c., within the terms of both the British and American statutes.

But I cannot accede to this conception of the legal characteristics of a privateer. *Whenever she is making war* or *pretending to make war*, which constitutes the question generally raised by a supposed violation of neutrality, *she is either serving in the employment of her sovereign, or pretending to serve*, in that employment; and, in either case, she must stand to the responsibility of her acts under the laws of the country which have imparted to her her semi-warlike prerogatives, or of that country whose jurisdiction she has violated by assuming them without due authority. At any rate, such a privateer is fairly estopped, *in that connection*, from denying her governmental employment, or, if only *preparing* for war, and not yet fitted out, that she proposes to make war *in the service* of that nation whose subjects are fitting her out.

Possibly Mr. Dana, together with General Banks, and (perhaps) Lord Curriehill, have all started wrong, upon this head, in supposing that the United-States statute of 1797, chap. 1, was the first and only statute of the United States prohibiting privateering. But the *gist* of that statute was not to prohibit privateering generally, but to prohibit American citizens from engaging in privateering from "*without the limits*" of the United States, i.e., in foreign parts, and against American commerce as well as foreign. Mr. Dana, in analyzing that statute, and in noticing its incorporation (in part) into sec. 4 of the present law, apparently overlooks this important feature in each instance.

"Alabama" unneutral outfit, — would it not be the uppermost answer, "But have you not said, yourselves, that the equipping without the arming, though the arming is afterwards effected as part of the scheme in a different jurisdiction, is no violation of neutrality? Can you expect of foreigners more than you require of your own citizens?"

There is another test of the indispensableness of this system of neutral legislation to our national welfare which I consider unanswerable. *Have we not always taken the ground, that, if a neutral nation omits proper precautions of neutrality, it renders itself liable to any belligerent power who suffers damage thereby?* And, unless we propose hereafter to meet all such demands when justly made upon us by belligerent nations entitled to redress with an answer of force, shall we not be righteously condemned out of our own mouths?

Thus, to give the test a practical illustration : It is said, that, at this moment (I know not how truly), we are presenting our *ultimatum* to Great Britain for satisfaction for the "Alabama" depredations. We found our claim largely upon our own precedents and practice, and insist, that, had the parties changed places, *we* should have unhesitatingly made reparation to Great Britain, *mutatis mutandis*. The claim is allowed, or disallowed, or submitted to arbitration, I care not which, nor with what result. This winter, Congress adopts the new project, and repeals the neutral code in part or in whole. Three years hence, when Great Britain is at war with France or some other European power or combination of powers, we repeat with gusto, for British benefit, the experiment of fitting out "Alabamas" to ruin her commerce, when there is no law to forbid the experiment. Great Britain suddenly finishes up her European quarrel, and turns upon us, — *unprepared for war, of course*, — with a demand for reparation. *Shall we not have to pay it to the uttermost farthing, and justly, upon our own principles, which we cannot repudiate with the bare repeal of our statutes?*

If you say, "But, in that case, we will fight, cost what it will," may I not justly reply, "Well, then, you confess that, without a neutrality code, you cannot get along without making war the normal condition of nations, and so compel a return to barbarism, — which was just my point"?

I submit thus, to any thinking American, with entire confidence, that the unwarlike condition in which the United States will always be found under ordinary circumstances, necessitates their adoption of, and their adhesion to, a just and well-developed scheme of neutrality, provided there were no higher considerations in the case to induce to such an end. If the suggested alternative is, that we shall always keep ourselves prepared to carry out the law of force, then I submit that the remedy is worse than the disease. This fairly leads me to a consideration of what is the true tenor and effect of a system of neutral laws.

CHAPTER XII.

Neutral laws are as permanent a civil necessity as extradition treaties and laws. — Illustration taken from the prohibition against one's making private war for his own gain. — The case of John Laird dwelt upon. — Laird builds the "Alabama" to the special order of the Confederate rebels, for a mission of cowardly buccaneering; enlists her crew in his ship-yard; tells the necessary lies to blind the Government and the Americans; falsely pretends that she is going out on a pleasure trip; and finally gets at the Government secrets about stopping her, through "treachery." — Is not such a transaction a crime to be permanently denounced and punished? — It is as bad as if Laird had planted his cannon at Birkenhead, instead of on board the "Alabama," and brought American ships to and rifled them. — This he has continued for months and years, and has besides hired one hundred and eleven men of the "Alabama's" crew to help him, thereby doing damage to more than $10,000,000 in value, and has bribed the Government officials to enable him to complicate the Crown with foreign powers. — No wonder Earl Russell has denounced him and his private warfare. — *Note* showing that Laird's doings are only a ground for a pecuniary claim, not for hostile feeling, considering that the United States have amnestied Semmes. — But the recognition of Confederate belligerency is no justification of Laird's doings, any more than it would be an excuse for wrecking by false lights. — Supposition of how such a plea would sound in court. — *Note* giving Laird his due. — Application of the wrecking illustration to the question whether neutrality laws are simply municipal and selfish in their scope. — Assertion that United-States neutrality laws have always had an international aspect. — Proved by Washington's proclamation, charges of Judges Jay and Wilson, Henfield's indictment, and Chief-Justice Marshall's declaration. — The point might be carried out to satisfy English publicists to the contrary; but enough to say that England has always acted upon the American idea, and asked for neutral favors accordingly. — Do not English statesmen contradict their own doctrine when they call upon an American minister to enforce a British law? — Extradition laws, however, afford the best illustration of the point that neutrality laws ought to be enacted in permanency. — If the obligation of a nation to pass these laws is denied, it may be asked, What nation will allow herself to be counted out of the association which adopts them. — Recent British debate on French extradition noticed. — The result, that an extraditionary crime is almost tantamount to a municipal one; and, though the last act was only limited to a year, the arrangement will no more be pretermitted than the act against larceny, if accidentally passed for a limited duration. — The people of the United States sufficiently alive to the importance of this kind of crime and its remedy. — Neutrality laws thus are not intended for temporary ends, to enable nations to play fast and loose in their foreign relations, but are a mode of permanently discharging international duties. — In this sense, the present head might more properly be called our "Neutral Duty" than "Our Neutral Policy."—On the whole, it would be as absurd to do away with the offence of piracy, because John Laird has not been punished for his *land piracies*, as to do away with all neutral laws out of antipathy to England. — And this conclusion is clenched by our civil-war experience.

CONTRARY to what is implied in General Banks's Report (p. 6), where it is said, "It [neutrality] is a temporary condition, not incident to the situation, and not necessarily permanent; . . . to make such a system permanent is impracticable,"—I maintain that a system of neutral laws in permanency is as essential a part of the code of any civilized nation as extradition laws, or any other statutory laws with an international aspect.

What, for instance, is it to forbid, statutorily, that any neutral subject shall fit out a vessel of war for belligerent use when his country is at peace with that belligerent? What, but to enact, that no private subject shall *make war, on his own account*, against that friendly power; or else that no private subject shall subject the Government to which he owes allegiance to the embroilments and disadvantages of war without his sovereign's consent? Does not the prohibited transaction amount to an offence which ought to be a standing one on a nation's statute-book? Not merely compromising the peace of the whole nation, and infringing upon its highest attribute of sovereignty, but inaugurating murder, arson, robbery, and the whole catalogue of crimes of violence, on the part of the offender himself?

To take an illustration afforded by our own recent bitter experience, let us consider whether the doings of John Laird, of "Alabama" fame, ought not to be made criminal at all events and for all time, as the acts of a British subject. The Confederate rebels have been recognized by the British Government as legitimate belligerents, and so entitled to belligerent rights. They apply to John Laird to fit out a ship of war for them, telling him expressly that it is for the public service of the Confederates, to be paid for with Confederate gold, and that it is to be fitted up in every way for immediate hostilities, except taking on board her guns and ammunition. The ship is to be fitted for the savage and unmanly mission which she afterwards so successfully fulfils by special qualities of speed, to *run after* unarmed merchantmen, and *run away from* fighting vessels of her own calibre. A special crew is to be provided for her, which Laird (as he pretty openly hinted in his reply to Earl Russell's Blairgowrie speech) recruited and pensioned on Confederate account. This crew, at any rate, is to be "enlisted or engaged to be enlisted" in his ship-yard, and they were accordingly so enlisted on his premises, and doubtless with his full knowledge and consent. Certain lies have to be told, such as that she was fitting up for the Spanish Government, that she had another destination than the Confederate service, &c.; and these lies were told by him or his partners to blind official scrutiny or American vigilance. Certain false pretences have to be used, or *professed* (!) to be used, to Collector Edwards,— such as that the vessel was going out on a trial trip with a pleasure party (consisting, among others, of his sons and daughters), and that Captain Bullock, and his twenty-five or thirty recruits on board the tug which followed her down to Moelfra Bay, were gentleman at large, or some other unobjectionable personages, &c.; and these false pretences were made or *acted out* by Laird, so far as a part in the plot fell to his personal intervention. Finally, it has to be managed to keep her out of the way of the mandate of seizure from the Foreign Office; and Laird, or his accomplices, have an understanding with a Cabinet employé, which secures, "*by treachery*," (*!*) her successful and triumphant departure from British waters.

Now, should such a transaction and series of transactions as this be branded by the law of any civilized state as a crime? I do not stop to ask whether British law did so brand it,— that has already been answered by Earl Russell, as above; but ought it to have been so branded by any civilized legislation in permanence?

Had John Laird fired at every passing American vessel with a cannon planted in his ship-yard at Birkenhead, and brought it to, and then robbed and burned it, would it have been any more a crime — which the statute of England ought to have prohibited and punished — than what he actually did?

First, he was making the shore of England the starting-point, not of one shot or a few shots, but of whole broadsides of cannonades, continued for months, and almost for years, against the peaceful merchantmen of a friendly power, allied to his own Government by most intimate and important connections. In the second place, not merely did he do as much as to touch off this multifarious and long-continued bombardment with his own hand, but he hired a ship's crew, — consisting, all told, of one hundred and eleven men and officers, — to aid him in assailing and plundering American commerce, sinking some sixty-nine steamers and sailing vessels, of the value of nearly $10,000,000,[1] and doing an injury to the American merchant service generally, of probably five times that amount, in the way of enhanced insurance and interrupted voyages. In the third place, not content with planning and organizing this expedition upon British soil, he or his sons personally intervene to effect its safe setting-forth, by imposing upon the British Government (as it alleges) with false pretences, and then bribing or otherwise seducing some ministerial official to betray the secrets of state, and expose the Government to the imputation of bad faith towards the American republic.[2]

No wonder that the combined elements of this transaction forced Earl Russell to speak of John Laird's "*having no right to go to war*" on his own account, and to demand of British legislators whether they deemed it expedient to permit him to embroil Great Britain in a war with the United States, for the sake of his own gains (Hans. Parl. Deb., April 29, 1864, vol. clxxiv. p. 1893). Viewed in the light of these two considerations, — viz., his levying war on his own account, and his compromising his Government into another and a greater one for the sake of his ship-yard's profits, — I might well make the inquiry here, whether these considerations are not enough to justify the permanent enactment — not to say honest and thorough enforce-

---

[1] Report of Mr. Wilson, Secretary of New-York Board of Trade, "New-York Evening Post," May 24, 1866.

[2] See a discussion of the final escape of the "Alabama" from British waters, by the present writer, in the "Boston Daily Advertiser" of Nov. 11 and Dec. 9, 1865.

ment — of a law suppressing such operations as these in question.[1]

But I pass by the levying-of-war and the compromising-into-a-war features of the transaction, and ask, whether John Laird should not be made accountable by British legislation for the offences of robbery, arson, breaking and entering, ship-sinking, underwriter-defrauding, &c., committed against American vessels from British soil, *just as much as if no war existed between the United States and its rebellious subjects?* How can the existence of that war justify him — a private subject, who has never had, and cannot procure, "Her Majesty's license" — for assailing one of the belligerents from British soil? Has he any more right to fire upon American ships, or fit out ships to cruise against the United States, from a British stand-point, because he happens to be in favor of perpetuating slavery, and hates the "Northerners," than he would have to set up false lights on a British headland, to allure American ships ashore, and cause their shipwreck, because all Yankees are odious to him?

Would it be any excuse for the said Laird, if he should be accused of wrecking under existing British laws, that he held out false lights only to lure *Northern* vessels ashore? Laws against wrecking and holding out false lights are sound in principle and commendable in practice, in all civilized codes, and for all times, — are they not? And would it be any justification for the wreckers of Birkenhead, that they made a judicious se-

---

[1] I hardly need say, that I have no desire to increase existing irritation on this side of the water, by thus reviving the story of British toleration of John Laird's equipment of the Confederate cruisers. Of course, Americans can hardly make it the ground of hostile antipathy to England, when their own Government have forgiven — at least, have embraced within their articles of amnesty — Semmes, the great hero of rebel naval warfare. What, again, has Semmes, —

"That mildest-mannered pirate that ever scuttled ship," —

as John Bright facetiously hit off the chivalrous rebel buccaneer, — what has Semmes ever done, in comparison with those who authorized the horrors of Andersonville and the Libby Prison? And yet these enemies of the republic, and foes to humanity, have been thought not unworthy of the country's forgiveness; and some are even now pressing their full restoration to political rights, and possibly to political honors. Can those who hold that line of political sentiment complain with any consistency of British unfriendly neutrality, or treat it as any thing worse than a mere question of civil and pecuniary damage?

lection of their victims? How would the plea sound, in the Queen's Bench, in the mouth of one of these wreckers, indicted for making his gains out of shipwrecked unfortunates, *that he was only taking cognizance of an existing war between Federals and Confederates, and that he confined his shipwrecking business to the destruction of the odious Yankee merchantmen?*[1]

If my position is a sound one, that Laird's business, in its external aspect, is no better than shipwrecking carried on from a British headland, then I would demand of our English exponents of neutrality, whether the legislation which enacts neutral statutes is merely municipal and selfish in its objects, or whether it has not also its international aspects, which justify foreign nations in interfering from without, to solicit its modification and progressive improvement. It may possibly be said to be no business of the United States, technically and politically, whether England should put out all the lights of her lighthouses, — those beacon-fires of civilization along her coasts, — and substitute for them the wreckers' signals, preparatory to embarking in a national enterprise of making her fortunes by wrecking; yet, would not all the nations of the earth feel justified in rupturing at once their treaties, and in suspending all relations with such a people, upon their turning themselves thus into a nation of land pirates?

In this sense, I deny that American neutral legislation was ever grounded exclusively, or even mainly, upon considerations of domestic good. The United States, I insist, have always had in view the protection and benefit of their belligerent allies, as well as the preservation of their own peace and quietude. So said all the early pioneers of the American neutral system; so have said succeeding legislators and jurists.

---

[1] Perhaps I ought to say, in justice to John Laird, that I have seen it stated that he withdrew as active partner from the Birkenhead ship-yard concern some time before the outfit of the "Alabama." But as I take it for granted, from his subsequent Parliamentary disclosures, that he afterwards continued to retain a pecuniary interest in his sons' partnership, and as he has since *fathered* the building of the "Alabama," and professed himself willing to go down to posterity on that reputation, in antagonism to John Bright as his condemner, I think it but fair to give him my humble aid towards securing his desired place in the world's history.

Washington's proclamation of April 22, 1793, gave notice that instructions had been given to the prosecuting officers of the Government to prosecute "all persons who shall violate *the laws of nations* with respect to the powers at war, or any of them" (1 Am. State Pap., 140). The charges of Chief-Justice Jay and Judge Wilson to the grand juries of their respective districts, in May, 1793 (Wharton's State Trials, p. 49), — intended to bear on the enforcement of that proclamation, and which the American Government caused to be printed and sent abroad for a definition of their position, — took the same ground. Henfield, as has already been noticed, was indicted *under the law of nations, and without a statute,* for breaking the peace of the United States by violating its treaties, and *by disturbing its friendly relations with other powers,* and also for combining with his warlike coadjutors *to attack, plunder, and burn the ships of British subjects, and to assault, imprison, and kill those subjects themselves,* they being portions of a friendly people (Wharton's State Tr., p. 66). Chief-Justice Marshall said in the "Santissima Trinidad" case (as already noticed), that the law of 1794 was "declaratory of the pre-existing law of nations, and was intended to aid the Executive in the enforcement of that law."

But it is not to my point to go on and substantiate this position by detailed citation of proofs, as I am confident I could do, to the satisfaction even of Sir Roundell Palmer, and those other leading British jurists who have asserted that American neutral legislation is founded upon the same selfish basis which they ascribe to their own. It is enough for me to show that the neutral laws of the United States started with seeking the good of friendly foreign powers, and not merely with aiming to preserve the domestic peace of the home jurisdiction, and vindicating the prerogatives of national sovereignty; and I trust that enough has incidentally appeared, in the course of the foregoing discussion, to at least render it probable that that original motive has not been lost sight of. Enough, certainly, has been shown to make it clear that foreign nations always took the United States at their word, as professing to have the protection of the rights of other powers at heart, by that constant intercession for improvement of the American code, which General Banks and his congressional coadjutors, in my judgment, so unjustly misinterpret.

If I have labored with any success to expose American regard for international rights, by demonstrating that a compliance with the reasonable requests of foreign governments to modify neutral laws has constituted a just feature of our traditional neutral policy, have I not, to the same extent, proved that the sphere of neutral legislation is international, and not municipal? How can England, for instance, for seventy years have praised our neutral code for its regard for foreign rights, and so often been a suitor for protection of her own belligerent privileges, and not be bound to admit that the sphere of her own neutral laws is not merely the peace and protection of her own insular dominions, or the good of British subjects wheresoever they may be?

I might go on to show how Englishmen of the most Anglican type, like Lord Palmerston, for instance, have belied their own doctrines, when they have admitted, that, if the British Government did not so handle the British Foreign-Enlistment Act as to afford international protection to American interests, the United States would have just occasion to complain. If neutral laws are a domestic institution, like the once-cherished "peculiar institution" of the Southern States, what voice, I pray, have the United States, or ought the United States to have, in enforcing them? Lord Russell, even, has left it to Mr. Adams to furnish the necessary evidence to initiate the governmental prosecutions in many, if not in most, of the great leading attempts to punish for infractions of British neutrality, which have been brought to the notice of the British courts during the late civil war. Is that a British institution which has to be set in motion and kept in operation by foreign appliances?

On the American theory, Secretary John Q. Adams might well have said to the Spanish minister, "Furnish the American Government with proof that privateers are fitting out in Baltimore, and we will see that they are stopped, and their equippers duly punished." But on what principle Earl Russell can have expected Minister Charles F. Adams to inform Her Majesty's

Ministry whenever John Laird was preparing to violate that insular Foreign-Enlistment Act, — intended solely for British protection, and for home use, and in whose enforcement or amendment the United States have no voice, — I cannot understand. On the other hand, is it not plain, even within the construction put upon the British theory in practice by the British ministers themselves, that neutral legislation, like international treaties entered into for the promotion of neutral rights, must have an external aspect, permitting of a certain amount of foreign intervention; or else that the Executive of the Government with which neutral relations are held must be so much of an autocrat and a despot as to be able to enforce international rights without the forms of legislation, or (I might almost say) without the forms of judicial procedure at all?

To come, however, to the analogy which seems most pertinently to explain the foreign aspect of any system of neutrality laws, I submit that these laws are as essentially external in their scope, and rest on the same ground of necessary permanency, as extradition treaties and laws designed in furtherance of such treaties.

If it be a well-settled feature of modern civilization, that one Government shall protect the rights of another Government, by giving up for deportation and trial its murderers, forgers, thieves, &c., and this feature constitutes that universal legislation which amounts to "one and the same law, prevailing among all the great powers of the world," and which ought to be established on a footing of permanency, so I conceive that the enforcement of neutrality calls upon every nation to say, that, in time of peace, she will not harbor within her limits those who are plotting the death, robbery, plunder, &c., of friendly belligerents. I do not say that the neutral nation must go the length of voluntarily giving up such belligerent refugees upon the foreign demand; but that she will not harbor their plottings, when those plottings manifest themselves in outward acts of enlisting soldiers, fitting out ships of war, and the other transactions usually denounced by neutrality statutes.

Will any one say, of these extraditionary laws, that they rest upon no foundation of a necessary duty, inherent in any nation, to enter into them? I ask, What nation, in these modern days, will willingly consent to dispense with them, or be counted out of the association which recognizes them? Is any country anxious to become the asylum of fugitive felons? Is any people willing to advertise that they hold to the carrying-on of felony from their borders, as a national institution? Is any people willing to say, that it is not a desirable object for themselves to recover and recapture, through a neighboring nation's courtesy, the numerous and various criminals, with their booty, which succeed in eluding their own municipal justice?

Quite recently, our British friends have had a parliamentary discussion over the dissatisfaction of their French neighbors with existing extraditionary laws, — founded on some supposed jealousy of French magistrates at the want of respect shown to their official certificates, or else on a real purpose, on the part of the French Government, to force the introduction of political offenders into the category of proscribed criminals, — which, I think, must have quite satisfied British thinkers with the general value and indispensable permanent necessity of such kind of laws. In that discussion, the general network of these extraditionary treaties and laws, among the most civilized portions of the globe, was brought into such prominent notice, and the intimate relations between the British Isles and the Continent of Europe, as affording easy intercommunication for the purposes of criminals and their evasion of justice, so plainly exposed to popular perception, that I fancy no Englishman can have read it without deciding for himself that England can no more do away with extraditionary crimes, than she can with the catalogue of her own municipal offences.

In the light of that discussion, I would venture to ask of my English readers, whether they do not think that the punishment of offenders who trust to a change of jurisdiction (not to a change of guilty intent, or to a restoration of their plunder for immunity from punishment) ought to be secured by a code of laws as efficacious and permanent as those forbidding the municipal crimes themselves which give rise to the application for extradition. Is it not essential to British security, that killing, forging, stealing, &c., should be summarily reached, and made surely and permanently justiciable, as much whether the murderer, &c., happens to be one side of the British channel, as on the other? And, if England and France have had treaties and laws providing for this discharge of the functions of government in protecting against crime ever since the fourteenth century (Ward's Law of Nations, vol. ii. pp. 318–20), can a British subject bring his mind any more to giving up such an arrangement in the nineteenth century, than he could to repealing all British laws against domestic crime, and letting the criminals go unprosecuted?

It is very true, that, in the late debate (see London daily newspapers of August 7), the law in aid of French extradition was only limited to a year's duration. But would the British Government any more omit to supply the necessary legislation before the year expired, than they would forget to make the act against larceny perpetual, if it had been left operative for only one year, with a view to some prison-discipline or transportation arrangement?

On this side of the Atlantic, I need not press the inquiry upon any well-informed American, whether, in view of the frequent absconding to foreign parts of defaulting bank-officers, clerks, and rogues and criminals of all sorts generally, we could consent to give up our extraditionary arrangements with European and other powers, any more than we could a portion of our own penal codes, whether State or Federal. From the first adoption of the practice, immediately after the organization of the Government, when we arranged only for the surrender of a few grades of the worst offenders, down to the Ashburton treaty of 1842, when we agreed with Great Britain for a tripled or a quadrupled extension of the catalogue, I think there can have been but one voice as to, and that in favor of, the temporary expediency, as well as the permanent necessity, of such arrangements. Certainly, all the law-abiding portions of the Union have hailed them as an enlargement of the domains of civilization.

I conclude, then, that an extraditionary arrangement, by treaty and statute, is, to some extent at least, as essential and permanent a feature of the criminal code of any civilized nation as its ordinary penal enactments. But, if it is impossible to frame any extraditionary project without giving to it an international aspect, so I contend that it is equally impossible to frame a code of neutrality laws without introducing into them an element of foreign protection, and so creating a stand-point for foreign intervention. I submit, also, that all neutral codes legislate against acts which, to some extent at least, are permanent breaches of the laws of nations; and which, therefore, can no more be treated as fugitive and temporary, than the offences of murder, robbery, and the like, in the municipal code.

To recur, then, to the assault of the Committee on Foreign Affairs upon our neutral system, as being a political and temporary expedient, which we are at liberty to retain or revoke at pleasure, I submit that it proceeds upon an entirely mistaken conception of the true office of neutral laws. *Their* function is not to enable us to play fast and loose in the game of international politics, but to discharge the duties of impartial neutrality, whenever they may happen to be imposed upon us, steadfastly and consistently, and the more steadfastly and consistently, when the pressure is strongest upon us to evade and nullify their provisions in order to gratify some national liking or some passing national antipathy. In this sense, I might justly have spoken of "our future Neutral *Duty*," rather than "our future Neutral *Policy*." I have retained the latter term, however, in the sense of our having the free choice of retrograding towards barbarism, if we will; but I trust that the decision in favor of civilization will commend itself to my readers as the most statesmanlike and most expedient *policy*.

I have thus discharged myself (imperfectly, I fear) of the idea that neutrality laws should rest on a basis of absolute and permanent principle. The conviction forces itself upon me, that one might as well recommend to the United States to abolish the crime of piracy, because British laws have not sufficiently punished John Laird's *land* piracies, as to do away with the whole neutral code towards all nations, because we are dissatisfied with British observance of neutrality during the past four years. And, if I have had any success in improving upon the moral of our civil-war experience, I trust that my readers have gone with me, in agreeing, that, instead of creating the occasion for blurring over and obliterating the lines of our past neutral enactments, and leaving a smooth tablet on which no feature of a neutral ordinance shall be traced hereafter, *that* experience has rather demonstrated the necessity of cutting out anew and deepening the letters of our old code, and adding to them new and improved commandments.

CHAPTER XIII.

But is not reciprocity as necessary in neutrality as in extradition ? — To this it is replied, that one nation is not to wait for another's neutrality, more than for its honesty. — Illustration taken from the Arguelles case. — But the analogy of extradition not wholly parallel. — Several reasons for our not waiting for neutral reciprocity. — First, we never have done so. — Second, we may have to wait in vain for reciprocity ; e.g., case of Spain. — Third, co-incident neutrality not always possible or desirable. — Illustration from British and American prize-court law, contrasted with the doctrines of the civilians. — Allusion to the opinions held by European publicists as to the "Trent" affair. — But is not British reciprocity a *sine qua non* for our action? — English concurrence certainly of vast consequence. — England and the United States, in accord, might give the law to the maritime world. — Would that English living publicists might join in the common undertaking ! — her Palmers, her Westburys, &c. ; yet the common sense of a Cobden the chief desideratum for the task. — At present, such concurrence out of the question. — Can England expect the United States to reform their neutral laws till she has done away with "the scandal and reproach" of the "Alabama"? — Attention called to the terms in which Lord Russell rejected the American proposition for arbitration. — Despatch of Oct. 11, 1865, cited. — The rejection only sets forth two reasons, — that it charges England with bad faith, or the Crown lawyers with bad law. — As to the first, it is, and has always been made (by Mr. Adams), a question of due diligence, and not of bad faith, on the part of England, that she let the "Alabama" escape. — As to the second, Mr. Adams has never said a word about the Crown lawyers, or their official advice. — If Mr. Adams *had* imputed bad faith to British conduct, it is what Earl Russell himself has set the example of doing. — But is it not an unjustifiable confusion of issues, to pretend that a question of due diligence is "in other words" a question of "good faith and honesty"? — Can Earl Russell any more take umbrage about British "honor," after his own declarations about Laird and Collector Edwards? — Suppose, too, that Mr. Adams had questioned the advice of the Crown lawyers, has not Sir Roundell Palmer himself said, over and over again, that the "Alabama" ought to have been stopped? — And has not Sir Hugh Cairns said that the subsequent stopping of the iron-clads gave the United States an unanswerable plea about the mistake of not stopping the "Alabama"? — But, if Earl Russell only means to refuse to let British law be drawn in question when the complaint is as to the law of nations, was ever denial of justice more insular and insufficient? — What is the Foreign-Enlistment Act to the United States? — Mr. Adams has always kept himself aloof from it, though Earl Russell has solicited his aid in enforcing it. — So that the United States really have the right to question British compliance with British law. — *Note* in reply to Americans "detesting" Lord Russell. — Earl Russell's request for United-States co-operation in amending the neutrality laws cited.

ITS EXPEDIENT FUTURE. 157

— Really a request to better the barn-door fastening after British connivance at the theft of the horse. — Earl Clarendon's more urgent and recent request for American co-operation also cited. — The latest phase of "the situation" noticed. — Opinion expressed, that, if no satisfaction is accorded by England, we ought, none the less, to go forward in the work of neutral codification.

But, granting my premises, it will at once be demanded of me, "But can we do this [i.e., revise and revivify the letter and spirit of our neutral code] without a mutual co-operation and acknowledgment of the principle of reciprocity on the part of other nations?" — "Are not neutrality laws, like extraditionary arrangements, dependent on the joint consent of two or more nations, and therefore incapable of being made efficacious by a one-sided or independent action?"

To this I reply, that there is no more occasion for a country to wait for its neighbors to attend to the discharge of its neutral duties under the law of nations, than there is for an individual to wait for his neighbors' conversion to the principles of moral honesty before he decides to become honest himself. The kingdom of Spain, to this day, has no extradition laws, for instance; but is that any reason why we should not make extraditionary compacts with other nations, who *are* willing to meet us on the score of well-defined written agreements, capable of being recognized by legislative forms, and thus avoid the strain which our laws were thought to have sustained by the recent surrender of Arguelles to the Governor-General of Cuba, without any such written formula of legislative sanction?[1]

But the analogy of extradition laws does not furnish an illustration altogether parallel on this point. Those laws are mainly external in their aspect. It is the foreign nation that makes the demand for the criminal. But, in the instance of neutral laws, the foreign *intuitus* is only secondary and subordinate. The neutral law is mainly to regulate our own conduct; and, if that is honest and impartial, the foreign duty is *ipso facto* performed.

Now, in reference to our waiting upon the movement of other nations to practise neutral impartiality before we resolve

---

[1] See particulars of this case, Dana's note to Wheaton, 8 ed. p. 183.

to become neutrally honest ourselves, or rather, in plainer terms, in reference to our postponing our neutral legislation till we can shape it in conformity with the laws of other concurring governments, I have several answers of a practical nature to urge : —

In the first place, the United States never have found it necessary or expedient to wait for the reciprocation of corresponding neutral legislation on the part of foreign nations, before proceeding to frame their own neutral laws for their own independent government. Neither in 1794, 1797, 1817, 1818, nor in 1838 did we ask, or expect, that Great Britain, France, Spain, Portugal, the Province of Canada, or whoever it might concern, should agree to give us a like enactment in return, before we put our new statute upon the statute-book. When we passed those laws, we were thinking of the performance of our own duties, and of the protection of our own Government against foreign complaints and foreign demands; and we took it for granted, that we should hereafter find a reciprocation, in kind, on the part of those nations to whose intercessions we were lending a compliant attention, if such reciprocation should ever become desirable. At any rate, on all of the five occasions named, it was motive enough for our legislative action, that those respective enactments were then expedient for our own good.

In the second place, it is not worth while to wait the movement of other governments before taking the initiative ourselves in neutral reforms, because, if we do so, we may never get the desired co-operation and reciprocity, and so our needed improvements may fail of consummation altogether. Thus, in the instance of Spain, I suppose she is as far behind the average march of civilization in point of neutral legislation and jurisprudence as she is in extraditionary arrangements. And yet we have neutral relations of the greatest consequence with Spain; probably, next to those with England and France, the most important that we have with any of the European powers. Shall we wait till the enterprise of the ancient Cortes has got ready to set itself in motion, before we think of mending the gaps in our statutes brought to light by the late ruthless and reckless experiments of our belligerent rebels?

In the third place, it does not seem expedient for us to make the co-operation of other powers a condition precedent to our own action, because — provided those powers were ever so willing to discuss and consider proposed neutral improvements in common — their circumstances, forms of government, local position, and other conditions, may be such as to forbid their co-operating with us to any great extent. Thus, take the case of most of the Continental nations of Europe, whose views of neutral rights and duties are shaped by the principles of the civil law, and who do not attribute to the judicial decisions of the courts that weight of authority which is usually accorded to them by the Anglo-Saxon race, under common-law jurisdiction; or, rather, take those European statesmen and publicists who have never yielded assent to the belligerent doctrines of the British and American prize courts. — Is it worth while to expect them to hold much in common with us on the great questions of the Right of Search, Commercial, or, (as Hautefeuille calls them) "Pacific" Blockades, and the Right of Neutrals to deal in Contraband of War, — which constitute so much of the debatable ground of reforms in neutral practice, and on which Englishmen and Americans have been educated to think so much alike?

For an illustration of this difference between the Anglo-Saxon and the Continental mode of viewing a question of neutral law, take the exposition of the right of search and other connected points urged upon us over the adjustment of the "Trent" difficulty, in the friendly communications of the European powers who advised us to surrender Mason and Slidell; were we not forcibly reminded by them, how little the Continental statesmen and publicists understand the spirit of maritime international law, as practised by us and our British ancestors? Even Earl Russell, I suspect, must have been greatly taken aback by some of the principles of international law propounded by his champions, so subversive as they were of some of the most cherished pretensions of the British maritime code. Yet, as to us, must not the thought have been uppermost in the mind of every instructed American, "Why! these Frenchmen and Prussians and Austrians, and even Russians, do not at all understand Anglo-Saxon doctrines and practice: they miss the very points in issue between us and our British antagonists, who profess to practise under the same common code"!

But, perhaps, more significantly than with reference to any other foreign coadjutors in the work of neutral reform, the question springs up, " Is it not, however, expedient or necessary for us to have the co-operation of Great Britain in that proposed betterment of the neutral code? And will any advancement of our own neutral laws be other than a one-sided legislation, of which she will reap all the benefit and we bear all the burden, unless, by a common understanding, England engages to put upon herself the same restrictions which we adopt?"

To this, I answer frankly, that, commercially and internationally speaking, I believe the reciprocation and common undertaking of Great Britain with us in the same line of neutral progress would be of almost inestimable value. As a commercial power, her example and co-operation are worth as much, or more, to us than the rest of the civilized world together. Indeed, England and the United States, in accord with each other on international maritime law, might well give the law to all other commercial nations; certainly so, if that accord is founded on liberal and high-minded notions of abstract justice, and respect for the rights of weaker maritime powers. Doubtless, too, they could go a long ways together in the same line of future neutral advancement, as is shown by the similarity of their respective codes, to which each has so long separately adhered thus far.

Then, again, what a flood of light, and what an abundance of valuable state precedents and of practical legislative expedients, might there not be contributed to the common stock, by the juridical and political ability and rich culture of her publicists and jurists, — her Palmers, her Westburys, her Cranworths, her Hugh Cairnses, her Colliers, her Phillimores, her Twisses, her Stuart Mills, her Harcourts, her Goldwin Smiths, and I know not whom, among friends and foes, who have been brought prominently forward in the recent neutral discussions, so earnestly and so warmly carried on in the courts, in Parliament, or through the English press! Would that we had, on our side, some of the Hamiltons, the Marshalls, the Storys, the Kents, and the Wheatons of former days, to meet and take part in such a congress of public law!

But the work to be done would not, after all, be that for shining public men. One such commissioner as Mr. Cobden, on the British side, to furnish the common-sense and broad international principles to be agreed upon, and one such master of the science of law-making and law-interpreting as Parliament and the British Bar (without naming) can furnish fifty, would be amply sufficient to represent Great Britain; and, on our own side, two men, if they could be found (and I doubt not that the race of born law-givers and legislators is not yet extinct among us), of like practical and yet far-reaching abilities and skill, would be enough to embody the requisite representation of our people. May such a conference yet be had!

Still, in the present state of public feeling on this side of the water, it is obviously impossible to suppose that such a commission can be held, without some preliminary action or concession on the part of our Trans-atlantic British friends and allies.

How can it be expected by Englishmen, that Americans shall agree to a joint undertaking for that reform of the maritime neutral code of the two countries, now pressed by England with so much urgency, and for her own good as they believe, while they are as yet smarting under the sense of injuries and injustice recently done them through an English code which they hold to have been amply sufficient to protect their rights? Grant that Americans are mistaken in this belief, and that the British statute was really so defective that it could not reach the difficulty, and that British neutral conduct has been as impartial and friendly as the nature of the case would permit of; would it not at least have been common international courtesy to give these American grievances a respectful hearing, and either refer them to a disinterested umpire for arbitration, or else, without such an umpirage, to attempt to remove them by some distinct concessions of principle for the future?

Can Englishmen expect Americans to go into a conference for future amendments of the law of nations, without an acknowledgment at least, on the part of the British Government, that they were in the wrong for what their own Foreign Secretary calls "the scandal and the reproach to our laws" of the "Alabama" business? If Earl Russell admits, in the face of the world, that the "Alabama" escaped by "treachery," and says that the Collector of Liverpool put a faith in John Laird's promises that he (Russell) would not have done, is it wonderful that Americans have adopted a conviction that some responsibility ought to fall on that Government which employs such treacherous and untrustworthy officials?

But how has this same British Foreign Secretary, who has made these irrevocable admissions, and who was himself responsible for the escape of the "Alabama," repudiated all approaches to an amicable adjustment of the American grounds of complaint?

I doubt if Englishmen have ever adequately canvassed Earl Russell's rejection of Mr. Adams's proposal to submit the questions between the two countries to arbitration, in the true light in which that rejection should really be made to stand; certainly, on this side of the water, I have never seen his lordship's misstatement of the true issue, and his unfounded claims on behalf of British honor and the supremacy of British law over the law of nations, held up to the rebuke which they justly deserve. If the question between the two nations is of future good understanding about past transactions, and a consentaneous movement together in the direction of reforming each one's separate neutral code for the future, then I submit that it must first be passed upon, whether the United States ought not to have received some different answer to their courteous and friendly proposition, from that actually given by the British Foreign Secretary in October, 1865, when he peremptorily declined to entertain any such proposal.

Says Earl Russell to Mr. Adams, in his letter of Oct. 11, 1865 (British Blue Book, "North America, No. 1, 1866, Correspondence respecting the 'Shenandoah,'" p. 31) : [1] —

"In your letter of the 23d of October, 1863, you were pleased to

---

[1] I am obliged to quote from the British publication, as our own Diplomatic Correspondence for the last year (1864-5) has not yet been published.

say that the Government of the United States is ready to agree to any form of arbitration.

"Her Majesty's Government have been thus led to consider what question could be put to any sovereign or state to whom this very great power should be assigned.

"It appears to Her Majesty's Government that there are but two questions by which the claim of compensation could be tested. The one is, Have the British Government acted with due diligence, or, in other words, with good faith and honesty, in the maintenance of the neutrality they proclaimed? The other is, Have the law officers of the Crown properly understood the Foreign-Enlistment Act, when they decline, in June, 1862,[1] to advise the detention and seizure of the 'Alabama,' and on other occasions when they were asked to detain other ships building or fitting in British ports?

"It appears to Her Majesty's Government, that neither of these questions could be put to a foreign Government with any regard to the dignity and character of the British Crown and the British nation.

"Her Majesty's Government are the sole guardians of their own honor. They cannot admit that they may have acted with bad faith in maintaining the neutrality they professed. The law officers of the Crown must be held to be better interpreters of a British statute than any foreign Government can be presumed to be. Her Majesty's Government must therefore decline either to make reparation and compensation for the captures made by the 'Alabama,' or to refer the question to any foreign state."

Now, here, it will be seen, are just two grounds, and only two, on which Earl Russell rejects the offer to afford some satisfaction for the "Alabama" and similar claims; viz., that the claims raise the question of the bad faith of the Government, or that they imply a misconstruction of the Foreign-Enlistment Act on the part of the Crown lawyers; and therefore (for conclusion), as "Her Majesty's Government are the sole guardians of their own honor," that Government will not entertain the proposal.

In contravention of this statement, I venture to assert, that,

---

[1] This date of "*June*, 1862," is probably a mistake for *July*, 1862. No opinion of any law adviser of the Crown (Customs' Solicitor or other) appears to have been furnished earlier than July 1st. The Solicitor of Customs gave the last legal opinion before the sailing of the "Alabama," which is in print, *July* 22, 1862 (Blue Book, 1863, "North America, No. 3, the 'Alabama,'" p. 2).

from first to last, Mr. Adams never undertook to impugn the good faith or honest purposes of the British Government, in any particular. Throughout, the complaint was of the facts as they had actually occurred, without the slightest imputation of motives on the part of the Government responsible for the occurrence of those facts. Subordinate officials were sometimes referred to as showing some partiality or slackness, but never any charge against the motives of Her Majesty's Ministry. No stickler for diplomatic etiquette could have more scrupulously guarded himself on this head than our well-instructed representative.

Then, as to the charge of imputing to the Crown lawyers a false or erroneous construction of the Foreign-Enlistment Act, nothing could have been further from Mr. Adams's intention or from the language actually employed by him. He never pretended to discuss the British statute at all; and it was no concern of his, from the outset, how the British authorities discharged their neutral duties, provided only that they actually *did* discharge them. As for the term "Crown lawyers," he never once used the words, or any thing equivalent to them; and I doubt if he has ever alluded to the legal advisers of the Crown throughout his five years' correspondence.

It is very true, that Earl Russell, at an early day, requested Mr. Adams to furnish evidence to aid in putting that law into operation; and also, that, at the time of submitting the preliminary depositions on which Mr. Adams asked for the detention of the "Alabama," he accompanied those depositions with an opinion of a British barrister and Queen's counsel. But Mr. Adams never volunteered an opinion, nor a criticism of any kind, whether this opinion (given by Sir Robert Collier, afterwards Solicitor-General, and ultimately endorsed by the action of the Crown lawyers as just and accurate) was right or wrong, or whether it ought to be weighed by the Crown lawyers at all. His contention was wholly with the Government of Great Britain alone. I have been carefully over the correspondence in this view, and am amazed — considering Mr. Adams's delicacy and reticence on the point — that Lord Russell should have made such an assertion.

The only point where the Foreign Secretary touches the true issue raised by Mr. Adams is, where he says, "Have the British Government acted with due diligence, or, in other words, with good faith and honesty, in the maintenance of the neutrality they proclaimed?" But when was it ever heard of in a court of law that "due diligence" was the synonymous equivalent of "good faith and honesty"? If a common carrier were sued for losing a parcel intrusted to his care, would it be said that the question "whether he took proper care of his charge" was synonymous with "whether he had stolen it, or converted it to his own use"? When the United States charge that the "Alabama" escaped by the negligence of the Liverpool customs officials, or by unwarranted delays at head-quarters, is that charging the British Government with bad faith and dishonest purposes?

Even if Mr. Adams had questioned the seeming good faith of Her Majesty's Government, would not that have been excusable, in view of what Earl Russell has himself said about the "treachery" and the scandal and reproach connected with the (so-called) "*escape*" of the "Alabama," and "the degree of credulity" with which the Liverpool collector, S. Price Edwards, listened himself, and persuaded the Crown lawyers to listen, to Mr. Laird's subsequent representations about the destination of the iron-clads? — representations which Earl Russell said in debate, in the House of Lords, he had satisfied himself were false, and which he only reproached himself with having noticed.

But will not the British as well as the American reader agree, that it is an unfair and unfounded mixing-up and confounding-together of entirely distinct things, to say, that a question of "due diligence" is, "*in other words*," a question of "good faith and honesty;" and that it is an equally unfair and unfounded misrepresentation of the true issue involved, to insist that neither *that* question (of the exercise of due diligence) nor *the other* question (whether the Crown lawyers have misconstrued the Foreign-Enlistment Act) — a charge never made, nor thought of being made, by the American minister — "can be put to a foreign government, with any regard to the dignity and character of the British Crown and the British nation"?

If (as Earl Russell further insists) "Her Majesty's Government are the sole guardians of their own honor," are "treachery" and custom-house proceedings — amounting to "a scandal and a reproach to our laws" — a part of the national honor, for whose vindication Earl Russell must shut the door in the face of a further hearing of the American complaint?

Suppose, too, that Mr. Adams *had* charged the crown-lawyers with misconstruing the Foreign-Enlistment Act in the case submitted to them, — has not Sir Roundell Palmer, while Attorney-General of England, over and over again, in Parliament and the courts of law, avowed that the "Alabama" ought to have been stopped on the true construction of that act, and that the only excuse for the British Government was, that Sir John Harding's consulting opinion, as Queen's Advocate, could not be had in sufficient season to act? Earl Russell and Sir Roundell Palmer state the thing differently on this head; Earl Russell ascribing it to the Cabinet secret (of issuing the order for the seizure of the "Alabama") being communicated to Laird or the Confederate agents, in advance, by "treachery," and the Attorney-General attributing it to Sir John's accidental sudden illness. Here, again, would it not be a fair question for umpirage, whether the loss of ten million dollars in value to American commerce, if attributable to such an accident as the illness of the Queen's Advocate, or to the treachery of some scampish official, should be borne by British or by American interests?

Furthermore, if the British Government found means and powers for stopping the iron-clads in September, 1863, in the same state of incomplete armament which the "Alabama" was in for at least five weeks before her departure (the American minister all the while pointing out her warlike character and hostile destination), and the present Attorney-General of England has declared that he could not see how the action of the Government in making that seizure could fail to compromise them into an acknowledgment of the omission of their duty in the instance of the "Alabama," ought the American minister to be blamed for imputing only what Sir Hugh Cairns asserts, upon his professional and parliamentary responsibility, is true, and what, he adds, the Americans will be sure to retort upon England?[1]

But leaving out of view the professional standing of the Crown's law-advisers, as drawn in question by Mr. Adams's proposal, and supposing that Earl Russell means to say that he is unwilling to leave to foreign arbitration at all the question of British interpretation of their own code, could there ever be a more insular and self-sufficient and (at the same time) *in*sufficient statement of the issue than the supposed case made up by the Foreign Secretary for the umpire's decision? Who pretends, except Earl Russell himself, that the controversy is about the proper interpretation of the British Foreign-Enlistment Act? What the United States want of a disinterested umpire is a decision outside of that act, under the law of nations.

The United States say that the "Alabama" (to take one of their chief grievances, for instance) took to the sea to make war against them from a British basis of preparation; and that such a transaction, with its attendant circumstances, was a violations of the law of nations, entitling them to redress under that law. To which Earl Russell replies, "England contends that she has fully and faithfully enforced her Foreign-Enlistment Act;" "he has asked of the Crown lawyers their opinion on this point, and they assure him that no complaint can stand against the Government on this head;" and, he adds, "shall I consent to submit the accuracy of British lawyers, and the goodness of the British statute, to foreign umpirage? Forbid it, the honor of England!" Was ever denial of justice more autocratic and Anglican?

It is very true, that Mr. Adams, when he could get no other governmental enforcement of the British act than what he interested himself to set in motion, lent a helping hand (with the aid of Consul Dudley) to do all there was effectively done towards stopping the "Alabama" under the Foreign-Enlistment Act. But, besides volunteering this at Earl Russell's special

---

[1] Since writing the above, the newspapers bring word that Sir Hugh Cairns has resigned as Attorney-General, and been appointed one of the Lords Justices of Appeals.

suggestion,[1] he always put himself outside of the scope of the British act, and insisted that he looked to the British Government for the performance of its duties, under whatever code they professed to justify themselves. And now, for the British minister to be constantly interposing what the laws of Great Britain can or cannot permit, and what opinion the law advisers of the Crown hold upon their own statutes, and, finally, when the mischief has happened, to say that he will submit no question of the goodness of British laws or British lawyers to the friendly arbitration of a third power, — what is it, but to turn aside the point of the American demand, and throw himself upon his dignity, with false pride and falser logic?

On his own principles, if he has referred Mr. Adams to the British act for his remedy, why should not the umpire take cognizance of whether the British law was properly interpreted, as well as whether it was diligently and vigilantly enforced?[2]

---

[1] See letter of Earl Russell to Mr. Adams, of July 4, 1862, "President's Message," &c., 1862, p. 129. See also Mr. Adams's despatch to Mr. Seward, of July 17, 1862. *ib.*, p. 137, in which Mr. A. speaks of Earl Russell's having dropped a suggestion to him in conversation about the best course to pursue.

[2] I take occasion to disclaim here, in the same spirit as in a recent earlier note, any intention of adding to the ill-feeling, so largely prevalent at the present moment in this country, against Earl Russell. The correspondent of the "London Times," however, who writes from Washington in the "Times" of Oct. 30, quite exaggerates that ill-feeling, when he says that Earl Russell "is detested" in the United States.

I insist, in justice to American intelligence and American candor, that that statement is not true, and is calculated to unfairly affect the reputation of one to whom Americans have been accustomed to look, during the late civil struggle, for greater consistency — not to say a certain sort of liberal-minded impartiality — than the majority of leading British statesmen, even of Earl Russell's own party. On three points at least, as it seems to me, — judging from external evidence, — Americans ought to hold Earl Russell's connection with the Confederate civil war in respectful if not kindly regard, — I mean his liberal and almost indulgent recognition of the sufficiency of our blockade, his uniform and sturdy resistance to the acknowledgment of Confederate independence, and his considerate and personally kind treatment of our national representative at the British Court, Mr. Adams.

On this latter head alone, judging from the tenor of Mr. Adams's despatches, and looking back to the dark crisis through which he had to pass, and in which he so frequently acknowledges the British Foreign Secretary's courtesy and good-will, I think there is ground enough for Americans to repudiate any such sentiment as that attributed to them towards Earl Russell, notwithstanding the many and grievous irritations of language and manner which he has allowed himself to be guilty of towards the United States. Americans certainly expected better things than they

In this view of the British refusal to submit the question raised by the outfit of the " Alabama " and other similar vessels to arbitration, with what countenance can Earl Russell have concluded his last discussion of the " Alabama " claims, while Foreign Secretary, with such a suggestion as the following, addressed to the United States, through their minister, Mr. Adams, for a mutual reform of the respective statutes of the two countries? —

" It appears to me, I confess, that, as neither the law of the United States nor our own Foreign-Enlistment Act have proved, upon trial, completely efficacious, it is worth consideration whether improvements may not be made in the statutes of both nations, so that, for the future, each Government may have in its own territory as much security as our free institutions will permit against those who act in defiance of the intention of the sovereign, and evade the letter of its laws." (Blue Book, 1866, " North America, No. 1, — The Shenandoah," p. 129.)

In other words, " Now that your horse has been stolen, and you are accusing us of having left the door open to the thief to steal it " [*carelessly*, of course], " will you not join with us in a mutual commission, to see how we may make both our barn-doors tight hereafter?" Is that a very taking form of address for the American people?

Earl Russell's successor in the Foreign Office, the Earl of Clarendon, repeats this same address to the American minister at London, six weeks later, under date of Dec. 26, 1865, — this time, however, in a much more conciliatory strain, and with a vast deal more of open urgency. The reader can judge, from the last six lines of the extract which follows (the italics of which are my own,) how real is the anxiety of England to

---

experienced at the hands of the liberal-minded British statesman, who had declared, in early public life, that the war of 1775 against them, on England's part, was " a war in which she had engaged for the suppression of liberty " (Hans. Parl. Deb., April 16, 1823, vol. viii. N.S., p. 1036), and who has always professed to rank himself among the friends of African emancipation; but I believe that they are willing to attribute rather to the supineness of his party, and to his own fear of proposing measures in advance of British public sentiment, than to any thing like unfriendliness towards their nation, that British neutrality, under his auspices as Foreign Secretary, made itself so little respected or respectable in American estimation.   22

unsettle the "Alabama" precedent as at present left standing. Lord Clarendon is repeating and reporting to Sir Frederick Bruce, the British minister at Washington, what had just occurred betwixt Mr. Adams and himself at London, and adds the concluding clause for Sir Frederick's own instruction and guidance (I quote, of course, from a British Parliamentary Blue Book, "The Shenandoah," &c., *ut sup.* p. 164) : —

"I asked Mr. Adams, whether it would not be both useful and practical to let by-gones be by-gones, to forget the past, and turn the lessons of experience to account for the future. England and the United States, I said, had each become aware of the defects that existed in international law; and I thought it would greatly redound to the honor of the two principal maritime nations of the world to attempt the improvements in that code which had been proved to be necessary. It was possible, I added, that the wounds inflicted by the war were still too recent, and that the ill-will towards England was still too rife, to render such an undertaking practicable at the present moment; but it was one which ought to be borne in mind, and that was earnestly desired by Her Majesty's Government, as a means of promoting peace, and abating the horrors of war; and a work, therefore, which would be worthy of the civilization of our age, and which would entitle the Governments which achieved it to the gratitude of mankind.

"Mr. Adams, in reply, said the law of England, in its international application, stood greatly in need of amendment; but he gave me no encouragement to expect that his Government would co-operate with that of Her Majesty in the course of proceeding which I had suggested.

"*You will, however, avail yourself of such opportunities as you may think fitting to bring the subject under the consideration of Mr. Seward or the President; and you can neither exaggerate the importance attached to it by Her Majesty's Government, or* [*nor*] *the satisfaction it would give them to co-operate with the Government of the United States in a work of which the benefit would be universal.*"

This is the latest diplomatic development of the position of the negotiation between the two countries at present, and, I suspect, has not as yet been reproduced in this country. Much more recently, the "London Times," — that important organ of British opinion, — recurring to the subject, under date of Sept.

1, 1866, while rejecting the idea of arbitration, and upholding Earl Russell for repudiating it, declares the urgent fitness and necessity of such a measure of joint reform as is above considered. And still more recently, under the date of this day's writing (Nov. 1), the cable telegraph informs us that the "Times" declares itself in favor of renewing the proposition to submit existing differences to arbitration.

On our own side of the water, newspaper statements, apparently authentic, indicate that some demand for satisfaction of the "Alabama" claims has recently been made by the Government of the United States upon England, outside of any proposition for arbitration or for a mutual reform of the neutral codes of the respective countries. If such shall prove to be the fact, and if the demand shall be acceded to by England, or if the result of making it shall be a submission of all difficulties between the two countries to arbitration, then the obstacle in the way of a joint consideration of legal reforms, which I have been considering, will have been removed, and the path will lie open for such a common undertaking. If, on the other hand, the British Government shall not show itself disposed to recede from its one-sided and self-sufficient attitude as to past occurrences, then the question, so long kept in abeyance in the past discussion, recurs, whether it is worth the while of the Congress of the United States to go forward separately in the work of reforming our own neutral code without British co-operation, and without any guaranty that England is not to reap the chief benefit which will result from our self-denying restrictions?

Adhering to all that I have before said on that topic, I would further add, that I have no hesitation in advocating the expediency of the forward movement, England to the contrary notwithstanding. I insist, that it is due to national consistency, to national protection, and, more than all, to international honesty, that we should enter forthwith upon the work of supplying those defects in our neutral code which have been shown to exist by the occurrences of the late civil war. I insist further, that not only should we make good these gaps in our statutes, but that we should go on, in the spirit of an honest neutrality, to show that we do not mean to do unto others what they have done unto us.

CHAPTER XIV.

Suggested improvements towards advancing neutrality. — Six heads, borrowed chiefly from the British Act : — (1) Prohibit effectually the fitting-out of privateers. — (2) Provide for "agreeing to enlist" as well as for an actual enlisting. — (3) Prohibit recruiting for a foreign ship of war from among foreigners. — (4) Authorize detention of vessel carrying away recruits; *note* showing that affidavits were not necessary for the seizure of the "Alabama." — (5) Adopt the better terms of sec. 7 of the British act, "or" for "and," "in order that," &c. — (6) Imitate the British prohibition against adding to the armament of a ship of war. — Then, for new independent legislation, (*a*) counteract Baron Bramwell's "evasion" of neutrality. — Quære whether it is worth our while to insist much upon our doctrine of the right of selling ships of war, as distinguished from building them "to order." — The bonding clauses seem a happy medium. — (*b*) Adopt the British doctrine of forbidding the fitting out transports and storeships. — Russia might have justly complained of us for furnishing transports for the allied troops in 1854. — General views about carrying traffic in arms, &c., into the scene of war. — It may be impartial, but it is not neutral, to sell to the two combatants alike. — B. Bramwell and Sir R. Phillimore cited. — (*c*) Reconsider our maxims about selling and carrying arms to belligerents. — The law at present well settled against the writer's view, and the practice of the United States has always been strenuously the other way. — Still the law and practice are both wrong. — It is hard to draw a just distinction between furnishing ships or arms to a belligerent. — Sir R. Phillimore, Lord Palmerston, &c., quoted. — Sir H. Cairns as to setting up a manufactory of arms in neutral territory. — What have we not suffered from our own principles during the late war ? — We cannot complain of England for furnishing Enfield rifles, &c., to the rebels. — What a blessed thing if we had had our statute of 1838 in force ! — The statute quoted. — Note showing that Mr. Everett moved to make it applicable to carrying arms by sea as well as by land. — (*d*) Improve the "bonding" clauses. — Reference to the United States requiring a bond of the German ship of war, "the United States," fitted out in New York, and to Baron De Cussey's praise of our conduct. — Various points of amendment to these clauses. — *Note* discussing the decision of Judge Betts in refusing to allow the "Meteor" to be bonded, except after condemnation. — (*e*) Extend the authority of district attorneys, &c., in making seizures. — Case of *Gelston and Hoyt* alluded to. — Provisions for preliminary detention and sequestration of ships fitting out like Laird's ironclads recommended. — (*f*) Make violators of the law like Laird responsible to the foreign Government. — *Note* on Mr. Lowrey's pamphlet. — (*g*) Take away from the jury the determination of neutral seizures, &c., and commit it to the admiralty judge. — Allusion to the case of the "Alexandra," and of Jefferson Davis, as beyond the scope of jury trials. — (*h*) Exclude by law an "Alabama" from hospitality on account of illegal outfit. — (*i*) Refuse her the privileges of a ship of war. — (*j*) Deny it on the score of burning whalers, &c. — (*k*) Perfect the machinery for restoring prizes. — These only some of the points of advancement. — But the question is, whether we shall go forward at all. — Final appeal in favor of the forward movement. — We are bound to it on religious, moral, and republican principles. — England may be a helper. — The two countries likened to travelling merchants in the desert who join their forces for mutual protection. — France and other belligerent powers will perhaps ultimately concur. — But, whether England concurs or not, the path is plain for us. — Needless to say that General Banks's Bill cannot be approved.

Am I asked, specifically, what amendments to existing laws, or what new fundamental reforms to our present neutral code, I have to suggest, I have to reply, on the first head : —

Let these defects, at least, of the existing laws be amended, — the same which, for the most part, have been drawn into discussion in connection with the superior completeness of the British code : —

(1). That the unneutral fitting-out of privateers for a belligerent's service shall be made a punishable offence, beyond the shadow of a cavil.

(2). That the unneutral "engaging or agreeing to enlist" shall be reached, as well as the "enlisting or entering one's self as a soldier," of the present statute.

(3). That the exception shall be struck out of the enlisting clause, which allows the recruiting within our territory for a foreign ship of war from among citizens of the same foreign nation as that to which the ship belongs; thus making all sorts of recruiting for a foreign service within our limits punishable.

(4). Authorize (as General Banks's Bill ineffectually proposes) the detention of any vessel or auxiliary tug-boat, &c., about sailing with persons on board, "enlisted or engaged to be enlisted," &c., for a foreign belligerent service.[1]

---

[1] On this head, it is perhaps quite unnecessary to imitate the strictness of the British law (sec. 5), in requiring the complainant to produce sworn affidavits as to the particulars of his reasons for believing that the offence is about to be committed. Probably, a general statement of belief of the attempted offence, as in the case of ordinary prosecutions for crime, will be sufficient. At any rate, if there is a provision inserted in the laws enabling the vessel to give bail in case of seizure, the formality of these particulars seems superfluous. Sir Roundell Palmer, in the debate on the seizure of the "Alexandra," in the House of Commons, April 24, 1863, pointed out, that, under the 7th section of the act (*that under which the "Alabama" should have been seized*), *no formality of affidavits is a pre-*

(5). Imitate the superior completeness of the British act, in inserting "or" for "and" in the important section of our own act against "fitting out and arming" ships of war. It would seem also, that the phraseology of "equip and furnish," of the British act, would add something to the bare use of the terms "fit out and arm," in the same section of our own. In the same view, the phrase "in order that" should be introduced into the new law, or the tenor and sense of those words in some manner formularized into it. To the same section should also be added, after the words, "colony [and] province," the words, "or exercising or assuming to exercise the powers of government," to correspond to the superior phraseology of the British statute. And, in a general way, this whole important section should be made *flaw-proof*, and receive the benefit of those great international discussions connected with the "Alabama," the "Alexandra," and other similar cases, so as to make it an efficient preservative of maritime neutrality.

(6). Imitate the British improvements before pointed out in connection with the section relating to the augmentation of the armament or equipment of a ship of war; viz., extend it to all ships of war *in time of peace;* to changing such a ship's guns for any other guns *whatsoever*, whether "of a larger calibre" or not; and forbidding the addition to such ships of *any* equipment of war, whether "solely [exclusively] applicable to war" or not.

So much for the amendments suggested by the Foreign-Enlistment Act.

Then for original or independent reforms, which the lesson of English recent practice of neutrality inculcates upon us, I have to urge, that we are manifestly called upon : —

(*a*) To intervene at the point between equipping to order a ship of war for belligerent use (which we now hold to be plainly unlawful), and selling the same as an article of merchandize (which our jurisprudence and practice have pronounced legitimate), so as to denounce, in unmistakable terms, that evasion of the law sanctioned by Baron Bramwell's opinion in the Eng-

---

requisite to seizure in British practice (Hans. Parl. Deb., vol. clxx. p. 751). If affidavits are not necessary where the forfeiture of the vessel is drawn in question, ought they to be any more insisted on where the purpose is only to detain?

lish Court of Exchequer in the "Alexandra" case; viz., the equipping of a ship of war in a neutral port so as to fit her all ready to receive her guns, and then sending out her guns by a separate vessel to join the war-ship, and complete the arming outside of the line of neutral jurisdiction.

Whether the establishment of this sharp line of demarcation is desirable, or whether it is expedient for us to haggle much about the right of selling ships to belligerents as articles of traffic at all, — considering (among other things) that we have so few steamers to dispose of, at any rate, — are doubtless points admitting of a good deal of discussion. For my own part, I think it very difficult to effectually interfere with and prevent such sort of transactions as we complain of in the instance of John Laird & Sons, as directed against us, except by forbidding the sale of war-vessels outright, or by putting them under such bonds, at the time of sailing out of port, as will prevent their taking part in hostilities, or, at any rate, secure the Government against being implicated in their warlike operations. Though I believe Judge Story's *dictum* of the "Santissima Trinidad" case to be the settled law and practice of the United States, I yet agree with Chief-Baron Pollock, that it is hard to set up a distinction between building a ship to order and selling one to a belligerent ready-made, which can be carried out into practical working efficiency, as a doctrine of neutral law.

In this light, I cannot but think that American legislators have hit upon a happy medium of prevention in adopting the bonding clauses, which I have already noticed, and upon which I shall presently say more; but, outside of this, I believe that we ought either to forbid the sale of vessels fitted for war or adaptable for war in the home port, outright, or to put the crews taking such vessels out of port under such surveillance and scrutiny as to prevent their constituting a warlike force or " hostile expedition."

(*b*) To reform our practice in the matter of furnishing transports or storeships to belligerent foreign powers.

This, to be sure, is an amendment suggested by the Foreign-Enlistment Act; but I prefer to treat it as a fundamentally new proposition for our adoption.

Though Russia may not have complained of us, at the period of the Crimean War, for furnishing this class of vessels to the allied armies, I cannot but think that she had serious grounds of dissatisfaction with the course of our ship-owners in this respect. Can there be a more direct intermingling with war than to transport armed soldiers to the field of battle? And, had a Russian vessel fallen in with one of these American transports before Sebastopol with French or English troops on board, could the United States have remonstrated against the Russians for firing into the vessel, or treating her crew, when captured, as prisoners of war? If a neutral resident should carry a wagon-ful of soldiers into the lines of a fighting army, is he not mixing himself up with war? This is the plain declaration of a great master of belligerent law, Bynkershoek;[1] and I do not see the difference of transportation by water from that by land.

I cannot sympathize with that defence of commerce which would justify the pursuit of neutral gain even to selling weapons of war on the battle-field to combatants whose hands are red with slaughter. If such sort of traffickers insist upon the right of plying their vocation, I say, let them be subjected to the hazards and hardships of war. In my view, a transport or a storeship is as much an auxiliary to war as a fighting-ship made such by means of the stores and troops which that transport is intended to supply; and if we forbid the furnishing of the latter, to preserve neutrality, why not the former as well?

Some may reply to this suggestion, perhaps, that the supplying of transports to a belligerent falls within that class of things which a neutral may lawfully do, provided he does it for both parties indiscriminately. That seems to have been President Pierce's point of view, in his annual message of December, 1854. But I protest against this whole notion of balancing a wrong done to one party, by holding out that we are ready to do the same thing impartially for the other. So far as Ameri-

---

[1] See his opinion to this point, cited by Earl Russell in his despatch to the American Government in the "Trent" case (Blue Book, 1862, "North America, No. 5," p. 34).

can law has lent an ear to this doctrine, it has been pretty well exposed in the "Alexandra" law hearing, in a discussion over the "Estrella" case between Baron Bramwell and Sir Roundell Palmer, — the latter of whom stood up for Judge Livingston's opinion in that case as long as he could ("Alexandra" Law Hearing, p. 328, &c.). Sir Robert Phillimore says very tersely and very truly of this sort of balancing of wrongs, "that it may be *impartial*, but it certainly is not *neutral*" (3 Com. Int. Law, p. 221).

(*c*) That we should reconsider our cherished tenet of the right of a neutral to furnish arms and munitions of war to belligerents, and either restrict it within narrower limits, or else altogether repudiate it, and put such material of war upon the same footing as armed ships.

This, I am quite aware, will be considered nothing short of a revolutionary proposition, and one, perhaps, falling entirely within General Banks's condemnation of "criminally restraining the rights of nations at peace, for the benefit of those at war." Yet, though the proposition is in itself one entirely contradictory of our past doctrines and practice, I feel very sure that, the more it is considered, the more it will commend itself to the acceptance of the American legislator.

Of course I agree, that, under the code of nations, — at least as declared and adhered to by England and the United States, — it has become settled law, that a neutral is at liberty to furnish, and even *carry*, arms and munitions of war to a belligerent; taking his chance, by the way, of forfeiting his commercial adventure, by belligerent capture, for contraband of war. I agree, too, that a distinction has always of late been carefully drawn between munitions of war and ships of war, in the views of the two nations; and that, while arming and equipping the latter for belligerent service is held to be a breach of neutrality on the part of the nation permitting it, the furnishing of arms to belligerents only subjects the private trader to loss, and is not imputed as a public wrong to the trader's Government. I further agree, that no nation has been more strenuous than the United States in upholding these doctrines, from the day of Mr. Jefferson's announcing it in 1793 — when he declared to the

French minister, "that it is the constant occupation and livelihood of some of our citizens" "to make, vend, and export arms," and that "to suppress their calling," in this respect, "would be hard in principle and impossible in practice" — down to President Pierce's re-iteration of the same dogma in 1854, in his message to Congress of December of that year, in the part touching our relations with Russia during the Crimean War.

But, on the other hand, I must frankly confess that I find it hard to answer the arguments of Sir Robert Phillimore (brought forward by him in his Commentaries on International Law, vol. iii. p. 321), and more recently urged (from a different point of view) by Lord Palmerston, Chief-Baron Pollock, and numerous other prominent British statesmen and jurists, to show that it is hard to draw the line in principle between furnishing ships or munitions of war to belligerents, — I mean, in the point of view as to what Mr. Phillimore says the law *ought to be*, not as to what *it actually is*. So, again, when Sir Hugh Cairns, the late Attorney-General of England, asserts, as he did in his argument for the defendants in the "Alexandra" case (Law Hearing, p. 147), —

"that there is nothing whatever, that I am aware of, in the law of this country [England] to prevent a belligerent power having a manufactory of arms in any seaport of this kingdom, such as the Government of this country have at Woolwich, and making guns and small fire-arms and shot and shells on a large, extensive scale, and afterwards putting those guns on board a freighting ship, and sending them to a foreign port," —

I cannot but feel, that, if such is the law, it is quite superfluous to make such an ado about the heinousness of fitting out ships.

It is very true that Sir Roundell Palmer denied that this was a correct statement of *international* law ("Alexandra" Law Hearing, p. 301), though admitting it in effect to be true of *municipal legislation and jurisprudence;* but this denial was made with such qualifications of its not being so, "*as between Government and Government*," and with its being, at all events, remediable by executive interference, that one is forced to believe that Sir Hugh Cairns's assertion is mainly correct, as the matter now stands. Need I ask, then, — taking warning from the late experience of the Confederate rebellion, and its almost indefinite prolongation through the aid furnished our secessionists by British Enfield rifles and British Whitworth and even Armstrong (!) cannons, — whether it is worth our while to any longer advocate a doctrine of neutrality, fraught with such pernicious consequences to us as belligerents?

Of course, we could lay no blame at the door of England; for had not Mr. Jefferson said that such sort of unneutral proceedings " made the constant occupation and livelihood of some of our citizens," and had not the United-States Supreme Court solemnly affirmed in the " Santissima Trinidad " case, that " there is nothing in our laws, or in the law of nations, that forbids our citizens from sending armed vessels, as well as *munitions of war*, to foreign ports for sale. It is a commercial adventure which no nation is bound to prohibit, &c."?

With such recorded doctrines and practice as this, no wonder that Mr. Seward and Mr. Adams had great difficulty in getting up a show of remonstrance against British blockade-running and British arms-selling in aid of the rebellion! What a case would they not have had, if they could have pointed to a statute in permanency on the American statute-book, like that temporarily enacted by the United States in 1838 to meet the case of the McKenzie rebellion in Canada? I quote from the first and second sections of that statute (St. 1838, ch. 31, § 1 ; U.-S. Statutes at Large, vol. v. p. 212) : —

" *Be it enacted, &c.*, That the several collectors, naval officers, &c., of the United States, shall be, and they are hereby, respectively authorized and required to seize and detain *any vessel, or any arms or munitions of war*, which may be provided or prepared for any military expedition or enterprise against the territory or dominions of any foreign prince or state, or of any colony, district, or people conterminous with the United States, and with whom they are at peace . . . and retain possession of the same until the decision of the President be had thereon, or until the same shall be released as hereinafter directed.

" Sec. 2. *And be it further enacted*, That the several officers mentioned in the foregoing section shall be, and they are hereby, respectively authorized and required to seize *any vessel or vehicle, and all arms or munitions of war, about to pass the frontier of the United States for any place within any foreign state or colony, conterminous with the United States,* when the character of the vessel or vehicle, and the quantity of arms and munitions, or other circumstances, shall furnish probable cause to believe that the said vessel or vehicle, arms or munitions of war, are intended to be employed by the owner or owners thereof, or any other person or persons, with his or their privity, in carrying on any military expedition," &c. [as in sec. 1].

Unfortunately, this law expired, by its own limitation, in two years. Had it been in force in 1863, could Sir Hugh Cairns or the Crown lawyers have reproached this country with having no provision to prevent the establishment of that belligerent manufactory of arms, like the royal arsenal at Woolwich, upon which so many changes were rung at the "Alexandra" trial? May I not also justly appeal to this law — though now defunct and dead — for corroboration of my point, that impartial neutrality, as well as national expediency, demand of us to put arms and munitions of war into the same category with ships of war, or else *to draw the temper* out of those dogmas of Mr. Jefferson and Judge Story, from which we have suffered (and that not once only) such incalculable prejudice?

I will only add, that the re-enactment of this statute (or its substance in an amended form) seems exactly pertinent to the exigencies of the present moment in reference to the fulfilment of our neutral obligations towards Canada, and towards supplying to the Executive prerogative some powers which have perhaps been rather questionably exercised. But, in reference to our neutral duties towards foreign powers *beyond sea*, the right of interference with the export of arms by water would obviously call for an extended application of the principle of the law of 1838 beyond its original scope. [1]

---

[1] Perhaps I ought to notice, that sec. 2 of the act of 1838, above cited, has appended to it the following proviso: "*Provided*, that nothing in this act contained shall be construed to extend to, or interfere with, any trade in arms or munitions of war, conducted in vessels by sea, with any foreign port or place whatsoever, or with any other trade which might have been lawfully carried on before the

(*d*) That we should make our bonding clauses efficacious by taking away from them that reproach which Earl Russell has justly cast upon them, of being useless to stop such sort of expeditions as the " Alabama " and the " Alexandra."

I have already pointed out that these sections only apply to vessels about being sent out by *American owners*, and not *by foreign*. Why should not foreigners be bound as much to respect our neutrality as our own citizens?

In the next place, it has been shown that the obligation of the bond is only upon the owners, that *they* shall not employ their vessel in a belligerent service. Why should not the vessel itself give bonds that she will not become a fighting-ship, or go into belligerent use, during the continuance of the war with reference to which she is supposed to be fitting out? In 1849, we refused to allow the German war-vessel, the " United States," to go to sea, except upon the footing that her bond should cover the entire duration of any existing war in which the Germanic Confederation should then be engaged. Why should not this principle be extended to include all *successive owners during any given war?* [1]

In the third place, the second of these bonding clauses (§ 11) plainly ought to be freed of that stumbling-block to its efficiency, which makes the presence of a cargo on board, " which shall consist principally of arms and munitions of war," a pre-requisite to detention. Neither the " Alabama " nor the " Alexandra," for instance, proposed to take their respective

---

passage of this act, under the law of nations and the provisions of the act hereby amended."

When the enactment of the law was under discussion, at the time of its adoption in 1838, Hon. Edward Everett, then a member of the House of Representatives, moved to strike out this proviso, but unsuccessfully. The reasons for his motion are not reported. See " Congressional Globe " for March 2, 1838, and 13 Bent. Ab. Deb., p. 368. Possibly they were grounded upon the views above contended for.

[1] See particulars of this case, Ex. Doc. House Rep., 31st Cong. 1st sess. vol. iii. part 1, Doc. 5, p. 18. Contrary to what General Banks thinks of the character of these bonding clauses, Baron De Cussey — an able and highly respectable, certainly an entirely impartial, French writer on international law — says of this conduct of the American Government (in reference to this German war-vessel just mentioned), " It affords a genuine proof of respect for the obligations of neutrality " (De Cussey's " *Phases et Causes Célèbres,*" vol. ii. p. 407).

armaments as a part of their own cargoes. Ought their evasive attempt to circumvent the law be any the less prohibitable on that account?

So, too, this same section ought to be rid of another fatal drag upon the full enforcement of its spirit and purpose, which makes the detention of the vessel to hinge upon the intent of "*the owners*" to employ her in hostilities. If no such intent of the owners is essential to authorize the seizure and *condemnation for a forfeiture* of a vessel "fitting out to cruise," &c. (under sec. 7), why should such intent be any more insisted upon on the part of the owners, in a case of mere *preliminary detention?*

In the same sense, this section ought further to be relieved of the rider (in an earlier clause), *of the vessel being "manifestly built for warlike purposes."* What a loop-hole is there here for dispute! The "Alexandra," according to the claimant's case, might have been fitting up merely for a gentleman's yacht![1]

---

[1] But, on the other hand, in connection with this subject of requiring bonds of vessels suspected of an intended violation of neutrality, it ought to be noticed that there is a mode of exacting a *judicial* bond in the instance of a vessel seized on suspicion and under adjudication, which may operate with great hardship on an innocent ship-owner and which ought therefore to be provided against by legislation. I refer to a decision made by the United-States District Judge of New York, in March last, in the case of the "Meteor," in which Judge Betts refused to allow court bail to be received for the arrested vessel, preliminary to the hearing of her case upon its merits. The effect was, that a vessel alleged by her owners to be entirely innocent, and which, as was essentially admitted by the counsel for the Government, was prosecuted in order to call in question the repeated rulings of the Supreme Court in the "Santissima Trinidad" and similar cases, was detained for nearly four months awaiting adjudication, at an expense to her owners of upwards of $50,000, and then, at the end of this long detention, the Court (though condemning the vessel) finally accepted bail, and restored the "Meteor" to the provisional custody of her owners.

Now, either the principle or the practice covering such a point as this ought to have been observed. As to the practice, Mr. Evarts, for the claimants, asserted, that, "after a practice of many years in his honor's court, he must say that he had never heard the right of the claimant of a ship questioned to substitute a bond in admiralty cases on the instance side of the court, — never. In the case of slavers, the vessels so seized are always given up on bonds being substituted; and there is no right or power in the Court to prevent it, — none whatever; and no ingenuity can draw a distinction between the object and purposes of the Slave-trade Act and the Neutrality Act," &c. So the universality of the practice was

(*e*) That we should extend the powers of the Executive and its subordinate functionaries, towards enabling them to administer prompt preventive remedies for the preservation of neutrality.

At present, as my readers are well aware, the United States insist that they have proved their superior good faith in enforcing neutral duties, more than in any other particular, by not waiting to be armed with proof *sufficient to convict*, before moving, but in setting the machinery of the law in motion on a *prima-facie case of intended violation*. This practice, I fancy, however, has grown up rather from the good disposition of the American authorities to compel neutral rectitude, than from any intrinsic superiority of their legislation over that of the British in this particular.

My present suggestion is, that, if any increase of powers needs to be conferred upon the United-States collectors of customs, district attorneys, &c., so as to furnish a technical justification of that exercise of official authority which has been habitually practised in past cases of detention, like those of the "United States," the "Maury," &c., such increase should be amply extended. Care, however, should be taken — I would add — to protect private rights, which, in some of these instances, seem

---

asserted and proved in several contemporaneous newspaper discussions of the case, condemnatory of Judge Betts's ruling, particularly in an able editorial of the "New-York Times" of March 26.

As to the principle involved, it seems to have been a strange inconsistency in the learned judge to have insisted that the public security required the vessel's detention in the first instance, when presumed to be innocent; and, after being found guilty and declared forfeitable, to have been restored to her owners on the same footing as that on which her liberation was asked for in the first instance.

Plainly, if Judge Betts's law holds good, that the admiralty judge *has no discretion* to accept bail *in limine* for a vessel accused of an infraction of the neutrality laws, a more biting clause is put into those laws than any thing dreamed of in General Banks's complaints. It is only necessary for the Government to seize the vessel, and for the district judge to refuse her bail, to enable the executive authorities to stop any vessel or any naval expedition till the longest war of the present day shall be over, — I mean with the use of appeals, &c., on the Government's part, to the upper courts. Ought not legislation to provide some protection for private rights against the wrongs which may be inflicted under such a doctrine as that ruled in this case of the "Meteor"?

to have suffered through the inequality of a contest between the Government and the individual.

In the case of *Gelston* v. *Hoyt* (decided February, 1818, 3 Wheat. Rep., p. 246), the Collector of New-York was cast in damages to the extent of $107,000, for making a seizure under the neutrality laws, which he could have proved if the evidence had been considered competent by the Court, was made by express orders of the President and the Secretary of the Treasury, and in good faith. Ought there not to be some further legislative sanction of a preliminary temporary detention of the suspected vessel, *for the purposes of examination*, short of the casting of the legal die, so as to render the collector, or other functionary, liable *in solido*, for the full value of the property detained?

Ought there not, further, — in view of the humiliating attitude in which the British Government was obliged to show itself in trafficking with the Lairds to buy off their rams, instead of daring to meet them in open court on the question of damages for tort, — ought there not to be, I ask, a provision authorizing the sequestration of any suspected vessel, — suspected of intending an infraction of neutrality, — so as to enable the Government to take it into its own custody, on an appraised valuation? We have plenty of laws now, by which private property is sequestrable to the public use, on paying compensatory damages; and can there be a better application of the principle of such laws, than to save a country from war by interfering with the private gains of such a private-war maker as John Laird? Suppose the Government *have* to pay a few thousands more than the value of "the vessel manifestly built for warlike purposes," — is not that a thousand times better than being forced into a general war by such an enterprising mischief-maker, or than having to pay the bill, in the long-run, for the consequences of his cupidity and love of strife?

(*f*) Adopt a provision giving the Government *pecuniary redress* against the citizen who renders the State liable to foreign powers for infractions of neutrality.

Possibly, had John Laird supposed that he was going to be ultimately vouched in by the British Government to respond to the claim of the United States for damages done to their commerce through his means, he would not have been quite so active in forwarding the creation of the Confederate navy. But is it not just that one who is ready to involve his own Government in war for his private gains, should respond out of those gains, as far as they will go, towards compensating for the injuries of his causing?[1]

(*g*) Take away from the forum of trial by jury all issues arising out of the enforcement of the neutrality laws, unless indictable offences, or involving personal punishment, and commit them to the admiralty jurisdiction.

How obviously improper, that the proceedings of a jury-trial should regulate the public relations of great nations! Ought issues like that in the "Alexandra" case, for instance, to depend upon the unanimous consent of twelve ordinary jurors, and then be subjected to the delays incident to the revision of the jury's verdict by the full Bench, or appellate Court, before the Executive of a nation can answer the demands of a foreign Government for neutral protection? Plainly, the function of a jury is municipal and administrative, and not international and political. As well submit the question of Jefferson Davis's right to organize revolution on the principles of State sovereignty, and whether, on the whole, he was not justifiable in waging civil war against the Union, to such a tribunal, as to lay before a jury the expediency or justifiableness of seizing a ship fitting out for war against the remonstrances of a foreign power! I mean in this latter case, where prevention, and not punishment, is the object proposed.

Who, that remembers the danger into which our foreign relations with England were drawn by the New-York State courts taking jurisdiction of the McLeod case in 1858, and by their submitting the question of his criminal liability for murder to a State jury, can doubt that the function of a jury is sometimes misapplied, when employed to administer a purely executive and political function?

---

[1] Mr. Grosvenor P. Lowrey has argued, with no little ability and ingenuity, in a pamphlet published in New York at as early a day of the rebellion as March, 1863, and entitled "English Neutrality: Is the 'Alabama' a British pirate?" that England ought to answer for the doings of the "Alabama" as authorized piracy.

Besides, if jurors are impartial as to private contentions, are they likely to be as much so, where national antipathies come into play, as the admiralty judge, who constantly decides with the responsibility of peace or war resting upon his shoulders?

(*h*) Codify the doctrine of American law, that no vessel built and equipped, or that has augmented its equipment (being already a ship of war), in violation of neutrality, shall be entitled to the hospitality of American ports, or shall receive provisions, fuel, or supplies of any sort, from American territory.

(*i*) So far define the status of a ship of war, as to deny recognition of that character to any vessel built or equipped in violation of neutrality, which has never touched the home territory of the power to which it professes to belong, or which has never been duly incorporated into the naval marine of a maritime power.

(*j*) Codify what is now, or what will surely become, a principle of the law of nations, that hospitality must be withheld from belligerent cruisers which plunder and burn their prizes at sea, without bringing them into the home port for adjudication; and further enact, that where such plundering and burning is practised against the peaceful and industrious " toilers of the sea," — the whalers and fishermen, — it shall constitute the offence of piracy, punishable in the courts of a neutral nation.

(*k*) Perfect the machinery of the law for restoring prizes captured in our waters, in violation of territorial sovereignty (§ 7, already commented on); and, under the same head, codify the established jurisprudence of the United-States courts affording a *judicial* restitution of the prize, when captured on the high seas, if brought again within United-States territory or control.

Doubtless many other points of improvement upon the existing neutrality laws might be added to the above, of equal or perhaps greater importance. I by no means pretend to have surveyed the whole ground with comprehensive and sagacious political wisdom, nor to have even arranged and distributed with scientific accuracy the detailed particulars which have been above brought forward. My object has been rather to indicate *the direction* in which movement should be made, not its amount.

For, after all, the question recurs, whether we are ready to go forward at all, not how fast or how far at present. Can it be, that, smarting under the sense of supposed recent injuries, we are willing to throw away the rich inheritance of our fathers, and voluntarily make shipwreck of our national fame? Can it be, that, proclaiming ourselves "a Government of laws and not of men," we are yet willing to declare our renunciation of obedience to the law of nations and natural justice, and announce that we have taken our stand with the Algerines of former days, professing to live hereafter under the law of might making right? Can it be, that, while professing to be an industrial and a commercial people, who reject the burdens and dangers of great standing armaments, and who rejoice that they are free from the complications of European connections, we shall yet proclaim ourselves ready to take the sword at any moment, as the arbiter of international justice, and play the part of international bullies and blusterers? Can it be, that, when Divine Providence has so plainly demonstrated to us, in our national growth and prosperity, that the ways of neutral equity and honesty, like those of wisdom, "are ways of pleasantness, and all her paths peace," we shall voluntarily refuse to accept the lesson, and put our trust in force rather than in the goodness of our cause?

In my judgment, national honor, national consistency, and national expediency, alike point to one and the same direction for our movement; and need I say that that direction is *forwards*, towards the advancement of civilization, *and not backwards*, towards the restoration of freebootery and savage warfare? Supposing that nations, like individuals, are not accountable to a higher law, is there not enough here to influence our conduct, on the score of the lower considerations of human expediency, and on the footing that we are simply seeking our own good?

But if there *is* a higher law, which proclaims that no *nation* "liveth to itself," as well as that "no *man* liveth to himself," can we reject the obvious prompting of the advanced opinion of the day, that we ought to do our part towards helping the whole family of nations adopt the law of natural equity and international justice? — that, " as far as in us lies, we should live at peace with all men," ourselves, and recommend to other nations the advantages of a national policy founded on principles which conduce to that end?

As citizens of a republic, we boast the possession of the best form of government extant. Are we not bound, by the possession of that privilege (if our boast is true), to prove to the world that a republic can conduct its foreign relations as commendably as its domestic? And if we have succeeded in this latter respect, in times past, to the general approval of the nations, as I hope my imperfect historical survey has in part demonstrated, shall we prejudice the cause of republicanism, henceforth, by changing our policy with our growing strength, and thereby admit that we were virtuous only because we were poor, and beginning life as a nation?

But we cannot consent to travel the same road (we say) with our English rivals and antagonists. Let me ask, if we have any friends or neighbors so near to us in the family of nations, politically, legislatively, or juridically, as the English? Are not the pursuits of peaceful industry, the development of material prosperity, the enlargement of the field of law and order, and the adherence as far as possible to the doctrines of non-intervention and neutral reserve and impartiality, the commonly distinguishing features of the two Governments? Are we not both great commercial nations, with a merchant marine far exceeding any naval armaments that we possess or intend to create, and therefore bound to cherish and extend the prerogatives of peaceful commerce? While we are each peculiarly suited to do each other harm by our extended line of seacoast and numerous harbors, by our capability of fitting out hasty expeditions, and by our having at command all the appliances of modern science to move quickly and act destructively at any given point, are we not, at the same time, peculiarly fitted to help each other along in maintaining the peace and security of the industrial world by our moral influence and reserved force?

What cannot the united English and American interests effect, for instance, in dealing with the great (so-called) semi-barbarous nations of Eastern Asia, — the Chinese and Japanese?

What weight cannot England and the United States give to their united declaration, in the face of (the so-salled) more civilized Europe, upon any point of internatioanl law or practice? What single nation, or combination even of the nations of the world, could resist their united navies, if they made common cause in enforcing a just code of the rights of commercial powers, with an ultimate appeal to hostilities in case of rejection?

To my apprehension, the United States have the same common interest with England in the prevalence of such a neutral code as I have above indicated, that caravans of travelling merchants in the Eastern deserts have in keeping each other comcompany through the savage districts. "In union there is strength;" and this is so true, that, if the numbers and moral force of the travellers are sufficient, there need be no occasion for the employment of arms at all. Let the other powers of Europe or the world be as belligerent as they may, they cannot resist the united moral force of England and the United States in accord upon any great principle.

But perhaps it is a reflection upon the other powers of Europe (saving, it may be, France, which cannot willingly forego its struggle for equality on the seas, and whose tonnage of warships almost equals its foreign commerce) to speak of those powers as belligerent or probably belligerent. They are, from their very condition and situation, inclined to the side of peace and upholders of neutral rights. Therefore the united voice of this country and England would have no opposing obstacle, if once declared outspokenly in favor of progressive civilization. And France, which I have seemingly excepted as normally antagonistic to England, will surely be found on the side of neutral commerce, for whose rights she has always contended.

But whether England follows suit or not to our example, or whether she will voluntarily put herself into such an attitude that we can consent to legislate in common or not, let *us*, at any rate, do the right thing, and the consistent thing, and the expedient thing, of our own independent motion. It may be that England *will* follow suit. I believe, that, with the enlarged and liberal-minded views taken of her best interests by her leading statesmen, she will not only imitate our improvements, but go beyond them, as she did in 1819. If so, so much the better. If not, we must perhaps wait for time to vindicate the expediency of keeping our integrity. But I cannot believe, that, in the rapid movement of the world's affairs at the present moment, that day of vindication will be far distant; or that, when it comes, we shall fail of being amply rewarded for keeping the faith first delivered us by the fathers of the republic.

I need hardly add, in reference to the congressional measure which has occupied so large a portion of my disquisition, that I trust it will neither become a law in its present shape, nor with any amendments whatsoever to better its efficiency, *in the same spirit;* but that, Congress, taking the present occasion to re-affirm their adherence to the traditions of Washington and the founders of the Government, will go on to advance and perpetuate (as far as may be) their principles, as one of the great works urgently demanded of them by modern civilization.

APPENDIX.

I.

THE NEUTRALITY ACT OF THE UNITED STATES.

Statute of 1818, chap. 88, United-States Statutes at large (Little & Brown ed.), vol. iii. p. 447.

[N.B. — The references to the statutes in the margin, added by the writer, are intended to show the original of the present law. The present statute is also referred to where it has at all varied the language of previous laws. The use of brackets — thus, [ ] — in the body of the statute, is to show the amount of departure (in general) from Hamilton's act of 1794, c. 50.]

An Act in addition to the "Act for the punishment of certain crimes against the United States," and to repeal the Acts therein mentioned. [*April* 20, 1818.]

That if any citizen of the United States shall, within the territory or jurisdiction thereof, accept and exercise a commission to serve a foreign prince, state, [colony, district, or people] in war, by land or by sea, against any prince, state, [colony, district, or people] with whom the United States are at peace, the person so offending shall be deemed guilty of a high misdemeanor, and shall be fined not more than two thousand dollars, and shall be imprisoned not exceeding three years. *[margin: Fine $2,000 and imprisonment for citizens accepting commissions within the United States, &c. to serve foreign states.]*

Sec. 2. That if any person shall, within the territory or jurisdiction of the United States, enlist or enter himself, or hire or retain another person to enlist or enter himself, or to go beyond the limits or jurisdiction of the United States with intent to be enlisted or entered in the service of any foreign prince, state, [colony, district, or people,] as a soldier, or as a marine or seaman, on board of any vessel of war, letter of marque, or privateer, every person so offending shall be deemed guilty of a high misdemeanor, and shall be fined not exceeding one thousand dollars, and be imprisoned not exceeding three years : Provided that this Act shall not be construed to extend to any subject or *[margin: For any person in the United States enlisting others, &c. to serve a foreign state, &c. 1794, c. 50, § 2. 1818, c. 88.]*

citizen of any foreign prince, state, [colony, district, or people,] who shall transiently be within the United States, and shall on board of any vessel of war, letter of marque, or privateer, which, at the time of its arrival within the United States, was fitted and equipped as such, enlist or enter himself, or hire or retain another subject or citizen of the same foreign prince, state, [colony, district, or people,] who is transiently within the United States, to enlist or enter himself to serve such foreign prince, state, [colony, district, or people,] on board such vessel of war, letter of marque, or privateer, if the United States shall then be at peace with such foreign prince, state, [colony, district, or people.]

<small>Fitting out or attempting to fit out.
1794, c. 50, § 3.
1817, c. 59, § 1.
1818, c. 88.</small>

Sec. 3. That if any person shall within the limits of the United States fit out and arm, or attempt to fit out and arm, or procure to be fitted out and armed, or shall knowingly be concerned in the furnishing, fitting out, or arming of any ship or vessel with intent that such ship or vessel shall be employed in the service of any foreign prince or state, [or of any colony, district, or people,] to cruize or commit hostilities against the subjects, citizens, or property of any foreign prince or state, [or of any colony, district, or people,] with whom the United States are at peace, or shall issue or deliver a commission within the territory or jurisdiction of the United States for any ship or vessel, to the intent that she may be employed as aforesaid, every person so offending shall be deemed guilty of a high misdemeanor, and shall be fined not more than [ten] thousand dollars, and imprisoned not more

<small>The vessel, &c. forfeited.</small>

than three years; and every such ship or vessel, with her tackle, apparel, and furniture, together with all materials, arms, ammunition, and stores, which may have been procured for the building and equip-

<small>Half to the informer.</small>

ment thereof, shall be forfeited, one-half to the use of the informer, and the other half to the use of the United States.

<small>For citizens fitting out or arming, &c., or aiding.
1797, c. 1.
1818, c. 88.</small>

Sec. 4. That if any citizen or citizens of the United States shall, without the limits thereof, fit out and arm, or attempt to fit out and arm, or procure to be fitted out and armed, or shall knowingly aid or be concerned in the furnishing, fitting out, or arming, any private ship or vessel of war, or privateer, with intent that such ship or vessel shall be employed to cruize or commit hostilities upon the citizens of the United States, or their property, or shall take the command of, or enter on board of any such ship or vessel for the intent aforesaid, or shall purchase any interest in any such ship or vessel, with a view to share in the profits thereof, such person so offending shall be deemed guilty of a high misdemeanor, and fined not more than ten thousand

<small>To be tried where apprehended or first brought.</small>

dollars, and imprisoned not more than ten years; and the trial for such offence, if committed without the limits of the United States, shall be in the district in which the offender shall be apprehended or first brought.

Sec. 5. That if any person shall, within the territory or jurisdiction of the United States, increase or augment, or procure to be increased or augmented, or shall knowingly be concerned in increasing or augmenting the force of any ship of war, cruizer, or other armed vessel, which, at the time of her arrival within the United States, was a ship of war, or cruizer, or armed vessel, in the service of any foreign prince, or state, [or of any colony, district, or people,] or belonging to the subjects or citizens of any such prince, or state, [colony, district, or people,] the same being at war with any foreign prince or state, or of any [colony, district, or people] with whom the United States are at peace, by adding to the number of the guns of such vessel, or by changing those on board of her for guns of a larger calibre, or by the addition thereto of any equipment solely applicable to war, every person so offending shall be deemed guilty of a high misdemeanor, shall be fined not more than one thousand dollars, and be imprisoned not more than one year. *Augmenting in the United States the force of foreign-armed vessels. 1794, c. 50, § 4. 1817, c. 59, § 4. 1818, c. 88.*

Sec. 6. That if any person shall, within the territory or jurisdiction of the United States, begin or set on foot, or provide or prepare the means for, any military expedition or enterprise, to be carried on from thence against the territory or dominions of any foreign prince or state, [or of any colony, district, or people] with whom the United States are (at) peace, every person so offending shall be deemed guilty of a high misdemeanor, and shall be fined not exceeding three thousand dollars, and imprisoned not more than three years. *Setting on foot within the United States any military expedition against a friendly power. 1794, c. 50, § 5. 1818, c. 88.*

Sec. 7. That the District Courts shall take cognizance of complaints, by whomsoever instituted, in cases of captures made within the waters of the United States or within a marine league of the coasts or shores thereof. *District Courts to have cognizance of. 1794, c. 50, § 6.*

Sec. 8. That in every case in which a vessel shall be fitted out and armed, or attempted to be fitted out and armed, or in which the force of any vessel of war, cruizer, or other armed vessel shall be increased or augmented, or in which any military expedition or enterprise shall be begun or set on foot, contrary to the provisions and prohibitions of this Act; and in every case of the capture of a ship or vessel within the jurisdiction or protection of the United States as before defined, and in every case in which any process issuing out of any Court of the United States shall be disobeyed or resisted by any person or persons having the custody of any vessel of war, cruizer, or other armed vessel of any foreign prince or state, [or of any colony, district, or people,] or of any subjects or citizens of any foreign prince or state, [or of any colo- *The President may employ the forces or the militia for suppressing such expeditions. 1794, c. 50, § 7. 1818, c. 88.*

ny, district, or people,] in every such case it shall be lawful for the President of the United States, or such other person as he shall have empowered for that purpose, to employ such part of the land or naval forces of the United States, or of the militia thereof, for the purpose of taking possession of and detaining any such ship or vessel, with her prize or prizes, if any, in order to the execution of the prohibitions and penalties of this Act, and to the restoring the prize or prizes in the cases in which restoration shall have been adjudged, and also for the purpose of preventing the carrying on of any such expedition or enterprise from the territories or jurisdiction of the United States against the territories or dominions of any foreign prince or state, [or of any colony, district, or people] with whom the United States are at peace.

<small>May employ the forces or the militia to compel the departure of vessels.
1794, c. 50, § 8.</small>

Sec. 9. That it shall be lawful for the President of the United States, or such person as he shall empower for that purpose, to employ such part of the land or naval forces of the United States, or of the militia thereof, as shall be necessary to compel any foreign ship or vessel to depart the United States in all cases in which, by the laws of nations or the treaties of the United States, they ought not to remain within the United States.

<small>Owners, &c. of armed vessels sailing to give bond not to commit hostilities, &c.
1817, c. 59, § 2.
1818, c. 88.</small>

Sec. 10. That the owners or consignees of every armed ship, or vessel sailing out of the ports of the United States, belonging wholly or in part to citizens thereof, shall enter into bond to the United States, with sufficient sureties, prior to clearing out the same, in double the amount of the value of the vessel and cargo on board, including her armament, that the said ship or vessel shall not be employed by such owners to cruize or commit hostilities against the subjects, citizens, or property of any foreign province or state, or of any colony, district, or people with whom the United States are at peace.

<small>Collectors to detain vessels built for warlike purposes and about to depart when probably they are intended against a friendly power.
1817, c. 59, § 2.
1818, c. 88.</small>

Sec. 11. That the collectors of the customs be, and they are hereby, respectively, authorized and required to detain any vessel manifestly built for warlike purposes, and about to depart the United States, of which the cargo shall principally consist of arms and munitions of war, when the number of men shipped on board, or other circumstances, shall render it probable that such vessel is intended to be employed by the owner or owners to cruize or commit hostilities upon the subjects, citizens, or property of any foreign prince or state, or of any colony, district, or people with whom the United States are at peace, until the decision of the President be had thereon, or until the owner or owners shall give such bond and security as is required of the owners of armed ships by the preceding section of this Act.

Sec. 12. That the Act passed on the 5th day of June 1794, entitled

"An Act in addition to the Act for the Punishment of certain Crimes against the United States," continued in force, for a limited time, by the Act of the 2d of March 1797, and perpetuated by the Act passed on the 24th of April 1800, and the Act passed on the 14th day of June 1797, entitled "An Act to prevent Citizens of the United States from privateering against Nations in Amity with, or against the Citizens of, the United States," and the Act passed the 3rd day of March 1817, entitled "An Act more effectually to preserve the neutral Relations of the United States," be and the same are hereby severally repealed: *Provided, nevertheless*, that persons having heretofore offended against any of the Acts aforesaid may be prosecuted, convicted, and punished as if the same were not repealed; and no forfeiture heretofore incurred by a violation of any of the Acts aforesaid shall be affected by such repeal. 5 June 1794, c. 50; 14 June 1797, c. 1; 24 April 1800, c. 35, and 3 March 1817, c. 58. repealed.

Sec. 13. That nothing in the foregoing Act shall be construed to prevent the prosecution or punishment of treason, or any piracy defined by the laws of the United States. Not to prevent the punishment of treason, &c. 1794, c. 50, § 9. 1818, c. 88.

II.

THE BRITISH FOREIGN-ENLISTMENT ACT.

An Act to prevent the Enlisting or Engagement of His Majesty's Subjects to serve in Foreign Service, and the fitting out or equipping, in His Majesty's Dominions, Vessels for warlike Purposes, without His Majesty's Licence.   [3d *July* 1819.]

Whereas the enlistment or engagement of His Majesty's subjects to serve in war in foreign service, without His Majesty's licence, and the fitting out and equipping and arming of vessels by His Majesty's subjects, without His Majesty's licence, for warlike operations in or against the dominions or territories of any foreign prince, state, potentate, or persons exercising or assuming to exercise the powers of government in or over any foreign country, colony, province, or part of any province, or against the ships, goods, or merchandise of any foreign prince, state, potentate, or persons as aforesaid, or their subjects, may be prejudicial to and tend to endanger the peace and welfare of this kingdom: And whereas the laws in force are not sufficiently effectual for preventing the same: Be it therefore enacted by the King's most excellent Majesty, by and with the advice and consent of the Lords spiritual and temporal, and Commons, in this present Parliament assembled, and by the authority of the same, that from and after the passing of this Act, an Act passed in the ninth year of the reign of His late Majesty King George the Second, intituled " An Act to prevent the listing His Majesty's subjects to serve as soldiers without His Majesty's licence ;" and also an Act passed in the twenty-ninth year of the reign of His said late Majesty King George the Second, intituled " An Act to prevent His Majesty's subjects from serving as Officers under the French King; and for better enforcing an Act passed in the Ninth Year of His present Majesty's Reign, to prevent the enlisting His Majesty's Subjects to serve as Soldiers without His Majesty's Licence ; and for obliging such of His Majesty's Subjects as shall accept Commissions in the Scotch Brigade in the Service of the States General of the United Provinces, to take the Oaths of Allegiance and Abjuration ; " and also an Act passed in Ireland in the eleventh year of the reign of His said late Majesty King George the Second, intituled " An Act for the more effectual preventing the enlisting of His Majesty's Subjects to serve as Soldiers in Foreign Service without His Majesty's Licence ; " and also an Act passed in Ireland in the nineteenth year of the reign His of said late Majesty King George the Second, intituled " An Act for the more effectual preventing His Majesty's subjects from entering into Foreign Service, and for publishing an Act of the Seventh Year of King William the Third, intituled ' An Act to prevent Foreign Education ; ' " and all and every the clauses and provisions in the said several Acts contained, shall be and the same are hereby repealed.

<mark>9 G. 2. c. 30.</mark>
<mark>29 G. 2. c. 17.</mark>
<mark>Irish Act, 11 G. 2.</mark>
<mark>Irish Act, 19 G. 2.</mark>
<mark>Recited Acts repealed.</mark>

<mark>Subjects enlisting or engaging to enlist or serve in foreign service, military or naval, guilty of misdemeanor.</mark>
2. And be it further declared and enacted, that if any natural-born subject of His Majesty, His heirs and successors, without the leave or licence of His Majesty, His heirs or successors, for that purpose first had and obtained, under the sign manual of His Majesty, His heirs or successors, or signified by Order in Council, or by proclamation of His Majesty, His heirs or successors, shall take or accept, or shall agree to take or accept, any military commission, or shall otherwise enter into the military service as a commissioned or non-commissioned officer, or shall enlist or enter himself to enlist, or shall agree to enlist or to enter himself to serve as a soldier, or to be employed or shall serve in any warlike or military operation, in the service of or for or under or in aid of any foreign prince, state, potentate, colony, province, or part of any province or people, or of any person or persons exercising or assuming to exercise the powers of government in or over any foreign country, colony, province, or part of any province or people, either as an officer or soldier, or in any other military capacity; or if any natural-born subject of His Majesty shall, without such leave or licence as aforesaid, accept, or agree to take or accept, any commission, warrant, or appointment as an officer, or shall enlist or enter himself, or shall agree to

enlist or enter himself, to serve as a sailor or marine, or to be employed or engaged, or shall serve in and on board any ship or vessel of war, or in and on board any ship or vessel used or fitted out, or equipped or intended to be used for any warlike purpose, in the service of or for or under or in aid of any foreign power, prince, state, potentate, colony, province, or part of any province or people, or of any person or persons exercising or assuming to exercise the powers of government in or over any foreign country, colony, province, or part of any province or people; or if any natural-born subject of His Majesty shall, without such leave and licence as aforesaid, engage, contract, or agree to go, or shall go to any foreign state, country, colony, province, or part of any province, or to any place beyond the seas, with an intent or in order to enlist or enter himself to serve, or with intent to serve in any warlike or military operation whatever, whether by land or by sea, in the service of or for or under or in aid of any foreign prince, state, potentate, colony, province, or part of any province or people, or in the service of or for or under or in aid of any person or persons exercising or assuming to exercise the powers of government in or over any foreign country, colony, province, or part of any province or people, either as an officer or a soldier, or in any other military capacity, or as an officer or sailor, or marine, in any such ship or vessel as aforesaid, although no enlisting money or pay or reward shall have been or shall be in any or either of the cases aforesaid actually paid to or received by him, or by any person to or for his use or benefit; or if any person whatever, within the United Kingdom of Great Britain and Ireland, or in any part of His Majesty's dominions elsewhere, or in any country, colony, settlement, island, or place belonging to or subject to His Majesty, shall hire, retain, engage, or procure, or shall attempt or endeavour to hire, retain, engage, or procure, any person or persons whatever to enlist, or to enter or engage to enlist, or to serve or to be employed in any such service or employment as aforesaid, as an officer, soldier, sailor, or marine, either in land or sea service, for or under or in aid of any foreign prince, state, potentate, colony, province, or part of any province or people, or for or under or in aid of any person or persons exercising or assuming to exercise any powers of government as aforesaid, or to go or to agree to go or embark from any part of His Majesty's dominions, for the purpose or with intent to be so enlisted, entered, engaged, or employed as aforesaid, whether any enlisting money, pay, or reward shall have been or shall be actually given or received, or not; in any or either of such cases, every person so offending shall be deemed guilty of a misdemeanor, and upon being convicted thereof, upon any information or indictment, shall be punishable by fine and imprisonment, or either of

All persons retaining or procuring others to enlist, guilty of the like offence.

them, at the discretion of the court before which such offender shall be convicted.

<small>Act not to extend to persons enlisted or serving before the times herein specified.</small>

3. Provided always, and be it enacted, that nothing in this Act contained shall extend or be construed to extend to render any person or persons liable to any punishment or penalty under this Act, who at any time before the first day of August one thousand eight hundred and nineteen, within any part of the United Kingdom, or of the Islands of Jersey, Guernsey, Alderney, or Sark, or at any time before the first day of November one thousand eight hundred and nineteen, in any part or place out of the United Kingdom, or of the said Islands, shall have taken or accepted, or agreed to take or accept any military commission, or shall have otherwise enlisted into any military service as a commissioned or non-commissioned officer, or shall have enlisted, or entered himself to enlist, or shall have agreed to enlist or to enter himself to serve as a soldier, or shall have served, or having so served shall, after the said first day of August one thousand eight hundred and nineteen, continue to serve in any warlike or military operation, either as an officer or soldier, or in any other military capacity, or shall have accepted, or agreed to take or accept any commission, warrant, or appointment as an officer, or shall have enlisted or entered himself to serve, or shall have served, or having so served shall continue to serve as a sailor, or marine, or shall have been employed or engaged, or shall have served, or having so served shall, after the said first day of August, continue to serve in and on board any ship or vessel of war, used or fitted out, or equipped or intended for any warlike purpose; or shall have engaged, or contracted or agreed to go, or shall have gone to, or having so gone to shall, after the said first day of August, continue in any foreign state, country, colony, province, or part of a province, or to or in any place beyond the seas, unless such person or persons shall embark at or proceed from some port or place within the United Kingdom or the Islands of Jersey, Guernsey, Alderney, or Sark, with intent to serve as an officer, soldier, sailor, or marine, contrary to the provisions of this Act, after the said first day of August, or shall embark or proceed from some port or place out of the United Kingdom, or the Islands of Jersey, Guernsey, Alderney, or Sark, with such intent as aforesaid, after the said first day of November, or who shall, before the passing of this Act, and within the said United Kingdom, or the said Islands, or before the first day of November one thousand eight hundred and nineteen, in any port or place out of the said United Kingdom, or the said Islands, have hired, retained, engaged, or procured, or attempted or endeavoured to hire, retain, engage, or procure any person or persons whatever, to enlist or to enter, or to engage to list or to serve, or to be employed in any such

THE BRITISH FOREIGN-ENLISTMENT ACT. 199

service or employment as aforesaid, as an officer, soldier, sailor, or marine, either in land or sea service, or to go, or agree to go or embark for the purpose or with the intent to be so enlisted, entered, or engaged, or employed, contrary to the prohibitions respectively in this Act contained, anything in this Act contained to the contrary in anywise notwithstanding; but that all and every such persons and person shall be in such state and condition, and no other, and shall be liable to such fines, penalties, forfeitures, and disabilities, and none other, as such person or persons was or were liable and subject to before the passing of this Act, and as such person or persons would have been in, and been liable and subject to, in case this Act and the said recited Acts by this Act repealed had not been passed or made.

4. And be it further enacted, that it shall and may be lawful for any justice of the peace residing at or near to any port or place within the United Kingdom of Great Britain and Ireland, where any offence made punishable by this Act as a misdemeanor shall be committed, on information on oath of any such offence, to issue his warrant for the apprehension of the offender, and to cause him to be brought before such justice, or any justice of the peace; and it shall be lawful for the justice of the peace before whom such offender shall be brought, to examine into the nature of the offence upon oath, and to commit such person to gaol, there to remain until delivered by due course of law, unless such offender shall give bail, to the satisfaction of the said justice, to appear and answer to any information or indictment to be preferred against him, according to law, for the said offence; and that all such offences which shall be committed within that part of the United Kingdom called England, shall and may be proceeded and tried in His Majesty's Court of King's Bench at Westminster, and the venue in such case laid at Westminster, or at the assizes or session of Oyer and Terminer and gaol delivery, or at any quarter or general sessions of the peace in and for the county or place where such offence was committed; and that all such offences which shall be committed within that part of the United Kingdom called Ireland, shall and may be prosecuted in His Majesty's Court of King's Bench at Dublin, and the venue be laid at Dublin, or at any assizes or session of Oyer and Terminer and gaol delivery, or at any quarter or general sessions of the peace in and for the county or place where such offence was committed; and all such offences as shall be committed in Scotland, shall and may be prosecuted in the Court of Justiciary in Scotland, or any other Court competent to try criminal offences committed within the county, shire, or stewartry within which such offence was committed; and where any offence made punishable by this Act as a misdemeanor shall be committed out of the

Justices to issue warrants for the apprehension of offenders.

Where offences shall be tried.

said United Kingdom, it shall be lawful for any justice of the peace residing near to the port or place where such offence shall be committed, on information on oath of any such offence, to issue his warrant for the apprehension of the offender, and to cause him to be brought before such justice, or any other justice of the peace for such place; and it shall be lawful for the justice of the peace before whom such offender shall be brought, to examine into the nature of the offence upon oath, and to commit such person to gaol, there to remain till delivered by due course of law, or otherwise to hold such offender to bail to answer for such offence in the Superior Court competent to try and having jurisdiction to try criminal offences committed in such port or place; and all such offences committed at any place out of the said United Kingdom shall and may be prosecuted and tried in any Superior Court of His Majesty's dominions competent to try and having jurisdiction to try criminal offences committed at the place where such offence shall be committed.

<small>Vessels with persons on board engaged in foreign service may be detained at any port in His Majesty's dominions.</small>

5. And be it further enacted, that in case any ship or vessel in any port or place within His Majesty's dominions shall have on board any such person or persons who shall have been enlisted or entered to serve, or shall have engaged or agreed or been procured to enlist or enter or serve, or who shall be departing from His Majesty's dominions for the purpose and with the intent of enlisting or entering to serve, or to be employed, or of serving or being engaged or employed in the service of any foreign prince, state, or potentate, colony, province, or part of any province or people, or of any person or persons exercising or assuming to exercise the powers of government in or over any foreign colony, province, or part of any province or people, either as an officer, soldier, sailor, or marine, contrary to the provisions of this Act, it shall be lawful for any of the principal officers of His Majesty's customs, where any such officers of the customs shall be, and in any part of His Majesty's dominions in which there are no officers of His Majesty's customs, for any governor or persons having the chief civil command, upon information or oath given before them respectively, which oath they are hereby respectively authorized and empowered to administer, that such person or persons as aforesaid is or are on board such ship or vessel, to detain and prevent any such ship or vessel, or to cause such ship or vessel to be detained and prevented from proceeding to sea on her voyage with such persons as aforesaid on board: Provided, nevertheless, that no principal officer, governor, or person shall act as aforesaid, upon such information upon oath as aforesaid, unless the party so informing shall not only have deposed in such information that the person or persons on board such ship or vessel hath or have been enlisted or entered to serve, or hath or have engaged or agreed or been procured to

<small>Oath to be made as to facts and circumstances.</small>

enlist or enter or serve, or is or are departing as aforesaid, for the purpose and with the intent of enlisting or entering to serve or to be employed, or of serving, or being engaged or employed in such service as aforesaid, but shall also have set forth in such information upon oath the facts or circumstances upon which he forms his knowledge or belief, enabling him to give such information upon oath; and that all and every person and persons convicted of wilfully false swearing in any such information upon oath shall be deemed guilty of and suffer the penalties on persons convicted of wilful and corrupt perjury.

6. And be it further enacted, that if any master or other person having or taking the charge or command of any ship or vessel, in any part of the United Kingdom of Great Britain and Ireland, or in any part of His Majesty's dominions beyond the seas, shall knowingly and willingly take on board, or if such master or other person having the command of any such ship or vessel, or any owner or owners of any such ship or vessel, shall knowingly engage to take on board any person or persons who shall have been enlisted or entered to serve, or shall have engaged or agreed or been procured to enlist or enter or serve, or who shall be departing from His Majesty's dominions for the purpose and with the intent of enlisting or entering to serve, or to be employed, or of serving, or being engaged or employed in any naval or military service, contrary to the provisions of this Act, such master or owner or other person as aforesaid shall forfeit and pay the sum of fifty pounds for each and every such person so taken or engaged to be taken on board; and moreover every such ship or vessel, so having on board, conveying, carrying, or transporting any such person or persons, shall and may be seized and detained by the collector, comptroller, surveyor, or other officer of the customs, until such penalty or penalties shall be satisfied and paid, or until such master or person, or the owner or owners of such ship or vessel, shall give good and sufficient bail, by recognizance before one of His Majesty's justices of the peace, for the payment of such penalty or penalties. *Penalty on masters of ships, &c. taking on board persons enlisted contrary to this Act, 50l. for each person.*

7. And be it further enacted, that if any person, within any part of the United Kingdom, or in any part of His Majesty's dominions beyond the seas, shall, without the leave and licence of His Majesty for that purpose first had and obtained as aforesaid, equip, furnish, fit out, or arm, or attempt or endeavour to equip, furnish, fit out, or arm, or procure to be equipped, furnished, fitted out, or armed, or shall knowingly aid, assist, or be concerned in the equipping, furnishing, fitting out, or arming of any ship or vessel, with intent or in order that such ship or vessel shall be employed in the service of any foreign prince, state, or potentate, or of any foreign colony, province, or part of any province or *Penalty on persons fitting out armed vessels to aid in military operations with any foreign powers; without licence.*

people, or of any person or persons exercising or assuming to exercise any powers of government in or over any foreign state, colony, province, or part of any province or people, as a transport or store ship, or with intent to cruize or commit hostilities against any prince, state, or potentate, or against the subjects or citizens of any prince, state, or potentate, or against the persons exercising or assuming to exercise the powers of government in any colony, province, or part of any province or country, or against the inhabitants of any foreign colony, province, or *or issuing commissions for ships.* part of any province or country, with whom His Majesty shall not then be at war; or shall, within the United Kingdom, or any of His Majesty's dominions, or in any settlement, colony, territory, island, or place belonging or subject to His Majesty, issue or deliver any commission for any ship or vessel, to the intent that such ship or vessel shall be employed as aforesaid, every such person so offending shall be deemed guilty of a misdemeanor, and shall, upon conviction thereof, upon any information or indictment, be punished by fine and imprisonment, or either of them, at the discretion of the Court in which such offender shall be convicted; and every such ship or vessel, with the tackle, apparel, and furniture, together with all the materials, arms, ammunition, and stores, which may belong to or be on board of any such ship or vessel, shall be forfeited; and it shall be lawful for any officer of His Majesty's customs or excise, or any officer of His Majesty's navy, who is by law empowered to make seizures, for any forfeiture incurred under any of the laws of customs or excise, or the laws of trade and navigation, to seize such ships and vessels aforesaid, and in such places and in such manner in which the officers of His Majesty's customs or excise and the officers of His Majesty's navy are empowered respectively to make seizures under the laws of customs and excise, or under the laws of trade and navigation; and that every such ship and vessel, with the tackle, apparel, and furniture, together with all the materials, arms, ammunition, and stores which may belong to or be on board of such ship or vessel, may be prosecuted and condemned in the like manner, and in such Courts as ships or vessels may be prosecuted and condemned for any breach of the laws made for the protection of the revenues of customs and excise, or of the laws of trade and navigation.

Penalty for aiding the warlike equipment of vessels of foreign states, &c. 8. And be it further enacted, that if any person in any part of the United Kingdom of Great Britain and Ireland, or in any part of His Majesty's dominions beyond the seas, without the leave and licence of His Majesty for that purpose first had and obtained as aforesaid, shall, by adding to the number of the guns of such vessel, or by changing those on board for other guns, or by the addition of any equipment for war, increase or augment, or procure to be increased or augmented, or shall be knowingly concerned in increasing or augmenting the warlike force of any ship or vessel of war, or cruizer, or other armed vessel which at the time of her arrival in any part of the United Kingdom, or any of His Majesty's dominions, was a ship of war, cruizer, or armed vessel in the service of any foreign prince, state, or potentate, or of any person or persons exercising or assuming to exercise any powers of government in or over any colony, province, or part of any province or people belonging to the subjects of any such prince, state, or potentate, or to the inhabitants of any colony, province, or part of any province or country under the control of any person or persons so exercising or assuming to exercise the powers of government, every such person so offending shall be deemed guilty of a misdemeanor, and shall, upon being convicted thereof, upon any information or indictment, be punished by fine and imprisonment, or either of them, at the discretion of the Court before which such offender shall be convicted.

9. And be it further enacted, that offences made punishable by the provisions of this Act, committed out of the United Kingdom, may be prosecuted and tried in His Majesty's Court of King's Bench at Westminster, and the venue in such case laid at Westminster in the county of Middlesex. *Offences committed out of the Kingdom may be tried at Westminster.*

10. And be it further enacted, that any penalty or forfeiture inflicted by this Act may be prosecuted, sued for, and recovered by action of debt, bill, plaint, or information, in any of his Majesty's Courts of Record at Westminster or Dublin, or in the Court of Exchequer, or in the Court of Session in Scotland, in the name of His Majesty's Attorney General for England or Ireland, or His Majesty's Advocate for Scotland respectively, or in the name of any person or persons whatsoever; wherein no essoign, protection, privilege, wager of law, nor more than one imparlance shall be allowed; and in every action or suit the person against whom judgment shall be given for any penalty or forfeiture under this Act shall pay double costs of suit; and every such action or suit shall and may be brought at any time within twelve months after the offence committed, and not afterwards; and one moiety of every penalty to be recovered by virtue of this Act shall go and be applied to His Majesty, His heirs or successors, and the other moiety to the use of such person or persons as shall first sue for the same, after deducting the charges of prosecution from the whole. *How penalties shall be sued for and recovered. Double costs. Limitation of actions.*

11. And be it further enacted, that if any action or suit shall be commenced, either in Great Britain or elsewhere, against any person or persons for anything done in pursuance of this Act, all rules and regulations, privileges and protections, as to maintaining or defending any suit or action, and pleading therein, or any costs thereon, in relation to *Former rules established by law to be applied to actions commenced in pursuance of this Act.*

any acts, matters, or things done, or that may be done by any officer of Customs or Excise, or by any officer of His Majesty's navy, under any Act of Parliament in force on or immediately before the passing of this Act, for the protection of the revenues of Customs and Excise, or prevention of smuggling, shall apply and be in full force in any such action or suit as shall be brought for anything done in pursuance of this Act, in as full and ample a manner to all intents and purposes as if the same privileges and protections were repeated and re-enacted in this Act.

<small>Penalties not to extend to persons entering into military service in Asia.</small> 12. Provided always and be it further enacted, that nothing in this Act contained shall extend or be construed to extend, to subject to any penalty any person who shall enter into the military service of any prince, state, or potentate in Asia, with leave or licence, signified in the usual manner, from the Governor General in Council, or Vice President in Council, of Fort William in Bengal, or in conformity with any orders or regulations issued or sanctioned by such Governor General or Vice President in Council.

III.

PROPOSED NEW LAW IN JUXTAPOSITION WITH THE PRESENT STATUTE.

[N. B. — As there is no official reprint of the new proposed Law, as finally amended, that I am aware of, I give the Bill as printed " in full " in the Congressional Proceedings of the New-York daily newspapers of July 27. I have assumed that this is the shape in which the Bill is now before the Senate. If it shall so happen that the official engrossment of the law corrects some of the etymological and grammatical errors which I have pointed out, I shall be heartily glad of it. My contention is certainly not directed against mere mechanical slips, or clerical blunders.

In regard to the annotations which are employed hereafter to enable the reader to take in the comparative amount of alteration upon the old law projected by the new, I would remark that the *added* or *corrected* matter of the text of the new law is enclosed in brackets. In regard to the *omitted* matter, attention is either directed to it by a note; or brackets, e. g. [   ], are inserted into the text, to indicate that something has been dropped out of the old.]

PROPOSED NEW LAW.

A Bill more effectually to preserve the neutral relations of the United States.	*An Act in addition to the "Act for the punishment of certain crimes against the United States," and to repeal the Acts therein mentioned.* [*April* 20, 1818.]

Be it enacted, &c., That, if any citizen of the United States shall, within the territory or jurisdiction thereof, accept and exercise a commission to serve a foreign prince, state, colony, district or people, in war, by land or by sea, against any prince, state, colony, district or people with whom the United States are at peace, the person so offending shall be deemed guilty of a [misdemeanor, and shall, on conviction thereof, be punished by a fine not exceeding $2,000, and imprisment not exceeding two years, or either, at the discretion of the Court in which such offender shall be convicted.]

SEC. 2. *And be it further enacted*, That if any person shall, within the territory or jurisdiction of the United States, enlist, or enter himself, or hire or retain another person to enlist, òr enter himself, or to go beyond the limits or jurisdiction of the United States, with intent to be enlisted, or entered, in[to] the service of any foreign prince, state, colony, district, or people, as a soldier, or as a marine[r] or seaman, on board of any vessel of war, letter of marque, or privateer, every person so offending shall be deemed guilty of a [misdemeanor, and shall, upon conviction therefor, be punished by fine not exceeding $1,000, and imprisonment not exceeding two years, or either of them, at the discretion of the Court, in case such offender shall be convicted:] provided that this Act shall not be construed to extend to any subject or citizen of any foreign power, state, colony, district or people who shall transiently be within the United States, and shall, on board of any vessel of war, letter of marque or privateer, which, at the time of its arrival within the United States, was fitted and equipped as such, enlist or enter himself, [and] hire or retain another

THAT if any citizen of the United State shall, within the territory of jurisdiction thereof, accept and exercise a commission to serve a foreign prince, state, colony, district, or people in war, by land or by sea, against any prince, state, colony, district, or people with whom the United States are at peace, the person so offending shall be deemed guilty of a high misdemeanor, and shall be fined not more than two thousand dollars, and shall be imprisoned not exceeding three years.

SEC. 2. That if any person shall, within the territory or jurisdiction of the United States, enlist or enter himself, or hire or retain another person to enlist or enter himself, or to go beyond the limits or jurisdiction of the United States with intent to be enlisted or entered in the service of any foreign prince, state, colony, district, or people, as a soldier, or as a marine or seaman, on board of any vessel of war, letter of marque, or privateer, every person so offending shall be deemed guilty of a high misdemeanor, and shall be fined not exceeding one thousand dollars, and be imprisoned not exceeding three years: Provided that this Act shall not be construed to extend to any subject or citizen of any foreign prince, state, colony, district, or people, who shall transiently be within the United States, and shall on board of any vessel of war, letter of marque, or privateer, which, at the time of its arrival within the United States, was fitted and equipped as such, enlist or enter himself, or hire or retain another subject or citizen of the same foreign prince, state, colony, district, or people, who is transiently within the United States, to enlist or enter himself to serve such foreign

subject or citizen of the same foreign prince, state, colony, district or people, who is transiently in the United States, to enlist or enter himself to serve such foreign prince, state, colony, district or people, on board such vessel of war, letter of marque or privateer, if the United States shall then be at peace with such foreign prince, state, colony, district or people.

SEC. 3. *And be it further enacted,* That if any person shall, within the limits of the United States, fit out and arm, or attempt to fit out and arm, or procure to be fitted out and armed, or shall knowingly be concerned in the furnishing, fitting out [and] arming of any ship or vessel, with intent that such ship or vessel shall be employed in the service of any foreign prince, state, colony, district or people, to cruise or commit hostilities against the subjects, citizens or property of any foreign prince or state, or any colony, district or people, with whom the United States are at peace, or shall issue or deliver a commission within the territory or jurisdiction of the United States for any ship or vessel to the intent that she may be employed as aforesaid, [or shall have on board any person or persons who shall have been enlisted, or shall have engaged to enlist or serve, or shall be departing from the jurisdiction of the United States with intent to enlist or serve in contravention of the provisions of this Act,] every person so offending shall be deemed guilty of a [misdemeanor, and shall, upon conviction thereof, be punished by fine not exceeding $3,000, and imprisonment not exceeding three years, or either of them, at the discretion of the Court in which such offender shall be convicted;] and every such ship and vessel, with her tackle, apparel and furniture, together with all materials, arms, ammunition and stores, which may have been procured for the building and equipment thereof, shall

prince, state, colony, district, or people, on board such vessel of war, letter of marque, or privateer, if the United States shall then be at peace with such foreign prince, state, colony, district, or people.

SEC. 3. That if any person shall within the limits of the United States fit out and arm, or attempt to fit out and arm, or procure to be fitted out and armed, or shall knowingly be concerned in the furnishing, fitting out, or arming of any ship or vessel with intent that such ship or vessel shall be employed in the service of any foreign prince or state, or of any colony, district, or people, to cruize or commit hostilities against the subjects, citizens, or property of any foreign prince or state, or of any colony, district, or people with whom the United States are at peace, or shall issue or deliver a commission within the territory or jurisdiction of the United States for any ship or vessel, to the intent that she may be employed as aforesaid, every person so offending shall be deemed guilty of a high misdemeanor, and shall be fined not more than ten thousand dollars, and imprisoned not more than three years; and every such ship or vessel, with her tackle, apparel, and furniture, together with all materials, arms, ammunition, and stores, which may have been procured for the building and equipment thereof, shall be forfeited, one-half to the use of the informer, and the other half to the use of the United States.

be forfeited [to the United States of America.]

¹ [SEC. 4. *And be it further enacted,* That it shall be lawful for any collector of the customs, who is by law empowered to make seizures for any forfeiture incurred under any of the laws of customs, to seize such ships and vessels in such places and in such manner in which the officers of the customs are empowered to make seizures under the laws for the collection and protection of the revenue, and that every such ship and vessel, with the tackle, apparel, and furniture, together with all the materials, arms, ammunition and stores which may belong to or be on board such ship or vessel, may be prosecuted or condemned for the violation of the provisions of this Act in like manner as ships or vessels may be prosecuted and condemned for any breach of the laws made for the collection and protection of the revenue.]

SEC. 5. *And be it further enacted,* That if any person shall, within the territory or jurisdiction of the United States, increase or augment, or procure to be increased or augmented, or shall knowingly be concerned in increasing or augmenting the force of any ship of war or cruiser, or other armed vessel, which at the time of her arrival within the United States was a ship of war or cruiser, or armed vessel in the service of any foreign prince, state, colony, district or people, or belonging to the subjects or citizens of any such prince, state, colony, district or people, the same being at war with any foreign prince, state, colony, district or people, with whom the United States are at

¹ This section is new, and borrowed from § 7 of the Br. For. En. Act. See *ante.* p. 113.
² Sec. 4 of the United-States Act is omitted bodily. See *ante,* pp. 35, 116.

² SEC. 4. That if any citizen or citizens of the United States shall, without the limits thereof, fit out and arm, or attempt to fit out and arm, or procure to be fitted out and armed, or shall knowingly aid or be concerned in the furnishing, fitting out, or arming, any private ship or vessel of war, or privateer, with intent that such ship or vessel shall be employed to cruze or commit hostilities upon the citizens of the United States, or their property, or shall take the command of, or enter on board of any such ship or vessel for the intent aforesaid, or shall purchase any interest in any such ship or vessel, with a view to share in the profits thereof, such person so offending shall be deemed guilty of a high misdemeanor, and fined not more than ten thousand dollars, and imprisoned not more than ten years; and the trial for such offence, if committed without the limits of the United States, shall be in the district in which the offender shall be apprehended or first brought.

SEC. 5. That if any person shall, within the territory or jurisdiction of the United States, increase or augment, or procure to be increased or augmented, or shall knowingly be concerned in increasing or augmenting the force of any ship of war, cruiser, or other armed vessel, which, at the time of her arrival within the United States, was a ship of war, or cruiser, or armed vessel, in the service of any foreign prince, or state, or of any colony, district, or people, or belonging to the subjects or citizens of any such prince, or state, colony, district, or people, the same being at war with any foreign prince or state, or of any colony, district, or people with whom the United States are at peace, by adding to the number of the guns of such vessel, or by changing those on board of her for guns of a larger calibre, or by the addition thereto of any equip-

peace, by adding to the number of guns of such vessels, or by changing those on board of her for guns of a larger calibre, or by addition thereto of any equipments solely applicable to war, [or shall have on board any person or persons who shall have enlisted or engaged to enlist or serve, or who shall be departing from the jurisdiction of the United States with intent to enlist or serve in contravention of the provisions of this Act,] every person so offending shall be deemed guilty of [misdemeanor, and shall, upon conviction thereof, be punished by fine or imprisonment, or either of them, at the discretion of the Court in which such offender shall be convicted].

[1] SEC. 6. *And be it further enacted*, That the District Court shall take cognizance of [all] complaints, [informations, indictments, or other prosecutions,] by whomsoever instituted, in cases of captures made within the waters of the United States, or within a marine league of the coasts or shores thereof.

[2] SEC. 7. *And be it further enacted*, That in every case in which a vessel shall be fitted out and armed, or in which the force of any vessel of war, cruiser, or other armed vessel shall be increased or augmented, [ ] in every case of the capture of a ship or vessel within the jurisdiction or protection of the United States, as before defined; and in every case in which any process issuing out of any Court of the United States shall be disobeyed or resisted by

[1] Sec. 6 of Act of 1818 is omitted bodily. See *ante*, p. 95. The addition of "informations," &c., is commented on, p. 119.

[2] For notice of the omissions in this section, see *ante*, pp. 95–6.

ment solely applicable to war, every person so offending shall be deemed guilty of a high misdemeanor, shall be fined not more than one thousand dollars, and be imprisoned not more than one year.

SEC. 6. That if any person shall, within the territory or jurisdiction of the United States, begin or set on foot, or provide or prepare the means for, any military expedition or enterprise, to be carried on from thence against the territory or dominions of any foreign prince or state, or of any colony, district, or people with whom the United States are (at) peace, every person so offending shall be deemed guilty of a high misdemeanor, and shall be fined not exceeding three thousand dollars, and imprisoned not more than three years.

SEC. 7. That the District Courts shall take cognizance of complaints, by whomsoever instituted, in cases of captures made within the waters of the United States, or within a marine league of the coasts or shores thereof.

SEC. 8. That in every case in which a vessel shall be fitted out and armed, or attempted to be fitted out and armed, or in which the force of any vessel of war, cruiser, or other armed vessel shall be increased or augmented, or in which any military expedition or enterprise shall be begun or set on foot, contrary to the provisions and prohibitions of this Act; and in every case of the capture of a ship or vessel within the jurisdiction or protection of the United States as before defined, and in every case in which any process issuing out of any Court of the United States shall be disobeyed or resisted by any person or persons having the custodia

PROPOSED NEW LAW.

any person or persons having the custody of any vessel of war, cruiser, or other armed vessel, of any foreign prince or state, or of any colony, district, or people, or of any subjects or citizens of any foreign prince, state, or of any colony, district, or people, in any such case, it shall be lawful for the President of the United States, or such other person as he shall have empowered for that purpose, to employ such part of the land and naval forces of the United States, or of the militia thereof, for the purpose of taking and detaining any such ship or vessel, with her prize or prizes, if any, in order to the execution of the prohibition and penalties of their act, and to the restoring the prize or prizes in the cases in which restoration shall have been adjudged [   ].

SEC. 8. *And be it further enacted,* That it shall be lawful for the President of the United States, or such person as he shall empower for such purpose, to employ such part of the land and naval forces of the United States, or of the militia thereof, as shall be necessary to compel any foreign ship or vessel to depart the United States in all cases in which, by the laws of nations or the treaties of the United States, they ought not to remain within the United States.

[1] SEC. 9. *And be it further enacted,* That offences made punishable by the provisions of this Act, committed by citizens of the United States beyond the jurisdiction of the United States, may be prosecuted and tried before any Court having jurisdiction of the offences prohibited by this Act.

[1] See p. 116 for comments on the superfluousness of this section.

tody of any vessel of war, cruiser, or other armed vessel of any foreign prince or state, or of any colony, district, or people, or of any subjects or citizens of any foreign prince or state, or of any colony, district, or people, in every such case it shall be lawful for the President of the United States, or such other person as he shall have empowered for that purpose, to employ such part of the land or naval forces of the United States, or of the militia thereof, for the purpose of taking possession of and detaining any such ship or vessel, with her prize or prizes, if any, in order to the execution of the prohibitions and penalties of this Act, and to the restoring the prize or prizes in the cases in which restoration shall have been adjudged, and also for the purpose of preventing the carrying on of any such expedition or enterprise from the territories or jurisdiction of the United States against the territories or dominions of any foreign prince or state, or of any colony, district, or people with whom the United States are at peace.

SEC. 9. That it shall be lawful for the President of the United States, or such person as he shall empower for that purpose, to emyloy such part of the land or naval forces of the United States, or of the militia thereof, as shall be necessary to compel any foreign ship or vessel to depart the United States in all cases in which, by the laws of nations or the treaties of the United States, they ought not to remain within the United States.

[1] SEC. 10. *And be it further enacted,* That nothing in this Act shall be so construed as to prohibit citizens of the United States from selling vessels, ships, or steamers built within the limits thereof, or materials or munitions of war, the growth or product of the same, to inhabitants of other countries or governments not at war with the United States: *Provided,* That the operation of this section of this Act shall be suspended by the President of the United States in regard to all classes of purchases whenever the United States shall be engaged in war, or whenever the maintenance of friendly relations with any foreign nation may in his judgment require it.

SEC. 11. *And be it further enacted,* That nothing in the foregoing Act shall be construed to prevent the prosecution or punishment of treason, or any piracy or other felony, defined by the laws of the United States.

SEC. 12. *And be it further enacted,* That all Acts and parts of Acts inconsistent with the provisions of this Act, or inflicting any further or other penalty or forfeiture than are hereinbefore provided for the acts forbidden herein, are hereby repealed.

[1] See p. 117 for extended comments on this new section.

SEC. 10. That the owners or consignees of every armed ship or vessel sailing out of the ports of the United States, belonging wholly or in part to citizens thereof, shall enter into bond to the United States, with sufficient sureties, prior to clearing out the same, in double the amount of the value of the vessel and cargo on board, including her armament, that the said ship or vessel shall not be employed by such owners to cruize or commit hostilities against the subjects, citizens, or property of any foreign province or state, or of any colony, district, or people with whom the United States are at peace.

SEC. 11. That the collectors of the customs be, and they are hereby, respectively, authorized and required to detain any vessel manifestly built for warlike purposes, and about to depart the United States, of which the cargo shall principally consist of arms and munitions of war, when the number of men shipped on board or other circumstances shall render it probable that such vessel is intended to be employed by the owner or owners to cruize or commit hostilities upon the subjects, citizens, or property of any foreign prince or state, or of any colony, district, or people with whom the United States are at peace, until the decision of the President be had thereon, or until the owner or owners shall give such bond and security as is required of the owners of armed ships by the preceding section of this Act.

SEC. 12. That the Act passed on the 5th day of June, 1794, entitled "An Act in addition to the Act for the Punishment of certain Crimes against the United States," continued in force, for a limited time, by the Act of the 2d of March, 1797, and perpetuated by the Act passed on the 24th of April, 1800, and the Act passed on the 14th day of June, 1797, entitled "An Act to prevent Citizens of the United States from privateering against Nations in Amity with, or against the Citizens of, the United States," and the Act passed the 3rd day of March, 1817, entitled "An Act more effectually to preserve the neutral Relations of the United States," be and the same are hereby severally repealed: *Provided, nevertheless,* that persons having heretofore offended against any of the Acts aforesaid may be prosecuted, convicted, and punished as if the same were not repealed; and no forfeiture heretofore incurred by a violation of any of the Acts aforesaid shall be effected by such repeal.

Sec. 13. That nothing in the foregoing Act shall be construed to prevent the prosecution or punishment of treason, or any piracy defined by the laws of the United States.

ERRATA.

Page 12, fifteenth line from top, for " with- " read without.
 ,, 15, fourth line from bottom, insert 1863 after " Nov. 4."
 ,, 25 and 27, for " John Ward " read Robert Ward.
 ,, 44, six lines from bottom, strike out two (" ") and read " Manchester Examiner and Times."

Printed in Dunstable, United Kingdom